The Complete Book of
Pottery Making

Other books by the author   **The Art of Papier Mâché**
Ceramic Design   Ceramic Sculpture   Design in Papier Mâché

Drawings by Carla Kenny

The Complete Book of Pottery Making

Second Edition

John B. Kenny

Chilton Book Company   Radnor, Pennsylvania

Manufactured in the United States of America
Cover photograph of Charlie Brown's Studio by Belton Wall

Library of Congress Cataloging in Publication Data

Kenny, John B
    The complete book of pottery making.

    (Chilton's creative crafts series)
    Includes index.
    1. Pottery craft.   I. Title.
TT920.K46   1976   738   76-302
ISBN 0-8019-5932-2
ISBN 0-8019-5933-0 pbk.

12 13 14 15 16   5 4 3 2 1 0 9

Contents

v

Foreword

The most widely known general text in the ceramic art and craft field for better than two decades has been *The Complete Book of Pottery Making,* by John B. Kenny.

We first met John Kenny in the late 1930s at Alfred University, and it was there we became lasting friends. During this period John began to compose this book. He used a method of selective photographs so that pivotal points in clay construction could be clearly illustrated. Pictures were accompanied by short descriptions relative to each illustration. His book was, we believe, the first in the pottery field to use this system.

John Kenny's enthusiasm for the crafts is reflected in his teaching and writing, which have covered a period of over fifty years. He and his wife Carla have authored several texts in the general craft field, and have traveled extensively in western Europe and Mexico visiting major pottery centers. During his long teaching career, John Kenny developed the firm belief that everyone has within himself or herself the making of an artist. In his teaching and writing he has stressed the importance of originality, exploration, and creation—while holding that everyone in ceramics must develop a wholesome respect for craftsmanship.

Over the past quarter of a century, *The Complete Book of Pottery Making* has been used by vast numbers of people in Europe, Latin America, and in this country. To many it was their introduction to the joys of working in clay. The contents have proven a valuable contribution to the field and their impact upon the reader remains high.

We are happy to welcome the second edition and we know that readers familiar with John Kenny's writing will share our enthusiasm.

Dorothy W. Perkins, Ph.D.
Curator, Art Slide Library
Art Department, University of Massachusetts
Amherst, Massachusetts

Lyle N. Perkins, Ph.D.
Professor in Art (Ceramics)
Art Department, University of Massachusetts
Amherst, Massachusetts

Preface to the  Second Edition

Since the first edition of this book was published in 1949, our world has changed; for potters it is a different world entirely—a better one.

There are many more potters now. Some say that twenty times as many people make pots today as did two decades ago. Other estimates by the manufacturers of equipment and supplies for potters (and they are the ones who ought to know) say that fifty times as many would be more accurate.

Why do we say the world is a better one for potters? One reason is the growth of appreciation, on the part of the general public, of pottery as an art form and the willingness of collectors to pay potters almost as much as their pieces are worth.

Another reason is the much greater freedom which potters enjoy. Contemporary movements in the fields of sculpture and painting have been reflected in ceramics so that potters, released from the bonds of classic tradition, have embarked upon explorations of new artistic concepts, creating pieces of startling originality. Some have fallen in love with the improvisational methods of raku. Much of the new work in ceramics is exciting, thrilling to behold.

Potters travel more today. They visit foreign countries. They go to exhibitions and they attend symposiums in this country and abroad. The names of leading potters are becoming known nationally and internationally.

One of the rewards of writing this book, perhaps the greatest reward, was the many, many friendships that developed. During its revision, old friendships were renewed and new ones were formed.

Potters are special people. Working with clay develops understanding and appreciation of the material's virtues. It develops appreciation of human virtues also, the basic virtues of integrity, generosity, friendship.

Thanks to all of you who helped, who welcomed us to your studios, and let us watch you at work, permitted us to photograph what you had done (or gave us photos taken by others). Thanks for the generous contributions of time, the sharing of information and experiences.

Mexico, 1975

Preface to the

First Edition

Welcome to the fraternity of potters! Come join the company of those who fashion things out of earth and fire, who work with materials old as time itself. Explore the mysteries of the kiln whose magic changes dull mud into objects as brilliant as jewels. Learn the secrets of the ceramic art—learn about clay.

A wonderful material, clay—probably the first to which man turned his hand when he felt the urge to make things, not for hunting or for war, but just for the pleasure of creating. Out of clay he contrived those first utensils for cooking and storing food which spelled the beginning of civilization. Out of it also he made ornaments, representations of natural forms, objects of religious veneration, even books.

If you learn its simple rules, clay will serve you well, obeying your slightest touch and giving tangible expression to your thoughts. It will remain plastic and responsive, changing as you command; yet when you achieve the form you wish and pass it through the fire, it will hold the impress of your fingers forever.

You may work clay with machinery or you may work it by hand. The experienced potter can use it to produce articles of exquisite design whose making will tax to the utmost his knowledge and his craftsmanship. A little child can use it, also, and make things of real utility and charm. It can be modeled, pressed, or stamped. It can be thrown on a wheel. It can be made into a liquid and cast in molds. It can be carved as a solid. It can be rolled, turned, scraped, incised, pulled, cut. When hardened by fire, it can be glazed with colors, brilliant or subdued, glossy or mat. It may be decorated with designs or given a variety of textures. Its range is almost limitless. It has something to offer to all tastes. It will lend itself to all degrees of skill.

It took a thousand centuries for forces of air and water working on granite rock to form the clay you work with. It took countless centuries more for winds and glaciers and running streams to deposit it in the bed where it was found. It is ready to serve you. Respect it for what it can do. If you are honest and sincere, it will reward you richly, not only in pieces of ware but in that deep satisfaction which comes from making something and knowing that you have made it well.

New York, 1947

List of Illustrations

Figure

Figure

List of Photo Series

The Complete Book of
Pottery Making

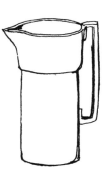

Chapter 1   Introduction to Clay

Making things of clay is good for the soul. From it we learn not only how clay responds, but also about the relationship between forms of objects and their materials. This is a subtle and beautiful relationship. Years ago when all utensils were made by hand and when nearly everyone made something, this relationship was understood and appreciated. Today, when practically everything is made for us by machine, we have lost much of our sensitivity to form and material. Our work with clay will help us to win it back.

Before we talk about buying clay, let's consider the problem of deciding what kind of clay to buy. Dealers offer such a variety of clays and clay bodies that the beginner will need help in making a choice.

Here is a suggestion: join a class or a ceramic workshop. Interest in pottery making has grown so in recent years that classes and work centers have been established in practically every locality. By enrolling with such a group you will be able to learn quickly about different kinds of clay and about the equipment potters use, and *you will have access to a kiln*!

Shaping clay is only part of the potter's job: pieces must also be fired. Owning one's own kiln is not nearly so difficult as it used to be; manufacturers offer a wide range of kilns—electric, gas fired, oil fired—that are simple to operate and moderately priced. Several examples are shown in Figures 1-1 through 1-3. But before buying a kiln it is good to do some work under the eyes of a more experienced potter.

Pottery must be fired to a temperature high enough to mature the clay; that is, to make it hard and dense, able to hold water.

1

Fig. 1-1   Gas fired studio kiln, Alpine.

The potter's term for this is *vitreous*. By starting with a group you will avoid the mistake of buying clay which requires a higher temperature than your kiln will reach.

In pottery classes you will be able to help with the loading and firing, and unloading of the kiln. You will also acquire practical knowledge of how to store clay; how to use a damp box or plastic bags to keep work in progress from drying out too rapidly; how to take care of tools and equipment: a valuable apprenticeship.

But the greatest advantage of joining a class is having a chance to work with others, sharing tasks and sharing experiences. From such fellowship comes enthusiasm and inspiration, a good feeling that helps produce good pots.

A Place to Work

Whether or not you join a pottery group you will need a place to do some work at home. Eventually you may have a complete home studio, but meanwhile you must have some area where you can turn ideas into forms.

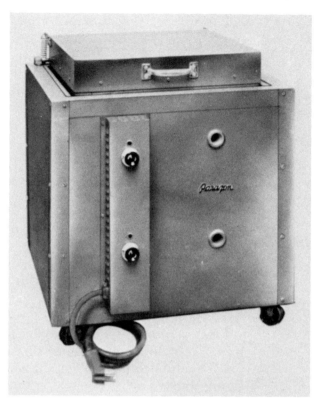

Fig. 1-2 Top-loading studio kiln, electric,
Paragon.

Fig. 1-3 Cylindrical type studio
kiln, electric, Paragon.

Pottery making is not an activity to carry on in a corner of the living room. You really need a place reserved for potting. If you have a cellar, a patio, or a carport, you are in luck. These make good studios, especially if there is running water nearby. You can work in the kitchen if no other place is available, but be careful not to get clay on the floor where it will be tracked into other rooms.

Buying Clay

Ceramic supply dealers sell clay and clay bodies in moist plastic form and also in dry powder form.

(A clay and a clay body are not the same thing. Clay is a natural product dug from the ground; a clay body is prepared according to formula by mixing different kinds of clays and sometimes adding other ingredients to achieve special properties. More about clay bodies in Ch. 11.)

Plastic clay

Dealers prepare moist clay by mixing it in pug mills. Sometimes a vacuum attachment on the pug mill removes all air pockets and produces a smoothness and density not obtainable in any other way. Clay which has been de-aired this way has superior working properties.

Moist clay is available in 50-pound cartons which contain two 25-pound units, individually packed in heavy plastic bags. Clay stored in such bags remains in good working condition.

Clay from a brickyard

Potters are sometimes able to buy clay, moist or dry, from a local brickyard. If you live near a brickyard, look into the possibilities of getting clay there.

Dry clay

Clay bought in a plastic form is ready for immediate use. Some potters, however, prefer to buy their clay as a dry powder. It is cheaper that way. (The price per pound may be the same, but you do not pay for the water.) Also when you are ready to make any special clay bodies for which the ingredients must be weighed out, you will have to have your clay in dry form.

One way of preparing powdered clay for use is to spread a layer about ½ inch thick on the bottom of a plastic pail and then sprinkle it with water until it is moist, but not soaking wet. Then spread another layer on top of the first and sprinkle again, continuing the process until the pail is nearly full. After an hour or two, the clay will be ready for wedging as described in the following section.

4

But there is an easier way. Most dealers supply extra-heavy plastic bags with the clay powder they sell. By adding the right amount of water and sealing the bag, one can mix the clay into good condition for wedging without even getting the hands dirty.

Wedging

Every time clay is used it should be wedged first. This is one of the oldest methods known for getting clay into good condition and it is still one of the best.

Wedging makes clay uniform in texture throughout and gets rid of air pockets. Clay that is too stiff can be moistened during the wedging process; clay that is too wet can be made less moist.

Using a wedging board

Many potters use a wedging board (Fig. 1-4). This is a heavy slab of plaster with an upright to hold a taut wire with a turnbuckle or some other device to keep the wire tight. A wedging board receives a lot of rough usage, so it should be constructed as solidly as possible. With use, the surface of the plaster will become scored and rough. For this reason some potters fasten canvas over the plaster surface.

To use the wedging board, take a lump of clay about the size of an orange; pass it beneath the wire, then grasping it in both hands lift it upward so that the wire cuts it in half. Throw one of

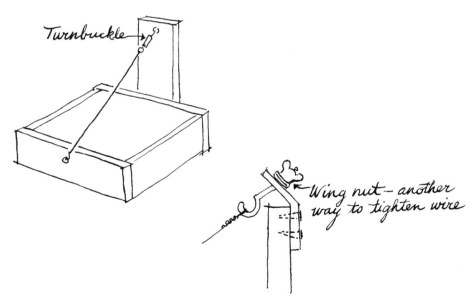

Fig. 1-4   Wedging board: two methods of
tightening wire.

5

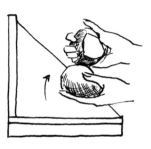

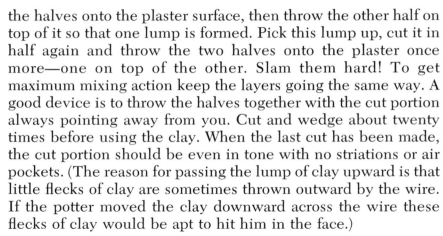

the halves onto the plaster surface, then throw the other half on top of it so that one lump is formed. Pick this lump up, cut it in half again and throw the two halves onto the plaster once more—one on top of the other. Slam them hard! To get maximum mixing action keep the layers going the same way. A good device is to throw the halves together with the cut portion always pointing away from you. Cut and wedge about twenty times before using the clay. When the last cut has been made, the cut portion should be even in tone with no striations or air pockets. (The reason for passing the lump of clay upward is that little flecks of clay are sometimes thrown outward by the wire. If the potter moved the clay downward across the wire these flecks of clay would be apt to hit him in the face.)

Wedging without a wedging board

Many potters prefer to condition their clay by kneading it almost the way a baker kneads his dough. A larger lump of clay —as much as ten pounds or more—can be conditioned this way and the method dispenses with the need for a wedging board. The kneading can be done on a heavy table with a bare wooden top or a top covered with canvas.

Large masses of clay—25 pounds or more—can be kneaded on the studio floor, or even trodden with bare feet.

Storing Clay

Moist clay can be stored in covered pails of galvanized iron or plastic; plastic is better.

Damp closet

A piece that is to be worked on for several days must be kept moist. For this purpose most studios have damp storage closets, zinc-lined, with shelves pierced by openings to permit circulation of air (Fig. 1-5). A large slab of plaster at the bottom of the closet kept soaked with water maintains humidity.

Small pieces can be kept moist in plastic bags.

Reclaiming Clay

Until it is fired, clay can be used over and over again. Dry clay should be broken into small pieces, tossed into a pail half filled with water and allowed to soak a few hours. After the clay has settled into the bottom of the pail, the water may be poured off and the clay emptied into drying bats. A drying bat is a large plaster bowl into which liquid clay can be poured and allowed to dry until it is firm enough for wedging.

6

Fig. 1-5 Sectional view of damp closet.

A Word About Tools

Don't buy too many tools, not at first anyway. We will see that many kitchen utensils make good potter's tools—paring knives, spoons, etc.

You will need a potter's knife. These are made of two kinds of steel: one is firm; the other is soft so that it can be bent into different hook shapes. You will also need some sponges, a wooden modeling tool or two (one with a wire loop end), a steel kidney-shaped scraper, and some type of turntable.

Good Housekeeping

Clay makes a lot of dirt, but it is easy to clean up. The best surface to work on is a plain wooden tabletop which can be wiped clean with a sponge. A wooden drawing board, a piece of plywood, or a piece of fiberboard will serve as a good working

7

surface. It is helpful to spread a piece of oilcloth, shiny side down, on the table and use a piece of board on top of that.

Care of tools

Clay will rust steel surfaces so the potter should clean knives and scrapers promptly. Wooden tools don't rust, but they deserve care also. Clean them as soon as you are through using them. Both steel and wooden tools should be rubbed occasionally with a cloth containing a few drops of oil.

The kitchen sink

Washing hands and tools and rinsing working surfaces under the faucet is risky—too much clay in the drain will cause trouble. A safer method is to have a pail half filled with water into which tools and hands may be dipped to remove surface clay. After this clay has settled to the bottom of the pail it may be reclaimed as described.

Kinds of Pottery

Ceramic wares are classified as earthenware, stoneware, china, and porcelain. These are not exact terms by any means but are merely generally descriptive.

Earthenware

Earthenware is usually made from natural clay, fired to some temperature between cone 08 and cone 2; most of it is fired in the neighborhood of cone 04. Cone 08 is a potter's way of saying 950° C or 1706° F. Potters rarely speak of temperature in any other way. When you fire a kiln you will use cones to measure temperatures, as described in Chapter 12, and you will soon find yourself thinking in those terms (See table 12-1).

The body of earthenware is nonvitreous, that is, comparatively soft and porous; it will not hold liquids unless it is glazed. Its color is usually buff or red, often quite dark. For this reason it is sometimes covered with a white or colored slip called *engobe* before glazes or decorations are applied.

Stoneware

Stoneware is sometimes made from natural clay and sometimes from prepared clay bodies. It is fired to higher temperatures than earthenware—usually between cone 6 and cone 8—and as a result is hard and vitreous, able to hold water even when unglazed. Not all natural clays can be used for stoneware, for many of them, especially the red ones, would melt at stoneware temperatures.

8

Pieces of sculpture or tiles made from natural clay and fired, but not glazed, are sometimes called *terra cotta*. The word means baked earth.

China

There is little common agreement on the dividing line between china and porcelain. In general, the term *china* refers to a type of ware made of a clay body composed of kaolin, ball clay, feldspar, and flint plus a flux (something to lower the melting point). The flux may be a natural ingredient such as talc or a prepared one such as ground glass. China is never made out of natural clay alone.

It is produced in two or more firings at different temperatures. The ware is formed and fired to bisque at a high temperature, about cone 10. The bisque ware is then glazed with a lower temperature glaze and fired again to about cone 2. After the second firing, china is sometimes decorated with overglaze painting or printed designs and fired a third time in a decorating kiln at a very low temperature, about cone 015. Some china is fired even more often than this for special decorative effects. The color of the body is usually white, although specially colored bodies are produced.

Porcelain

Porcelain requires the highest fire among all pottery wares. It is always made from a specially prepared body composed of kaolin, ball clay, feldspar, and flint. This is true porcelain, sometimes called *hard paste*. Ware made of a body with additional fluxes is sometimes referred to as *soft paste*. Porcelain is made in one fire, the body and the glaze maturing together at about cone 13. The product of such a fire, as you might expect, is extremely hard and vitreous.

Porcelain has always held a special place in the thoughts of man. The desire to possess it has sent ships around the world and the search for its formula has kept potters busy for centuries. The Chinese knew how to make it first and interesting stories have been told of the efforts made to win the secret from them, stories for example of Père d'Entrecolles, the missionary, who visited the great porcelain city of Ching-te-chen in an effort to convert the porcelain workers and at the same time learn how porcelain was made. His letters were interesting to read. The Chinese are a poetic people. In one of his letters, the good Father recounts a conversation with a Chinese potter who explained that porcelain must have muscle and bone, the muscles being ka-o-lin and the bones, pi-tun-se. We know now that the potter was talking about kaolin and feldspar, but those who read

9

the letter took his words literally and actually mixed some ground-up bones with their clay. The legend has it that this accounts for the discovery of bone china.

Stories could be told, too, of how the dukes of Italy, envious of the wares Marco Polo brought back, ordered their potters to get busy and produce the same thing. The potters, in desperation at being unable to turn out anything but yellowish or brown ware from clay at their disposal, finally hit upon the expedient of covering their plates with an opaque white glaze containing tin. In this way they imitated the surface, if not the body, of porcelain and so produced the ware we know as *majolica*. Stories could be told too, of the final discovery of kaolin in Germany by Heinrich Boettger. One legend has it that white clay on his horse's hoofs led to the discovery, and another that he found it in the powder he used on his wig. Another tale is told of the first porcelain factory set up at Meissen: the workers were all locked up to guard the secret.

Yes, porcelain has always been a subject of romance and glamour. It has even been used as a medium of exchange in place of money. It is worthy of note, however, that the Chinese, the fathers of porcelain, who knew more about it than anyone else, did not regard it with such exaggerated awe. To them a good earthenware pot honestly made and serving its purpose well was just as worthy of respect. So take a lesson from the Chinese: work your material well and your pottery will have merit, be it porcelain, stoneware, or low-fired earthenware.

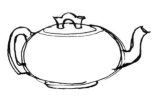

Chapter 2   Getting Started

The potter loves the feel of clay in his hands. So the first thing to do is get some clay and handle it in order to learn what it feels like.

   Grasp a lump of clay. Squeeze it; roll it; make a ball; flatten the ball into a pancake. Press your fingers into the pancake to

Fig. 2-1   Form.

Fig. 2-2   Movement.

11

create textures. Press other things in for variety—the end of a block of wood, the tines of a fork, a dried seedpod, a pine cone, a seashell, a scrap of rough toweling.

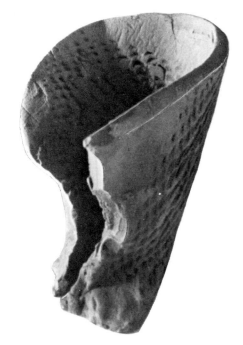

Fig. 2-3   Shape.

Fig. 2-4   Texture.

Experiment with some abstract designs, slice masses of clay into cubes, cut holes with a knife. Try combinations of masses; see what happens to a form when it is paddled with a block of wood into a different form. Make lots of shapes. (No representational forms yet, we'll come to those later on.)

Now we'll begin by making a pottery form: a round cup.

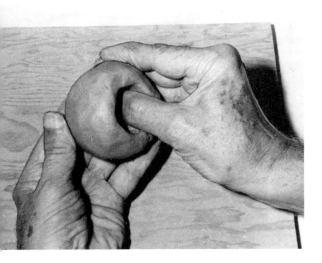

Photo Series 1

Making a Pinch Pot

1. Take a lump of clay about the size of a small orange and roll it into a ball. Holding the ball in the palm of the left hand, press the right thumb into the center of the clay. Rotate the ball as the thumb goes in. Push the thumb in far enough so that a thickness of about ¼ inch is left at the bottom.

12

Continue to rotate the clay while you gently press the wall between the thumb on the inside and the first two fingers of the right hand on the outside.

2. Fingers press from the inside, thumb from without. Turn the clay constantly as the wall is gently squeezed into an even thickness slightly less than ¼ inch.

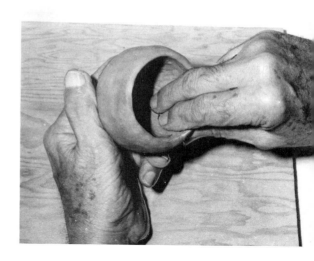

As you work this way your tactile sense will develop; you will begin to "see with your fingers." They will tell you where a portion of the wall is slightly too thick, warn you when it starts to become too thin, help you to keep the shape symmetrical.

If the wall starts to crack as you work on it, moisten a finger and press the crack closed. Use a damp sponge to smooth the sides and the top edge, but don't let the work get too wet.

3. The top of the cup will be somewhat ragged. It can be made even by using a sharp-pointed kitchen knife. Brace the knife on some solid object like a block of wood or a tumbler so that it is at the right height; rest the cup on the table and rotate it against the knife so that a straight score line is made all around the top.

4. The rim may be cut off with a knife but it is easier to use a pair of nail scissors.

13

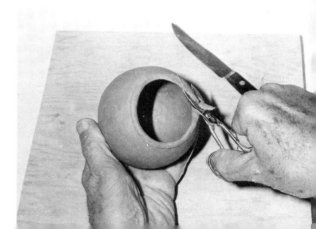

5. The top edge is smoothed with a dampened sponge. Now we are ready to add a foot.

When two pieces of clay are joined together, care must be taken to make sure the joint holds. The two surfaces must be roughened slightly, then moistened with water or slurry (clay in a thick liquid state, see Ch. 9), then welded firmly together.

6. The cup is supported upside down while the portion to which the foot will be attached is roughened with a plastic fork. A thin coil of clay has been rolled for the foot.

7. Welding the foot into place with the handle of a spoon.

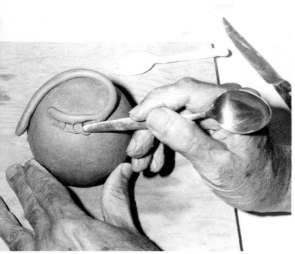

8. Smoothing the foot using a wooden modeling tool.

At this point, stop. We have worked long enough; clay gets tired after 45 minutes or so. We may consider our cup finished—it is crude, but it is honest. It looks like what it is, a cup modeled of a plastic material; its form shows how it was made. If we were to let it dry, then fire and glaze it, we would have a functional piece of pottery. But we'll not let it dry just yet.

A second look

If we put our cup aside for an hour or two, or better still overnight, when we look at it again we will see things we did not see before (we were too close). We may decide that the piece is not worth preserving and so mash up the clay and put it back into the clay bin, or we may decide it is just right the way it is and needs nothing more done to it. Or we may decide to carry the work further and change the form. So we'll put our cup into a plastic bag to keep it from drying out while we try another project.

Modeling a Rectangular Planter

1. We start with a lump of clay that has been pressed into a rough block form.

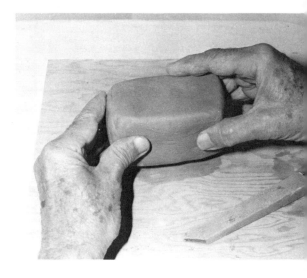

15

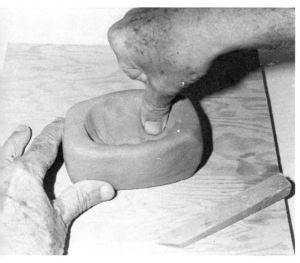

2. The thumb begins to press the block of clay into the form of a box.

3. Fingers and thumb of the right hand press the wall to make it taller and thinner.

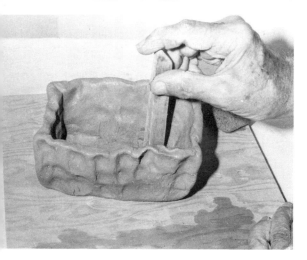

4. A block of wood is pressed inside to make the bottom even in thickness. After this step the box was allowed to dry upside down on two strips of wood. When the box had dried thoroughly it was bisque fired and a commercial glaze was brushed on.

5. The finished piece after its second firing: a planter.

Forming a Small Pitcher

1. Now for another look at the cup; it has been in a plastic bag overnight. The clay is firmer but still plastic so the shape can be altered. We'll make a cream pitcher out of it.

A spoon is used to smooth the inside surface of the cup.

2. Cutting a shape to use for a spout from a pancake of clay.

17

3. Trying the spout on the cup for size and position.

4. Roughening the clay where the spout is to be attached.

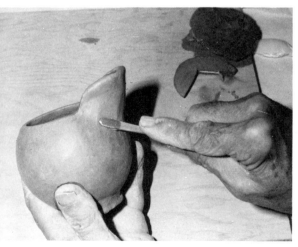

5. Welding the spout into place with a wood modeling tool.

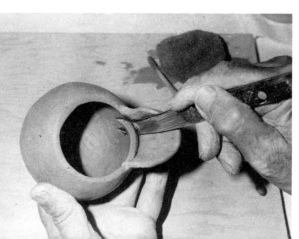

6. Cutting out the portion of the wall behind the spout attachment.

18

7. Shaping a handle.

8. Attaching the handle. The portions being joined were roughened and moistened first. Now the joints will be welded.

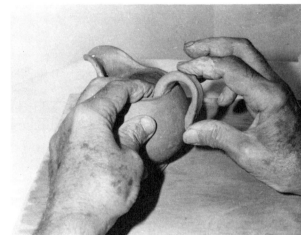

Shrinkage

Clay shrinks as it dries and it shrinks some more when it is fired. For that reason, two pieces of clay which are to be joined together should have the same moisture content. A handle of wet plastic clay stuck onto the side of a partially dried pot would fall off even before the piece was put into the kiln. The handle and spout that were just attached were somewhat moister than the body, so to make sure that all parts become firmly welded together the pitcher will be put into a plastic bag to remain damp for 24 hours.

19

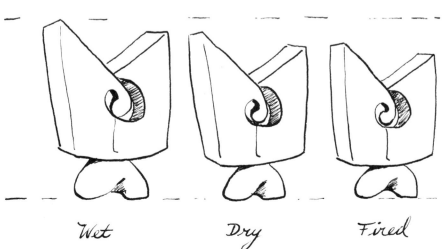

Wet   Dry   Fired

9. Clay forms should dry slowly and as evenly as possible.

The pitcher was removed from its plastic bag and stood for a while on two strips of wood so that air could reach the bottom, then it was turned over. Since the top is too delicate to permit the pitcher to stand on its head, it was placed over a temporary support made by stuffing a paper napkin into the end of the core of a toilet paper roll.

Note the addition of a small lump of clay to the top of the handle: this makes the pitcher easier to lift.

10. As clay dries, it goes through the condition potters call *leather hard,* when it becomes firm, though not yet completely dry. No modeling is possible in this state, but finishing touches can be made with a knife or a scraper.

11. The pitcher has been fired to the bisque state; now a commercial glaze is being brushed on (firing and glazing are described in later chapters).

20

12. The finished pitcher.

Forming a Globular Shape

1. Two hemispherical pinch pots have been made. The top edges have been smoothed, then roughened and moistened.

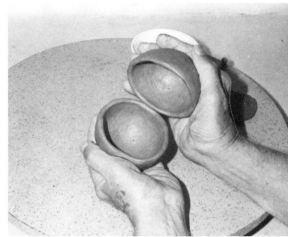

2. The two halves have been pressed firmly together. The air trapped inside makes it possible to weld the joint with a modeling tool.

3. If we want a ball shape, the form can be rolled in a circular motion on a board. Again, the air trapped inside makes this possible. Here a paring knife is used for a final smoothing of the surface. We shall see this globular form again in Photo Series 7.

21

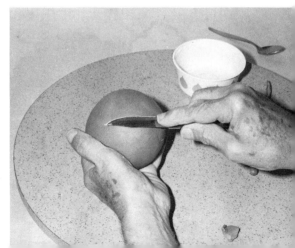

Fig. 2-5   Martini Bird, a pinch pot.

Finishing Ware

The surface of a piece of pottery may be smoothed by sponging it before it is fired. This can be done when the piece is

Fig. 2-6   Moon Pot by Charlie Brown; two pinch pots joined, raku, 7" x 7".

Fig. 2-7 Vase by Charlie Brown;
two pinch pots joined, coiled base
and neck, added strips textured with
bits of driftwood, raku, 11″.

leather hard or even when it is bone dry, provided care is taken
not to let too much water soak in. A silk or elephant's-ear sponge
is the best type to use. Avoid too much sponging, it destroys
character.

Grinding tops and bottoms

The tops and bottoms of green ware (unfired pieces) may be
made perfectly level by grinding them on a smooth board or on
a sheet of glass, as shown in Figure 2-8. To do this, put a few
drops of water on the board or glass and rub the piece over it,
upside down, using a circular motion. Have a sponge handy so

Fig. 2-8 Grinding the top of an unfired piece.

23

that, after the top has been ground for about 5 seconds, the piece can be lifted up and the rim wiped dry with the sponge. The grinding action is very fast. This is why a few seconds will suffice.

The operation must be done rapidly and the piece of green ware must be kept in constant motion. If you allow it to stand still for a moment, it will glue itself fast to the board and break when you try to loosen it.

Burnishing

Rubbing leather-hard ware with a smooth stone, a wooden modeling tool, or a special burnishing tool made of bone gives a shine to the surface which remains after the piece is fired. The effect is seen only in unglazed ware.

Decorating in Clay

Incising designs

The simplest way to ornament clay is to incise a design with a pointed tool. Experiment with this kind of decoration. Try using a three-pronged fork to scratch a crisscross pattern on a pot, as shown in Figure 2-9. Or try almost any kind of notched stick. The possibilities of variation here are infinite. Irene Batt is shown in Figure 2-10 making an incised decoration on a slab-built pot. Ornamental clay ribbons have been attached to the bottom (at top in photograph); such ribbons are made in Photo Series 5.

Fig. 2-9   A fork is used to incise decorations in ware.

Fig. 2-10   Irene Batt incises design in leather-hard coil
and slab-built sculptured pot.

Adding coils

Try rolling a thin coil of clay and pressing it onto a leather-
hard piece of pottery in a decorative way as shown in Figure
2-11. Such coils can be applied as bands around a pot or as

Fig. 2-11   Using coils to decorate ware.

vertical lines on the sides. They will need to be moistened before being applied and must be firmly pressed against the pot in order to stick. This very act of pressing may give them a decorative quality.

Carving and piercing

Clay can be decorated with carved figures as shown in Figure 2-12. This is a more formal kind of decoration than that just described. When a piece is leather hard, a design may be drawn on it and the background cut away to leave the design in low relief. When you do this kind of work, remember that you are a potter, not a sculptor, and that the decoration is good only if it enhances the beauty of the form. This means that the design must not be so prominent and demand so much attention that we fail to see the shape of the pottery itself.

Fig. 2-12   Examples of carved and pierced ware.

Carving in leather hard clay can be carried further to produce pierced ware (Fig. 2-12). This is an extremely elaborate kind of decoration: be cautious about trying it. Pierced ware is suitable for certain kinds of purely decorative pieces, such as lamp bases or ornamental lighting fixtures. You may be interested in trying it. Plan the design and draw it on the surface of the pot, then cut out the background. Do not cut out so much that what remains is thin and weak. Remember, too, that the remaining portions will need to be modeled slightly and given a satisfactory finish.

Some of the first porcelain tableware imported from China was shipped from the city of Gombroon and was known as "Gombroon ware." Later the name was replaced by "china." Today some ceramists use the term *gombroon* to describe a type of porcelain which is decorated with a pierced design, then covered with a flowing glaze which fills up the openings so that after the firing they appear as translucent windows.

26

Photo Series 5

Working with Clay Ribbons

Irene Batt demonstrates

1. A slab of clay has been rolled with a rolling pin. No guide strips were used, the artist merely pounded the clay flat on layers of newspaper and then rolled with a rolling pin from the center outward, not going over the edge. A ruler is used to cut strips of equal width.

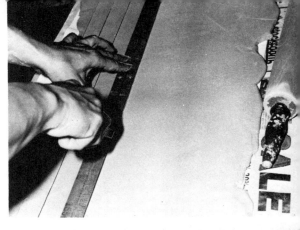

2. Moistened thumb and forefinger smooth the edge of the strip and make grooves.

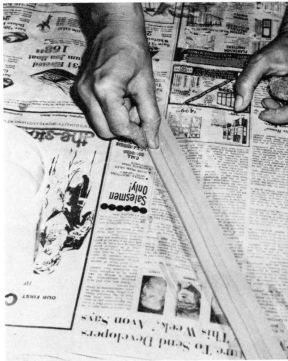

3. Attaching the ribbon to a wheel-thrown form. The area of attachment was roughened and dabbed with slurry.

27

4. Forming a loop in the ribbon.

5. Forming a second loop in the ribbon.

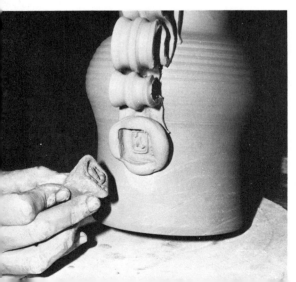

6. Completing the ornament by pressing in the potter's signature stamp.

Chapter 3  Sketching in Clay

Say the word *sketch* and one thinks of a quick drawing made with pen or pencil on a sheet of paper: a representation of something or a design. But a sketch can have a third dimension if it is made in clay.

We were sketching back in Chapter 2 when we tried abstract shapes and arrangements. Now, for a different approach, we shall seek inspiration from life.

Fig. 3-1 Swan.

29

Fig. 3-2 Cat.

Fig. 3-3 Pony.

30

First, some *setting-up exercises.* Start with a ball of clay and squeeze it into various shapes. Make a fish, a cat, a bird, a tree.

Make an animal with four legs by rolling two balls of clay, one slightly larger than the other, and then rolling a coil about as thick as your middle finger. Cut the coil into four pieces to serve as legs. Use the smaller ball as a head and stick them all together. Add ears, nose, eyes, and mouth.

Now make some more animals. Your hands and the clay itself will guide you. There are no rules to follow; work for realism if you wish, or stylization or even semiabstraction. Create some creatures of pure fantasy.

These animal figures are merely exercises to acquire freedom and confidence, so don't save them. Mash them all up and throw them back into the clay bin—unless there is an especially amusing one worth keeping. If so, check to see that all parts are well fastened together. Legs that have simply been pushed onto the body will drop off in the kiln. Follow the procedure we used in Photo Series 3 (Ch. 2): roughen the surfaces to be joined, moisten them, then press them firmly together and weld the joint all around with a modeling tool.

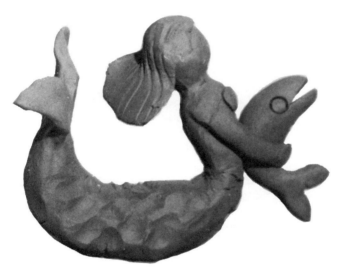

Fig. 3-4   Mermaid.

Hollowing Out

Clay, even when it is bone dry, contains chemically combined water which must escape during the firing. A solid lump of clay an inch or more in thickness, with no openings to let the water out, will break apart when it is fired, an accident that can ruin everything in the kiln. A small piece of sculpture must be made hollow by scooping out the insides so that no portion

31

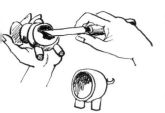

remains more than ⅜ inch thick. If the piece has a flat base this can be done from underneath. An animal with four legs must be cut in half, scooped out, then put together with the joint welded thoroughly.

Grog

When modeling small figures, wedge some grog into the clay. Grog is clay which has been fired, then ground up and screened. Added to clay, it provides openings through which moisture can escape so that thick pieces will not crack during drying and firing. It also prevents thin pieces from warping.

For most work, 30–60 mesh grog is used, that is, grog fine enough to go through a screen with 30 meshes to the inch but

Fig. 3-5   At ease.

too coarse to go through one with 60 meshes to the inch. This is medium grog. Coarse grog, 20–40 mesh, is needed for heavy sculpture. Grog can be bought in 10-pound quantities. Use one handful of grog to two of clay, and wet the grog thoroughly so that the two will mix more easily.

People Sketches

Now model some representations of people. Try a man sitting on a bench, a woman with a basket of flowers. Make a hole in a block of wood by driving a nail into it, then stick a piece of

Fig. 3-6   Pals.

33

coat-hanger wire into the hole. This can serve as a temporary support for a dancing figure, a ballerina, or a clown balanced on one toe.

The woman in Figure 3-9 holding the basket of flowers seems to have possibilities. Let's use this idea to make a figurine.

Fig. 3-7. Sisters.

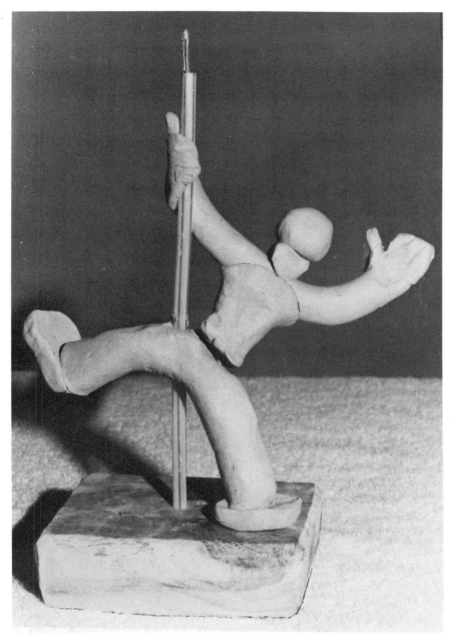

Fig. 3-8   Clown.

35

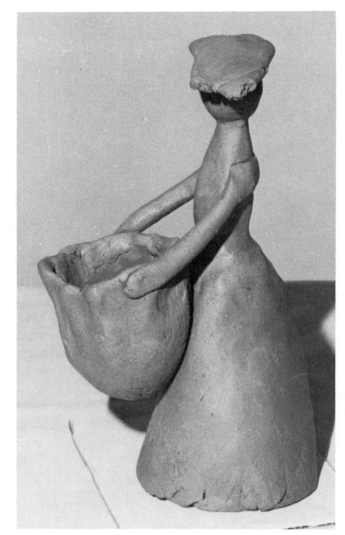

Fig. 3-9   Flower girl.

Photo Series 6

Making a Flower Girl Figurine

1. A hump on which to model our figurine has been made out of an empty cottage cheese container with half a ball of clay on it as shown.

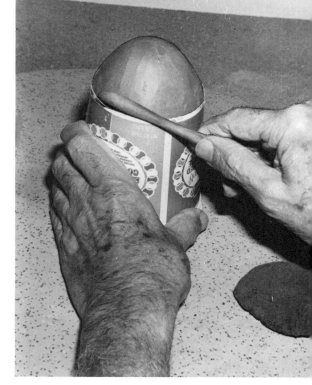

2. The hump has been wrapped in damp paper towels. Now a large pancake of clay rolled out with a rolling pin is wrapped around the hump. This will form the skirt and torso of the figure.

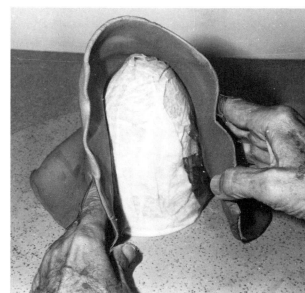

3. Trimming the edge of the skirt.

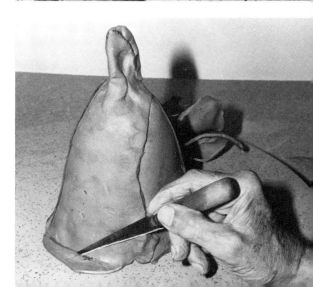

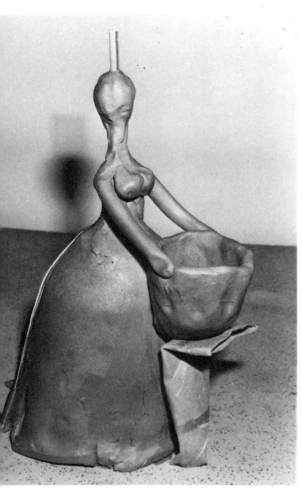

4. Starting to model the upper part of the figure. A piece of a drinking straw has been pushed downward through the head and the neck to serve as a temporary armature. The flower basket—a pinch pot—is propped in position.

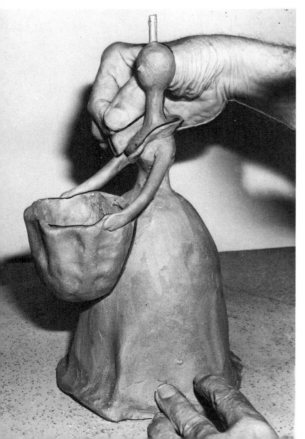

5. Completing the modeling by adding a collar to the dress. Finger marks in the basket will remain. The drinking straw will be rotated gently and pulled out before the clay hardens and the hole will be covered by a topknot. As soon as the clay is firm enough to stand unsupported, the figurine will be lifted off the hump and allowed to dry standing on two strips of wood.

6. The finished figurine.

Armatures

Sculptors who model large figures of clay use armatures, supporting frames made of pipe and metal wire (usually flexible aluminum). But such sculpture is intended for casting in materials other than clay. Clay with a metal wire inside cannot be fired. However, we can model a figure over a temporary armature which will be removed before the clay is allowed to dry. This is how it can be done.

Photo Series 7

Modeling a Clown

1. Let's see if we can make a clown able to balance on either hands or feet. For this we shall need two pieces of coathanger wire, one of them bent as shown. Both wires are pressed into holes in a block of wood. Before we start modeling, pieces of drinking straws slit lengthwise will be slipped over the wires.

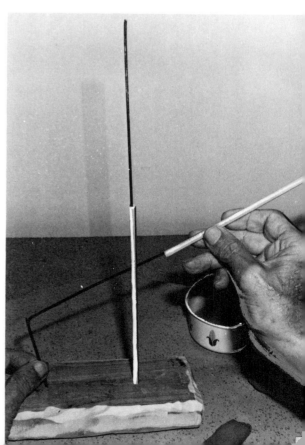

39

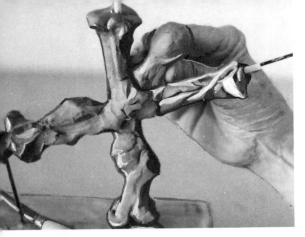

2. The form of the clown is begun by pressing clay onto the armature to make legs, arms, feet. Here a roughly constructed head is being put into place.

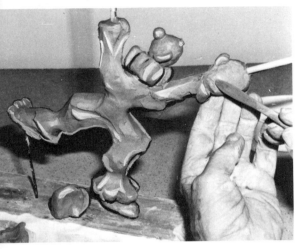

3. Modeling the figurine. When this is done, the clown will be lifted up off the vertical wire. The second wire will slip out of its hole and remain in the clown until the clown has been removed from the vertical wire. Then the figure will rest on a cushion made of crumpled paper towels while the second wire is removed and the straws are rotated gently and pulled out of the clay.

The straws are necessary so that the holes, after firing, will not be too small to slip over a coat-hanger wire

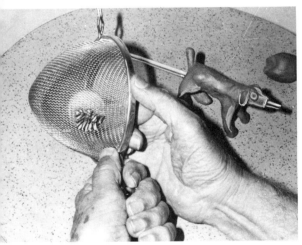

4. A companion for the clown. A straw pierces the figure of a dog. A lump of clay is pressed through a sieve to make poodle hair.

5. Attaching the poodle's topknot.

6. The clown and the poodle performing their act using the ball made in Photo Series 4 (Ch. 2). The figures and the ball have been bisqued, but not glazed. They are supported on a longer piece of coat-hanger wire which allows them to change their poses.

Clay sketches are frequently used for planning larger pieces of sculpture. They can serve also as studies for paintings. Some of the old masters, Degas, Renoir, and Daumier among them, made clay sketches of people or animals in action poses before touching a brush to canvas.

Marguerite Drewry, a contemporary artist who learned about clay at a crucial time in her life, is now a potter as well as a painter (the story is in Ch. 16). Some of her clay sketches have been executed as large garden sculpture in cast stone; others have been produced commercially as figurines.

Figurines

Little figures of clay have been objects of enchantment ever since the dawn of history. Terra cotta people and animals have been found in the ancient tombs of China, Siberia, the Middle East, and the Western Hemisphere. The term *enchantment* applied to tomb figures is literally true for they had a magic purpose—to accompany some powerful person on his journey to the other world as servants or companions. In the tombs of later

41

Fig. 3-10   Sketches in clay, Marguerite Drewry.

periods terra cotta was replaced by faience, glazed stoneware, and porcelain.

In later centuries figurines were made to delight the living. During the Renaissance wealthy patrons vied for the work of the makers and decorators of figurines. The palaces of the baroque period which survive today with some of their furnishings intact show what an important part of the culture of the time was played by figurines from the potteries of Europe and China.

The production of figurines is a big industry today, as a glance at the advertising pages of some magazines will show. Many gifted artists are employed in the manufacture and the decoration of these works so avidly sought after by collectors. Unfortunately they are not as well known as their counterparts in earlier centuries.

Drawing

While you sketch in clay, do not neglect your drawing. Keep a sketchbook and get in the habit of filling a page every day. Draw people, animals, trees, flowers. Draw objects, too: coffee pots, chairs, autos, boats. Draw things you see. Draw from memory, draw from imagination.

42

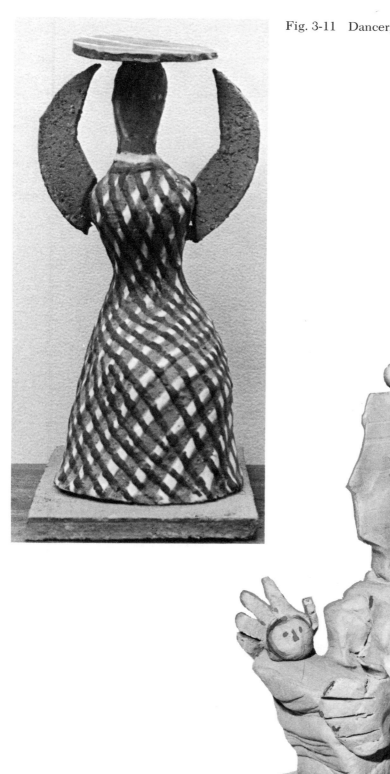

Fig. 3-11   Dancer, Marguerite Drewry.

Fig. 3-12   Earth Mother, Carla Kenny.

43

Experiment with different ways of drawing. Try scribbling—doodling. Make some drawings in pencil where erasing is possible. Draw others with pen and ink. Draw in outline. Experiment with shading. Try putting pen on paper and completing the drawing without lifting the pen.

Draw on a blackboard (every pottery studio should have one). White lines on black give a different point of view and drawing at arm's length develops strength. After completing a sketch in chalk, see how many lines you can erase and still have a drawing which says what you want it to say.

Seek design in what you draw. Turn a sketch of a flower into a design for a tile, something which could be carved into clay. Sketch pottery forms and plan decorations for them.

As you continue to draw you will develop your own style, your own way of saying things; you will become fluent in a new graphic language—a way of expressing your thoughts. Your sketchbook will help you to develop ideas and to record them. It will become a reservoir, a source of constant inspiration.

Fig. 3-13   Model for porcelain figurine, David Micalizzi.

44

Chapter 4  Coil Building

Before the invention of the potter's wheel, people made vessels by rolling coils of clay and laying them on top of one another in spiral fashion. As the work progressed, the coils were welded together; when the form was completed, the whole surface was rubbed with smooth stones until the joints between the coils were concealed. Sometimes the surface was decorated by pressing carved sticks into the clay to impart texture. Vessels of good size and considerable beauty were made this way. The method seems to have been used in every part of the world where pottery was made.

It is a mistake to think that coil-built pottery need look crude or clumsy. Quite the opposite. With time and care, one can produce pieces to be proud of. Nor is the method limited to simple shapes. Teapots and vases can be made this way, as well as nonsymmetrical forms. Let's make a coffee pot with a spout, a handle, and a lid.

Photo Series 8

Coil Building a Coffee Pot

1. Before starting, make a full-size sketch of the piece to be built; then trace one side of it on a piece of cardboard and cut out a shape to use as a template or pattern.

Roll a ball of clay and flatten it into a disk ¾ inch thick to serve as the base.

45

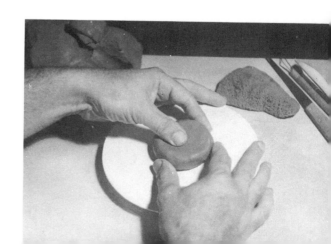

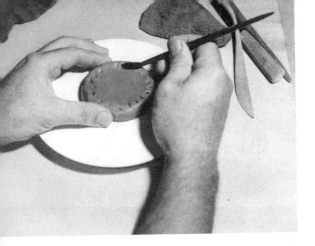

(This piece will have a foot rim. If you prefer a flat base, start with a disk ½ inch thick and omit step 8.) For greater ease in working, lay the disk on a plaster bat (a round slab of plaster, cast in a pie tin).

2. Roughen the top outer edge of the disk and moisten it with a soft brush.

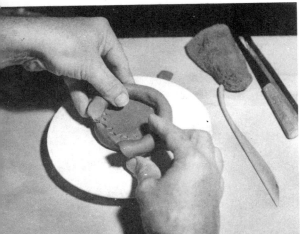

3. Next roll a coil of clay and lay it on the outer edge of the base. Cut the ends of the coil at a slant so that they will join without making a thick spot in the wall.

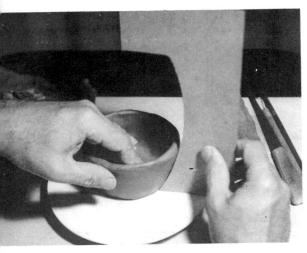

4. Weld the coil firmly into place and press the form with your fingers until it is about ½ inch thick and uniform throughout. Then hold the template against it to see how the shape is progressing.

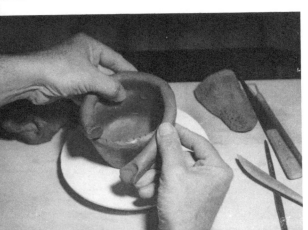

5. When the first coil is finished, roughen the top and moisten it. Then roll a second coil and put it in place on top of the first, welding the joint thoroughly as before. Then roll a third coil and add it in the same manner. While

46

you are laying the coils you are also forming the piece, so watch the shape closely. Compare it with the sketch you made. Keep turning your work, and hold the template against it, not as a scraping tool but as a gauge of your progress. Look at the piece from the top at frequent intervals to see that the coils form concentric circles.

6. Sometimes you may find it helpful to roll a very thin coil of clay and press it into the joint between the pot and the coil you are adding.

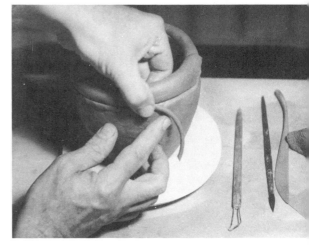

7. After you have put the fourth coil in place, the walls may be too weak to support more weight. If so, set the work aside for a while. You may let it harden for an hour or two and then continue, or you may cover it with a plastic bag and leave it overnight.

When you resume building, take care that the top edge of the piece is thoroughly roughened and moistened before the next coil is added. Continue adding coils until the shape is completed. If necessary, trim the top edge with a knife or a pair of nail scissors as you did with the cup made in Photo Series 1 (Ch. 2).

If you want the surface of your piece to be quite smooth, rub it with the flat side of a wooden modeling tool. Don't try to achieve a machined finish, however: let the work bear the mark of your hands.

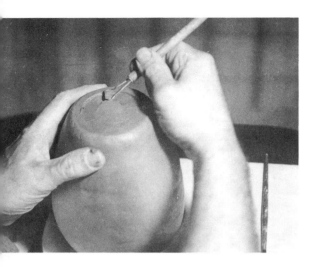

8. After the last coil has been put in place and the top edge finished, let the piece dry for an hour or two, then shape the foot. When you made the base you allowed a thickness of ¾ inch. This was so that a portion could be cut out with a wire loop tool, leaving a foot or rim for the piece to stand on. Hold the piece carefully while you do this, so that you don't spoil the top edge while it is standing upside down.

It may be necessary to support the piece on something tall, such as a fruit juice jar, allowing it to rest on the inside of the base. Fold a paper napkin over the top of the jar to form a cushion. The foot should be cut so that in cross section it looks similar to the one shown in Figure 4-1. Now for the spout and the handle.

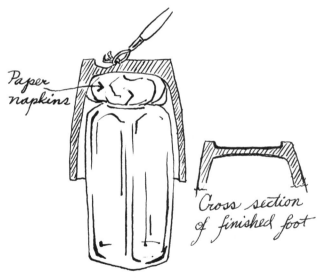

Fig. 4-1 Cutting the foot of a pot with wire loop tool.

9. Roll a ball of clay, flatten it, and cut out a fan-shaped piece. This can be folded to make the spout.

10. Cut an opening in the pot where the spout should be.

11. Take the spout which you have folded and hold it against the piece to see how it looks. If it is the right size and shape, roughen the edges, moisten them, and weld the spout into place.

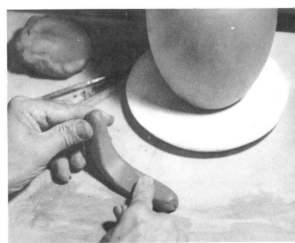

12. Roll a coil of clay and flatten it into a strip with your thumb.

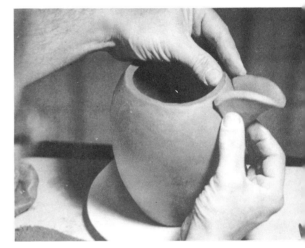

13. Bend the strip into a handle shape and attach it, welding both ends completely.

49

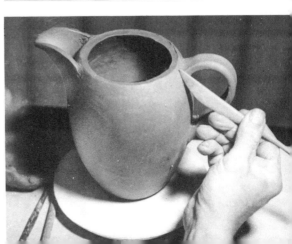

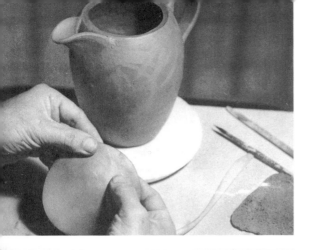

14. Roll another ball of clay and flatten it into a disk about the right size for a lid. Make it slightly dome shaped.

15. Hold the lid against the pot to see if the two go well together.

16. Make a flange for the underside of the lid by first rolling a coil. Flatten it into a strip, then cut the ends and join them to form a circle. Be sure that this circle is the right size to fit into the opening of the pot.

17. Next, fasten the flange in place on the underside of the lid.

18. Now roll a small ball of clay to serve as a knob. Fasten it in place on the top of the lid, using a very thin coil of clay to weld the joint.

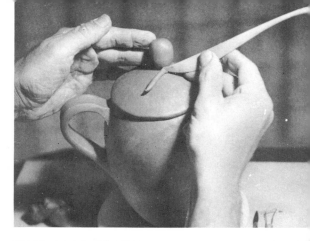

19. A little sponging on the outside surface and our coffee pot is done. Before putting it aside to dry we should place it in a damp closet or a plastic bag for a day or two. This is called *curing*, a process of slow aging which makes cracking less likely to occur. (Some potters put a damp paper towel over spouts and handles before putting the work aside to cure.)

Fig. 4-2 Coil-built teapot, Irene Batt.

Fig. 4-3 Coil pot, 11½″, Jane Russell Bates.

Sometimes, in spite of all precautions, a piece will crack as it dries. When that happens it is almost impossible to save it, so don't waste clay by putting it in the kiln, hoping that some miracle will occur during the firing to make the piece whole again. Such things don't happen. Consider the loss as experience gained, break up the piece and prepare the clay for reuse.

The coffee pot we just made has a traditional shape, but the coil-building method may be used to make almost any kind of ceramic form ranging from the classic to the ultra modern. Large pots for the garden can be made this way and so can sculpture.

Coil-Built Sculpture

We know now that any ceramic sculpture bigger than a tiny figurine must be hollow. The best way to achieve this is to make a solid clay model first, then cast a mold in plaster and either pour or press the final piece which is to be fired. If, however, you want to work more directly and fire the original model, you may build it hollow by using the coil method. Make a small sketch in clay and decide upon the ratio of enlargement needed, then proceed to copy the sketch by building clay walls to conform to its outlines, as shown in Figure 4-4. Take care to weld the coils firmly together. Use clay with a heavy mixture of grog (one part grog to two of clay) and make the walls about ¾ inch thick throughout, slightly thicker if the sculpture is to be over 12 inches high. Walls may be built inside the piece to brace it.

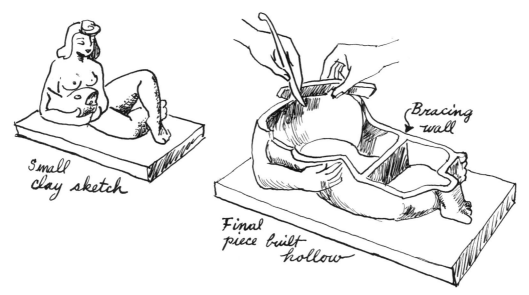

Fig. 4-4 Coil building full-size sculpture: clay sketch is used as a model.

Model the form as the walls grow, referring constantly to the sketch to make sure that proportions are right. A pair of sculptor's proportional calipers will be useful here, but if you don't own such an instrument you may make a fairly good substitute out of two strips of wood of equal length, pointed at the ends and fastened together with a bolt and wing nut to serve as a pivot, as shown in Figure 4-5. If the pivot is placed so that distance AC is one-half of distance CB, then no matter how the

53

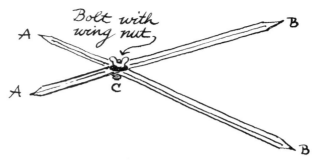

Fig. 4-5   Proportional calipers, homemade.

sticks are moved, the distance between points AA will always be half that between points BB. To enlarge a small sketch to a figure twice as big, measure the length of a portion of the sketch with the small end of the calipers and lay off the corresponding portion in the enlargement with the other end. By changing the position of the pivot, a different ratio of enlargement may be obtained.

But it is not really necessary to work for extreme accuracy when enlarging a clay model. A sketch captures an idea, an inspiration which changes as clay and fingers work together to create a larger form. Thus a sketch and the final product may resemble each other without being identical.

The late Vali Wieseltier, a pioneer in the field of large terra-cotta garden sculpture, used coils to fashion life-sized

Fig. 4-6   Tattooed Ram, coil built, incised
design, 17" x 20", Ann Paul.

Fig. 4-7   Patio Candle Lamp, variation of coil method; small bits of clay with open spaces between, 12″.

Fig. 4-8   Coil-built vase, raku fired in fireplace, 11″.

figures—gay, amusing, filled with spirit and movement. Through an arrangement with a brickyard she was able to do her work at the plant and fire it in a brick kiln.

Ann Paul coil builds her sculpture but does not roll coils. Instead she pounds or rolls her clay into a layer 2 inches thick, then cuts it into strips an inch wide. As she builds and models a form, the strips are melded together to make the shape and the wall becomes an even thickness of about 1 inch. Small coils of clay are pressed into the joints on the inside of the figure as shown in Photo Series 8, step 6.

Artists can modify the process of coil building to suit their own tastes. Coils need not be smoothed together but may retain their original shape. Instead of being built up in a succession of horizontal rings, coils can be arranged so that they form a pattern. (One of the glaze samples in the color section showing a blue glaze over a red body was made this way.) Sometimes, as in the case of patio lamps, open spaces are left between the coils.

Charlie Brown's adaptation of the coil method uses flattened strips of clay about 4 inches long, 2 inches wide, and ¼ inch

55

Fig. 4-9 Charlie Brown at work.

thick. Out of these he fashions thin-walled pots 12 inches or more in height which are amazingly light.

Coil-making equipment

Mechanical extruders for making clay coils and tubes of various shapes and sizes are available. The sculpture in Figure 4-12 by David Silverman shows the use of an extruder.

56

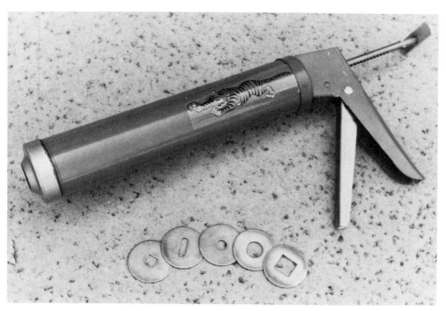

Fig. 4-10 Hand-held coil extruder, Menco.

Fig. 4-11 Clay extruder for coils, tubes,
and slabs; Craftool.

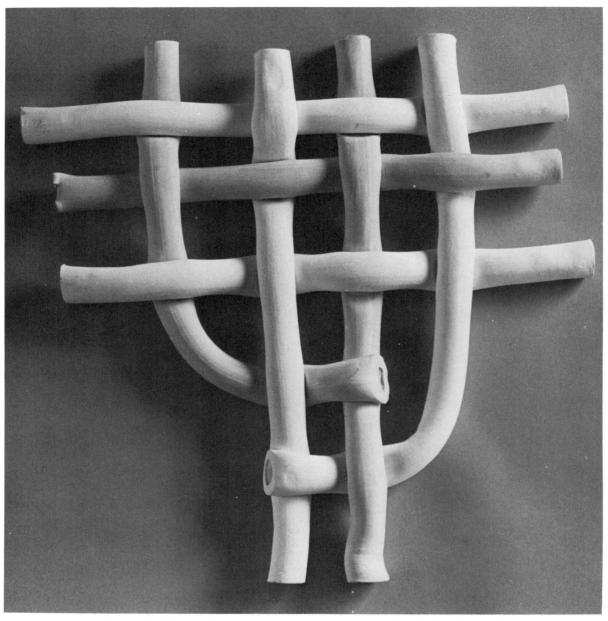

Fig. 4-12   Woven Form, porcelain extruded tubes, 2′ x 2′, by David F. Silverman.

It may be a mistake to try to classify techniques of forming clay because all sorts of combinations of methods are possible. Many ceramists, particularly those who make large abstract sculptural forms, find their work is simplified if they form the clay into slabs and build with these. We'll consider this and other methods in Chapter 5.

Chapter 5　Slab Building

For slab building, clay is rolled or pressed or cut into layers or slabs which are then cut into patterns, folded and joined together to make various ceramic objects. Originally the method was used mainly for rectangular shapes, square vases, boxes, or similar objects, but as potters became interested in the abstract shapes of contemporary art, they found that through combina-

Fig. 5-1　Travelling Nuns, 18″ slab sculpture,
Marguerite Drewry.

59

Fig. 5-2 The General, 14″,
coil and slab built, Lyle
Perkins.

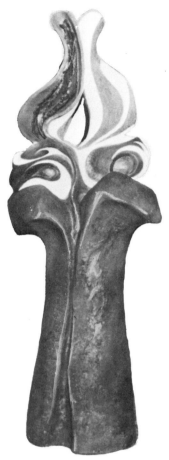

Fig. 5-3 Labyrinth, coil and
slab built, 43″, Marie
Nishimura.

tions of slab and coil building they could create almost any shape imaginable.

We'll begin our exploration of slab building by making a box with a lid.

Building a Box

1. Add some grog to your clay to make it work better, then roll it out using a rolling pin and two strips of wood ⅜ inch thick to serve as guides. Two wooden rulers are good for this purpose. Take a ball of clay the size of a large orange and flatten it into a disk; then place the rul-

60

ers beside it and roll the clay with the rolling pin. Roll from the center out, lifting the layer of clay from time to time. If the clay sticks to the rolling pin, wipe the surface dry and dust it with a little flint or talcum powder. Continue rolling until the rolling pin rides on the two strips of wood. Then you will have an even layer of clay just as thick as the wooden guides.

2. Cut a pattern for the box in one piece, shaped like a cross.

3. With the pattern cut in one piece, the sides will have to be folded up; as a result, the bottom edges will be rounded, not square. There is no allowance for the thickness of the slab, which means that the sides can be firmly squeezed together, making a ridge of excess clay at the corners. The portions to be joined should be roughened and moistened before they are brought together.

4. To make the joints extra secure, roll a thin coil of clay and work it into each inside corner when you squeeze the sides together.

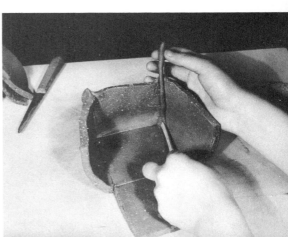

61

5. When all the sides are joined, trim off the excess clay at the corners with a knife. (What if we did not trim the corners? We'd have a different kind of box—maybe one more interesting.)

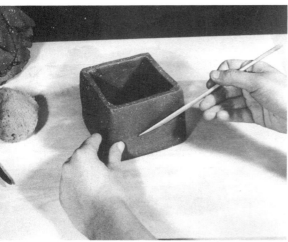

6. The contours of the box will have a soft, claylike quality. The shape will be the result of modeling with your fingers—not cut-and-dried fitting—and that is the way it should be. Finish the surface with a wooden modeling tool.

7. The lid for the box is easy to make. Cut a piece slightly larger than the box.

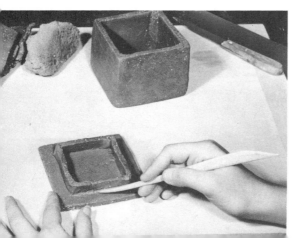

8. Then cut a long strip ½ inch wide for the flange and bend it to shape. Try it in the box for size (make it a little too small rather than too big), and then fasten it on the underside of the lid.

9. Make a knob for the lid by rolling a ball of clay and flattening its sides, then attach it and weld it into place with a modeling tool.

If you prefer, the handle may be made from a strip of clay or from a thin coil bent into a loop. Some suggestions are shown in Figure 5-4. The lid will need support while you are attaching

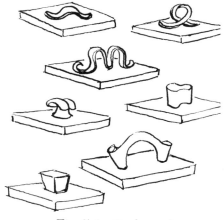

Fig. 5-4   Knobs and
handles.

the handle. Cut a little piece off a plaster slab and place it under the lid inside the flange as shown in Figure 5-5.

Slab-built pieces must be allowed to dry slowly; leave your work in the damp box for a day or two after it is finished, then let

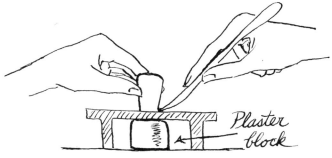

Fig. 5-5   Plaster block supports lid
underneath while pressure is applied to
weld on the handle.

it dry in the room. When the box and the lid are thoroughly dry, see how they fit together and make any necessary adjustment before you fire them. When you put them in the kiln for the bisque fire, have the lid in place. This tends to prevent warping and assures better fit. In the glaze fire, the box and the lid must be put in the kiln separately.

Slab-built pieces lend themselves to gay decoration, majolica, slip painting, or some of the other methods described in Chapter 15.

10. The little box whose progress we have watched had a design trailed on in slip, and was then covered with transparent glaze and fired. The body of red clay makes a pleasing contrast to the white slip design.

11. Note how the grog which was added to the clay to give it better working properties produced an attractive texture in the final piece.

Tall pieces may be made by the slab method if some temporary support is provided to hold the clay until it becomes strong enough to stand by itself. For example, a 1-quart milk carton would help in forming a tall rectangular vase or the base for a lamp. The milk carton would have to be wrapped in several layers of newspaper first so that the clay would not shrink to such an extent in drying that it would crack. The next project is the making of a lamp by a combination of coil and slab building.

Fig. 5-6   Slab-built lamp, 13″,
pierced design.

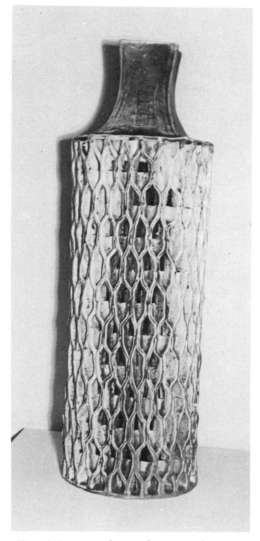

Fig. 5-7   Lamp base of woven clay, 26″,
Boxley-Ramos.

Photo Series 10

Coil and Slab Building a Lamp

1. A box has been wrapped on five sides with newspaper and a layer of clay has been shaped into the form of another rectangular box on top of it. The clay is still moist. Openings to form a pattern have been cut. A drinking straw is used to make perforations.

65

2. A base for the lamp was made out of coils welded together, but not smoothed on the outside. (A paper cup wrapped in paper toweling served as a temporary support.) Here the base is attached to the body of the lamp. Since considerable pressure must be exerted to make sure that the base adheres, a milk carton covered with newspaper serves as a temporary support inside the body of the lamp. A spirit level is used to check the accuracy of the attachment of the base. The notch cut in the back rim of the base is for the electric cord.

3. The finished lamp in use. A socket for the light bulb was inserted where the base is attached to the body and a piece of fiberglass has been set inside the body of the lamp. The fiberglass diffuses the light.

A lamp of this type lights up an area of wall in back of the lamp (indirect light) and also gives an interesting pattern in light on the front and sides.

Embossing Dies and Rollers

Roll a coil of clay about 1 inch in diameter; cut a section 2 inches long and incise a design on one end. When the clay hardens (or has been bisque fired) it becomes a stamping die which, when pressed into plastic clay, will produce the design in relief.

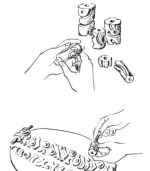

Embossing rollers can be made from a coil of clay about 2 inches in diameter, cut into sections of varying lengths and pierced longitudinally by a drinking straw. After bisque firing, an axle of coat-hanger wire or a narrow paint brush provides a handle for rolling. In the next two projects we shall see how embossing dies and rollers are used.

Making a Fruit Dish

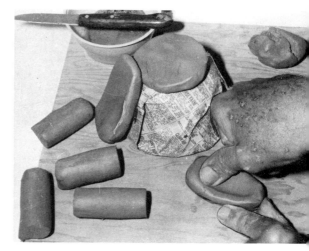

1. An empty cottage cheese box has been covered with newspaper to serve as a drape mold. A coil of clay has been rolled, then cut into pieces about 4½ inches long. A ball of clay rolled and flattened has been placed on top of the mold. Sections of the coil are flattened, shaped, and laid on the side of the mold in such a manner that they can be welded firmly against the clay circle.

2. Flattened coils are added to the construction until the whole surface is covered.

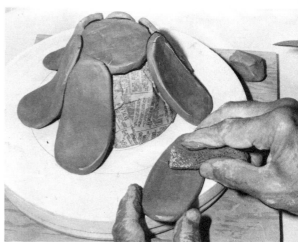

67

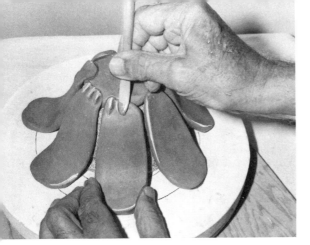

3. The side slabs are welded firmly into the circle. Note that space has been left between the slabs.

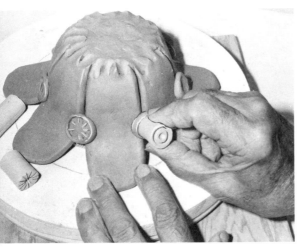

4. Small balls of clay have been pressed over the openings between each pair of slabs. These are now being pressed firmly into place with an embossing die.

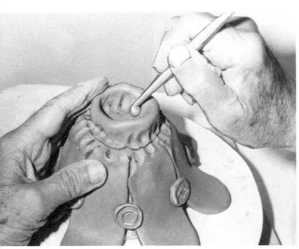

5. Attaching the base using a series of coils. Here the first one is being welded firmly into position.

6. Pressing a design as the final coil is welded onto the base.

7. The completed fruit bowl in use after firing and glazing.

Modeling a Wall Planter

1. An embossing roller is used to make a design in a slab of clay which forms the pocket for the planter. A long-handled paintbrush serves as an axle. (A better axle could be made out of coat-hanger wire.)

2. The embossed layer is folded over a pad to form a pocket. The padding was made of crumpled newspaper covered with paper towels and stuffed into a plastic bag.

69

3. Corners of the pocket have been pressed together; thumbprints remain. Top edge of the pocket is formed.

4. Stamping dies have been pressed into the thumbprints along the pocket sides. Holes for hanging the planter on the wall are punched with the metal cap of a breath freshener. This completes the construction.

Fig. 5-8 Vases, roller-embossed slabs, 15″, Anne Kraus.

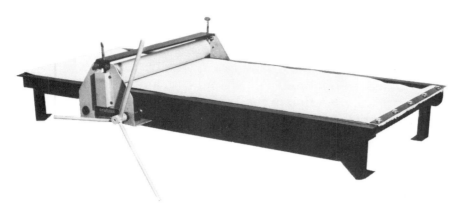

Fig. 5-9   Slab roller, Craftool.

Slab Rollers

Potters who do a great deal of slab building find it convenient to have mechanical slab rollers (Fig. 5-9). Some ingenious ceramists have built their own, but rollers can be bought from manufacturers. They are adjustable for rolling slabs of varying thicknesses. Heavy burlap on the roller bed gives slabs an interesting texture.

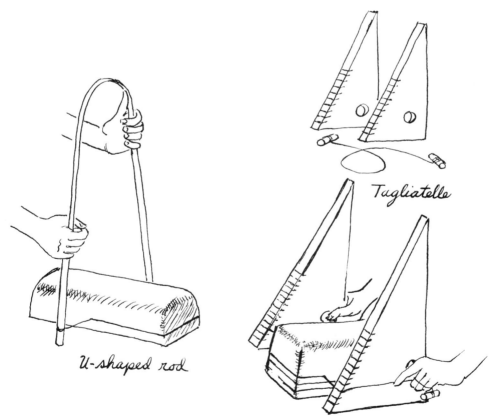

Tagliatelle

U-shaped rod

Fig. 5-10   U-shaped rod and tagliatelle: instruments used to cut, rather than roll, slabs of suitable thickness.

71

Slab Cutting

Some potters prefer to cut slabs rather than roll them; they find that fewer tensions are set up in the clay this way. A steel reinforcing rod bent into a U- shape, with a piano wire fastened across the open portion of the U 1 inch from the ends of the bar, can be used to cut layers of clay 1 inch thick as shown in Figure 5-10. A large mass of clay thoroughly wedged is pounded into a block. Then the wire is drawn through it, with the ends of the rod touching the table. The top portion of the clay is lifted off, leaving a clay slab 1 inch thick. The process is repeated until all the clay has been sliced into slabs. The slabs may be piled one on top of another with sheets of plastic in between until the potter is ready to use them.

Potters in Italy use a device called a *tagliatelle* for cutting layers of clay (Fig. 5-10).

Slab Pressing

A device like the one shown in Figure 5-11 can be used for pressing clay slabs. The clay is pounded into the space between the guide strips, then a board is drawn along the top, resting on the guides, to make a slab. A knife loosens the sides of the slab from the guide strips. The removable piece of canvas makes it possible to lift the slab with ease.

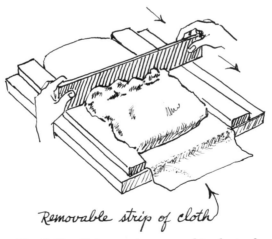

Removable strip of cloth

Fig. 5-11 Slabs can be pressed to desired thickness, an alternative to rolling or cutting.

Slab Building Tall Cylinders

Steven Kemenyffy, creator of "Black Presence #1" (Fig. 5-13), uses a bedsheet to help him form tall cylinders. Slabs are thrown onto the sheet, crumpled newspaper is prepared as a cushion or stuffing, the sides of the sheet are brought together so that the clay becomes a cylinder with the paper inside.

72

Fig. 5-12   Black Angel Captured, 19″, Pat Casad.

The construction is cradled in an aluminum stovepipe until the clay becomes leather hard. Then it is raised to a vertical position, the stovepipe is lifted off, the sheet is removed, and clay wings are attached. The pieces in this series are sprayed with soluble glaze, then fired once to cone 10. The end result resembles salt glazing.

Reinforcing Clay Slabs

Cheesecloth or burlap

Large slab-built clay constructions are apt to crack or come apart at the joints during the drying period. To guard against this danger, cloth of open weave such as cheesecloth or burlap can be used as a reinforcement. The clay must be worked into the cloth so that it is thoroughly embedded. This increases the strength of unfired pieces considerably. The cloth burns out during the firing, leaving voids which weaken the piece to some extent, usually not enough to be serious.

73

Fig. 5-13   Black Presence #1, 6′ by Steven
Kemenyffy; permanent collection, University
of Notre Dame.

Fig. 5-14   Slab Sculpture, 38″ x 24″ x 15″,
Irene Batt; collection of Dr. and Mrs. Robert
Cornfield.

Fig. 5-15   Guardian, 6′, ceramic with fiberglass by Daniel
Rhodes; Huntington Gallery, Huntington, West Virginia.

Slip-impregnated cloth

A strip of cheesecloth or burlap, or a strip of fiberglass, dipped into a thick deflocculated slip will form a thin layer of clay. Several such layers combined will make a slab suitable for slab building. (Deflocculation is described in Ch. 9.)

Fiberglass

Daniel Rhodes, known for his large slab-built sculpture, pioneered in the use of fiberglass cloth as reinforcement for clay slabs. Fiberglass does not burn out during the firing, but melts and actually increases the strength of the final piece.

Plaques

Plaques made of clay are used in interior decor as well as on the outsides of buildings. Potters who make plaques report that reinforcing with fiberglass reduces warping.

Fig. 5-16   Zocolo, sketch for a mural, Boxley-Ramos, 31″ x 28″.

Fig. 5-17 Karakul Sheep, tile, Marguerite Wildenhain; collection,
Luther College.

Fig. 5-18 Mock-up for large fountain, exposed terra cotta, cone 6, 12″ x 18″,
Charlene deJori.

Fig. 5-19 Harbor, Betsy Stoinoff.

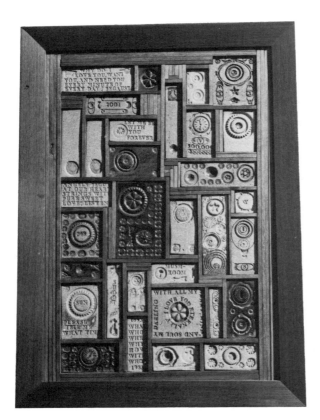

Fig. 5-20 Assemblage, plaque
by Gig Greenwood.

78

Fountain, by the author

Concerto, Franconeri Lo Scricciolo.

Wizzard, by Marie Nishimura.

Mushroom Fountain, by Lee Magdanz.

Bull, by Armand Henault. Photo courtesy Community Gallery, Hanover, New Hampshire.

Birth of a Nation, discussing how they'll feed themselves; by Warren Angle.

Fig. 5-21　Hand-textured mural, Lee Rosen; reception area of Oliver Tyrone Building, Pittsburgh.

"Zocolo," the sketch by Boxley-Ramos in Figure 5-16, became a large ceramic mural in a bank. The word *zocolo* means the town square or center of a city in Spanish.

The amusing panel "Harbor" by Betsy Stoinoff (Fig. 5-19) is made of a number of small slabs cut, textured, colored, fired, then glued to a piece of driftwood.

The ingenious decorative plaque by Gig Greenwood shown in Figure 5-20 is an assemblage of clay slabs with designs pressed in with oddments of type, matrixes, bits of hardware, showerheads, and keyholes.

The hand-textured mural in Figure 5-21 by Lee Rosen is made of slabs rolled in her factory. The mural uses flaps of clay plus a strong linear texture which moves throughout the wall.

Principles of Slab Design

What is good design in pottery? That's a difficult question; so much depends upon taste. We know that tastes change in cultures as well as in individuals. Some things made and admired a century or so ago have, a generation later, lost popularity and been discarded, only to regain favor and once more be treas-

79

Fig. 5-22 Tree Pot, 20″, Tommy
Thurmond; Delta State College Art
Department, Cleveland, Mississippi.

Fig. 5-23 Nature as Designer: Poppy Seedpods, patio lamps by Ann Paul.

ured. Despite the fact that people are fickle in their tastes, there are a few guiding principles which remain unchanged.

Well-designed pottery shows how it is made and what it is made of. Ware, though hardened by fire, should still suggest the plastic quality of clay.

Not all pottery is functional. But that which is must be designed to serve its purpose well.

Embellishment must enhance form—not conceal it.

As one grows in experience, artistic judgment grows also. A potter must not hesitate to use a hammer on any pieces which no longer seem good. (Some call the hammer a potter's best friend.)

Be yourself. If you prefer the more enduring classical shapes, make them. If you prefer the exciting, explosive styles of the ultra modern trend, make your pottery that way.

Whatever you do, be honest! Clay is quick to reveal insincerity.

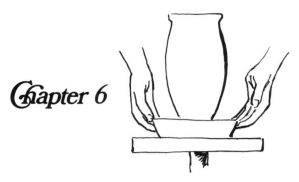

Chapter 6

The Potter's Wheel

When a potter works or "throws" on his wheel there is magic in his touch. The clay comes to life in his hands as it rises from shapeless mass to forms of grace and elegance.

There is some doubt about the origin of the term *throwing*. Most potters believe that it comes from the first step in the process—throwing a lump of clay forcefully onto the wheel head. Some scholars, however, maintain that it is a variation of an old English word *thrawan*, meaning to twist. This does seem a likely explanation.

The potter's wheel is probably one of the first machines ever invented. We know that it existed 4000 years ago, for there are pictures of Egyptian potters of that period using it.

For many centuries the wheel was the potter's true love, one might say his only love. With it he made beautiful symmetrical, classic shapes not obtainable in any other way. Today, however, with great interest in contemporary art movements and a heightened appreciation of abstract art forms, more and more potters use slab building and other hand forming processes in addition to throwing on the wheel. When they do work on the wheel the shapes of their pieces are usually altered, distorted in some way, paddled, even deliberately thrown off-center. As we shall see later in this chapter, some potters use the wheel to produce sculpture.

No matter what kind of work you plan to do, some experience on the wheel will help you to learn more about clay, and that is important.

82

Fig. 6-1   Kick wheel, Craftool.

Foot-Operated Wheels

There are several different types of wheels. With a kick wheel the potter kicks a heavy horizontal disk connected by a shaft to a wheel head (Figs. 6-1 through 6-3). Once he gets it going,

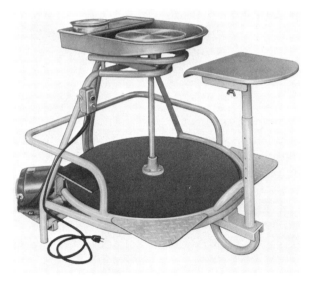

Fig. 6-2   Kick wheel, Amaco; separate motor assembly available, furnished with flat or recessed wheel head.

83

Fig. 6-3   Kick wheel, Randall, motor attachment available.

Kick Wheel

Treadle Wheel

momentum keeps the wheel turning for a minute or so, after which he must kick it again.

In other types, the potter moves a treadle back and forth with his foot, operating a crank on a shaft and so turning the wheel head. This type allows full coordination of hands and feet with the speed of the wheel always under control.

Electric Wheels

There are many different types of electric wheels on the market built in a wide variety of designs (Figs. 6-4 through 6-6). Before considering the purchase of one, learn as much about wheels as you can. If you are in a class you will, of course, have an opportunity to try out a number of wheels there. If not, make a point of visiting such a class for a bit of advice. Consult the advertising pages of such magazines as "Ceramics Monthly" or "Craft Horizons" and write to manufacturers of wheels for their catalogs.

You will find that there is little agreement among potters as to which types of wheel are best. As a rule, a potter likes best the kind of wheel on which he learned to throw. Better put off buying a wheel until you have had an opportunity to try several.

84

Fig. 6-4 Electric wheel, 13″ wheel head, variable speed with foot control, Max Corporation; can be furnished with drilled wheel heads and pins to hold bats.

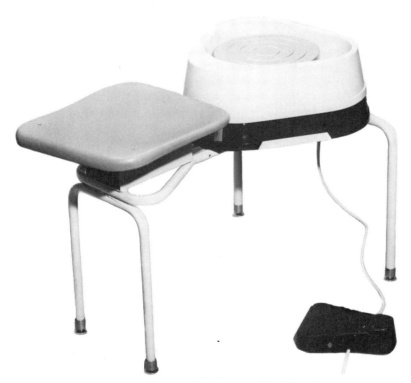

Fig. 6-5 Electric wheel, 10″ wheel head, variable speed, foot control, Craftool.

Fig. 6-6 Shimpo wheel; courtesy Westwood Ceramic Supply Company.

Wheel Heads

Most potter's wheels have flat heads, usually of metal though sometimes of wood, on which ware may be thrown directly or on which plaster bats can be fastened to receive the clay. Work thrown directly on the wheel head must be cut free with a wire and lifted off, a difficult trick to do without spoiling the shape. (Dealers sell pairs of stainless steel pottery lifters which make lifting a wet piece off the wheel much simpler.) Throwing on a plaster bat makes it possible to lift the ware by lifting the bat.

Some wheels have a recessed type of head, that is, a head with a depression to hold specially shaped bats. With this type of head one can take work off the wheel and put it back on again with the work still attached and still centered. Some manufacturers furnish wheels with either flat or recessed heads. With the latter they supply casting rings for casting plaster bats to fit the wheel head.

Tools for Throwing

Provide yourself with a bowl of water large enough to dip your whole hand into; a sponge, elephant's ear, if possible; a potter's knife; a wooden modeling tool; a rubber or wooden rib;

86

a stick sponge—a small piece of sponge tied to the end of a stick; a scraping tool; and a pricker. The pricker is a tool you will make for yourself by driving a needle into the end of a small stick of wood so that ¾ inch of the needle remains exposed. This will be useful in measuring the thickness of the wall or the bottom of a piece and it will come in handy for trimming the top edge. Have these tools within easy reach.

Using the Wheel

Preparing the clay

Wedge the clay thoroughly; otherwise you will have trouble. A tiny air bubble can ruin your work and any hard lumps will throw it out of true. Wedge at least twenty times, and do not stop then unless the portion of your clay which is cut by the wire looks smooth, even, and clean. Prepare five or six balls of clay, each as big as a baseball. Pat each ball of clay until it is round, with no cracks or folds in the surface.

Centering

If your wheel has a recessed head, set the bat in place; if it has a flat head, put a plaster bat in the center and fasten it in place with wads of clay—*keys*. Wet the clay keys and press them firmly against the bat and the wheel head, then start the wheel turning counterclockwise. Moisten the bat slightly and throw a ball of clay briskly onto the center of the bat as it turns. (For some reason, throwing the clay onto the wheel while it is in motion makes it hold better.)

Wet your hands and wet the clay. Brace your left arm firmly against the frame of the wheel or against your body and push the heel of your left hand against the side of the clay. Put your right hand on the other side of the ball, opposite your left, and pull the clay toward you while your left hand pushes against it. Keep the wheel turning rapidly during this operation and moisten the clay from time to time by squeezing the sponge over it.

The heel of your left hand does most of the centering, so keep the left arm firmly braced. Grasp the clay in both hands, with the thumbs resting on top, and press it into a cone-shaped mound. This mound must be absolutely true, with no bumps or irregularities. You will know by the feel when the clay is centered. When it is, remove your hands gently. The mound of clay should now look as though it were standing still even when it is turning.

Some potters like to work the clay up and down at this stage by grasping the mound in both hands and pressing toward the center as the wheel turns. This forces the clay to rise into a

87

Fig. 6-7   Working clay up and down.

taller, thinner cone. The heel of the left hand is then pressed down on top, pushing the mound back into its original shape. Doing this two or three times improves the texture of the clay. Beware, however, of getting the clay too soft.

Perfect centering is essential for all work on the wheel, so practice it until you have mastered it. If you are using a kick wheel, practice so that the motion of your leg will not interfere with your hands. Feet, hands, and body must all work together. We will go through the steps of opening a ball of clay and raising the wall to form a cylinder in Photo Series 14, after watching a potter at work on the wheel, throwing a vase.

Learning how to throw

Facility on the potter's wheel requires practice, practice, and more practice—and you must have help from someone who knows how. Whenever you have the chance, watch a potter working at his wheel. Note how he holds his hands, how he controls the clay and shapes it to his will. Let's watch right now as Lyle Perkins gives a demonstration.

Photo Series 13

Throwing a Vase

1. The potter has set the bat in place in the wheel head. In his hand, he has a ball of clay, thoroughly wedged and ready for throwing. He will toss this onto the center of the bat after he has started the wheel.

88

2. Centering. The potter's elbows are pressed firmly against his body. His hands have been dipped in water and he holds them against the clay, forcing it into the shape of a truncated cone. His thumbs ride on top.

3. Opening. The thumbs press downward to make a depression in the top of the clay.

4. The potter's left hand is held against the outside of the clay while the fingers of his right hand push down in the center, enlarging the opening made by his thumbs. His right hand is braced against the left.

The soupy clay that sticks to his hands is *slurry*.

5. Raising the cylinder. The knuckle of the right index finger presses against the outside of the clay while the left index finger pushes outward against the inside of the clay wall. Note how the left thumb is braced against the right hand

89

so that the two index fingers will be kept an even distance apart. Starting at the bottom, the potter will bring his two hands straight up, shaping the clay into a cylinder.

6. The cylinder has been raised. The potter's hands have moved up, squeezing the clay into a wall of even thickness.

7. Shaping. The left hand presses from the inside while the right hand shapes the outside.

8. The shaping is finished. Using a scraper, the potter cuts away excess clay from the base of the vase. After this step, the bat with the vase attached will be put in a damp box overnight.

9. Next day. Before returning the piece to the wheel, a circle was drawn by holding a pencil against the bat as the wheel turned.

The potter fastens the piece upside down on the bat, centering it in the circle. Three keys of clay will hold the piece firmly on the bat while he uses the loop tool shown to finish the base and the foot.

10. Turning the foot. The potter's hands rest on a turning stick (described in this chapter, under *Turning*). Using the loop tool, he cuts away excess clay from the foot and makes a depression in the bottom of the piece so that it will stand on a raised ring.

11. The piece is finished. The potter will now put it aside to dry for two or three days, after which it will be ready to fire.

Now let's practice!

Photo Series 14

Centering a Cylinder

1. Opening. When the ball is centered, press downward with the thumbs to make a depression in the top.

91

2. Then brace the left hand against the mound of clay and, resting the right hand on the left, press the fingers of the right hand down on the middle of the mound to enlarge the opening.

3. The opening should go down far enough to leave a ¾ inch thickness at the bottom of the piece. Don't go too far. Until you are able to judge, use the pricker as a gauge to measure the thickness of the bottom. Plunge the needle directly downward; if the wood goes into the clay, you will know that the base is too thick by that amount. The hole made by the needle will close up as you continue working.

4. The clay is now shaped like a low, squat bowl with a thick wall. Let this wall turn in your hands for a minute or two, your left hand on the outside and the fingers of your right hand on the inside. Feel it as it turns, smooth and true.

5. Pulling up. Next raise the wall to form a cylinder. The wheel should turn a little more slowly for this operation. Put your right hand on the outside of the piece and your left hand on the inside, with the thumb of the left hand braced against the right wrist.

92

6. Then, pressing the clay between the index finger of your left hand and the first knuckle of your right, bring your hands straight up. Your left thumb, braced against the right wrist, will help you keep your hands the same distance apart so that the wall of the cylinder will be even in thickness.

7. Repeat this process two or three times, each time making the wall thinner and higher. Use enough water to keep the work lubricated, but do not use any more than is necessary; if you do, the walls will weaken and slump. From time to time remove the water which collects on the inside of the piece with the stick sponge.

8. Keep the piece cylindrical. The top will have a tendency to become wider and turn the cylinder into a bowl, but don't let this happen. Using both hands, pull the top together to keep it the same width as the base. Try to make the cylinder 6 inches tall (taller, if possible). You should be able to pull it up to the proper height in three or four pullings. If you work on it too long, the piece will collapse.

9. Trimming the top. The top edge of your cylinder will probably be uneven, so it will be necessary to trim off a narrow strip. The pricker is the best tool for this, although you can use a knife. Brace both hands in position and hold the left index finger against the inside of the rim

93

while you press the point of the pricker or the knife blade toward it from the outside.

10. Keep the wheel turning at a moderate speed and press the point in slowly until it goes all the way through; then raise both hands quickly and lift up the strip of clay which has been cut off.

The top of the cylinder will now be perfectly level but slightly rough. Moisten the fingers and hold them against it to smooth it. Then clean excess clay off the bat as shown in Photo Series 13, step 8.

The finished cylinder

Let's see what you have accomplished. Measure the height of the cylinder. Were you able to raise it to six inches? Good! Eight inches? Excellent! More than eight? You're an old hand and ought not to be reading this chapter at all!

11. Now put your knife on the top edge and cut straight down to the bottom. Then do the same thing on the opposite side.

12. Cut through the base and remove one-half of the cylinder, so that you can look at the cross section. (It will take courage to do this, but remember this cylinder was practice—you did not intend to keep it anyway.) Is the wall even in thickness, only slightly heavier at the bottom? Is it free from thin spots? This inspection will tell you what to work for next time.

94

Don't be discouraged by your first results. Throwing on the wheel sounds a lot simpler than it is. The ease with which a potter does it is highly deceptive, but as you practice your skill will increase. Don't save any of your first attempts. Keep on throwing cylinders and cutting them in half until you are able to make one 9 inches high, with walls no thicker than ⅜ inch throughout.

Shaping

When you are able to throw a cylinder, you are ready to begin forming special shapes. Most pieces made on the wheel, with the exception of plates and shallow bowls, start out as cylinders, for this form can be easily modified.

To make a vase with a narrow neck, throw a cylinder and raise it to full height. Then, pressing on the inside with the left hand and supporting the outside with the right, bring the wall out to the contour you desire. Finish the lower portion before you bring in the neck, because afterward it will be impossible to get your hand inside the piece.

Photo Series 15

Forming a Narrow-Necked Vase

1. When the lower portion is finished, grasp the top of the cylinder in both hands and, using a gentle even pressure, reduce the size of the opening.

2. Then with the fingers of the left hand supporting the inside, press in with your right hand until the desired shape is obtained.

95

3. Reinforcing the rim. Thrown pieces are less apt to warp during the firing if they are slightly reinforced at the rim. Fold over a small portion of the top so that it makes a thicker rim at that point.

Bowls and Plates

To throw a bowl or a plate, you do not need to form a cylinder. Center the clay and open it as usual; then, instead of bringing the wall straight up, start to make a bowl shape by widening the opening, bringing the walls upward and outward at the same time. Let's watch Lyle Perkins again while he throws a large bowl.

Throwing a Large Bowl

1. The potter uses the heel of his right hand to enlarge the opening and force the wall outward. His left hand supports the clay on the outside. Note how the fingers of the two hands are locked together.

2. Bringing up the wall. The potter makes the bowl wider and taller by pressing the clay between the fingers of both hands.

3. The wall is brought to full height.

4. Shaping the foot. The index finger of the right hand presses in from the outside. Note how the left thumb rides on the rim.

5. Removing excess water with a sponge.

6. Smoothing the inside with a kidney-shaped rubber rib.

97

7. Shaping the rim with a sponge.

8. The throwing is finished. The potter lifts the bat out of the wheel head and puts the bowl aside to dry. Later he will turn it over and finish the foot.

Pitchers

Forms

To make a pitcher, throw the body exactly as you would a vase, allowing a little extra thickness at the top rim. Shape the spout by supporting the rim with the first two fingers of the left hand, at the same time pulling the top rim outward with the index finger of the right hand until a spout is formed. The clay will need to be coaxed during this step. If you do not handle it gently the rim will crack. Keep the fingers wet.

Spouts

Making a spout which will pour well is a challenge to the potter. It is annoying to have a cream pitcher which drips every time it is used. To keep liquids from running down the side, the spout must be made with a sharp curve downward, as shown in Photo Series 17 and the edge of the lip should be quite sharp so that there will be no place for a drop to hang on when you stop pouring.

Handles

Handles for thrown pieces may be rolled, as shown in Photo Series 8, or pulled.

Pulled handles are made by grasping a longish lump of clay in the left hand, so that one end protrudes, and pulling the exposed end with the right hand. Pulling is not exactly the word to describe this operation, for the action is similar to milking a cow. The clay is coaxed into shape by squeezing and pulling simultaneously, a process which must be repeated a dozen or more times. The right hand must be kept wet.

When the clay is drawn out thin enough for a handle, it will be quite pliable; if the left hand is turned, the clay will bend into a loop of its own weight. It can be set aside to harden for two or three hours, after which a portion of the loop suitable for a handle can be cut off and attached.

This process is not easy; it will take practice. But once you have mastered it, you will be able to make handles in full harmony with your thrown ware. When clay takes shape through its own bending action, the result is more pleasing than anything accomplished by pressing or rolling. A handle which looks as if it had been worked over laboriously spoils the appearance of a thrown piece.

Handles look better when they are not perfectly round in cross section, but rather flattened; they are more pleasing when not uniform in thickness throughout the entire length. Remember, too, that handles must be grasped by hands, so allow room for the fingers and a place for the thumb. Practice making lots of handles before you actually fire one.

Photo Series 17

Making a Pitcher

1. The centering and the opening have been completed. The potter is bringing up the wall to form a cylinder.

2. Both hands press gently when narrowing the top.

3. Reinforcing the edge by folding over a small portion of the top to make a thicker rim.

4. Making ridges in the neck with the fingernail while the left hand provides support from inside.

5. Starting to pull the handle.

100

6. Pulling the handle.

7. Turning the left hand so that the clay bends of its own weight.

8. Forming the spout. The first two fingers of the left hand press against the outside while the right index finger pulls the clay out between them. Meanwhile the handle is drying.

9. The spout is finished. The potter cuts off a piece of the loop to use for the handle.

10. Attaching the handle. It is then welded firmly into place at each end.

11. The finished pitcher. The potter lifts the bat out of the wheel head and puts the pitcher aside for a while.

12. The potter has put the pitcher back on the wheel upside down and has turned the foot. With a brush he applies a layer of colored engobe to the lower portion.

13. Slip trailing a decorative band (this process is described in Ch. 15). We shall see the firing of the pitcher in Ch. 12.

102

Teapots

Here is where the potter meets a real challenge to his skill. Throwing a teapot presents technical problems which call for expert craftsmanship, but at the same time the potter has much freedom in his choice of design. If he is an artist as well as a craftsman, he can create something truly original, graceful, light, easy to hold and to pour. It's a big order.

Forms

The body of a teapot is thrown in the same manner as a vase. First a cylinder is formed, then shaped. Then it is brought in at the top to form a seat for the lid. Care must be taken to make the wall thin enough and even throughout, and to finish the outer surface in its final form; after spout and handle are attached, no changes are possible

There are two ways in which the lid may fit (Fig. 6-8). Whichever is chosen, the seat at the neck of the pot must be made accurately. Use a straight piece of wood with a square end in shaping it, as shown in Figure 6-8.

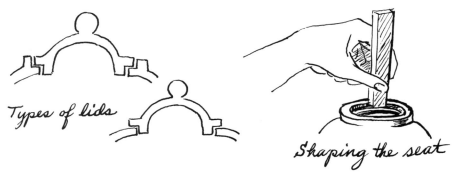

Types of lids

Shaping the seat

Fig. 6-8   Using a block of wood to shape a seat in the teapot for the appropriate type of lid.

Spouts

To make a spout, take a ball of clay, center it, and open it as if you were going to make a cylinder. Instead of bringing the walls straight up, draw them upward and inward until you have formed a cone-shaped tube. Be careful not to make the opening too small. Use a wooden tool, as shown in Figure 6-9, to smooth the inner surface of the tube and make the opening the right size. Allow this tube to harden for an hour or two, then cut off a piece of the proper length for the spout.

It is good to roll some coils of clay first and roughly shape a number of spouts from them. By holding these against the body of the pot you will get a good idea of proper size and placement.

When you have decided on the position, mark it and cut a
103

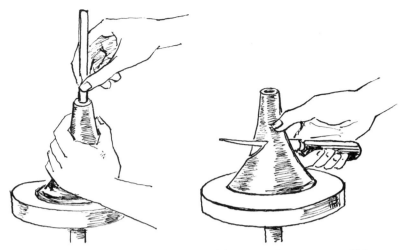

Fig. 6-9   Smoothing the inside of the cone, then cutting off the portion to be used as a spout.

hole equal to the opening of the spout, leaving a rim to which the spout may be fastened with slurry.

Take care not to mar the surface of the pot when you attach the spout. Better let the pot and the spout harden for an hour or two before putting them together. Weld the joint carefully, using a long modeling tool with a ball-shaped end to close the seam on the inside as shown in Figure 6-10.

Fig. 6-10   Welding the inside seam where the spout joins the pot form.

Be sure that the top of the spout is higher then the top of the pot; otherwise the tea will spill out when the pot is filled (Fig. 6-11).

Fig. 6-11   The top of the spout should be higher than the opening of the pot.

104

Handles

The handle for the teapot may be made in the same manner as the handle for the pitcher, either rolled or pulled.

Some people prefer the bail type of handle, made out of a piece of split bamboo and fastened to two clay loops on the pot. If you want to make the handle this way, roll two small coils of clay and fasten them to the shoulder as shown in Figure 6-12.

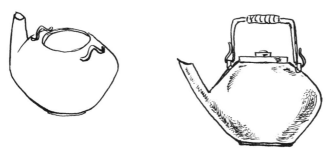

Fig. 6-12   Attach coils of clay to the pot for holding a bail handle.

Lids

The lid for a teapot presents a special problem because both the top and the bottom must be shaped. It may be thrown right side up or upside down: in either case, it will need turning after it is leather hard to form the other side. If it is thrown right side up, its shape and that of the knob may be formed in the plastic clay and the turning limited to forming the underside of the flange where appearance is not so important. Usually better design results this way. Throw the lid as a solid, as shown in Figure 6-13.

Fig. 6-13   If the lid is thrown solid, right side up, tools are used to shape underside.

Use calipers to get the size of the flange equal to the size of the opening in the teapot. Allow the solid lid to become leather hard, then set it in a clay cradle; center it carefully. The inside of the flange and the inner portion of the lid can then be cut with turning tools.

105

If the lid is thrown upside down, the flange may be formed and finished with a rib. In this case the lid will have to be finished without a knob. After it is leather hard some kind of coil or rolled knob may be attached.

Before the teapot is fired, make sure that the lid fits properly. When both pot and lid are bone dry, put the lid in place and twist it carefully, thus grinding it to a perfect fit. Remember that the glaze will add thickness; hence, the lid should be rather loose in the raw state. When the teapot is put into the kiln for its first firing, the lid should be in place.

As a final step before firing, make a small hole with the pricker in the lid. (When the pot is glazed, make sure the hole remains open.) This makes it possible to pour tea smoothly without bubbling and spitting.

Surface Treatment

Much of the charm of thrown ware is due to the marks of the potter's fingers on the finished piece. At times you will want smooth surfaces, and it will be necessary to remove the ridges with a rib (Fig. 6-14). The rib is a piece of wood, either straight or curved, which is held against the side of the piece as the wheel turns. A kidney-shaped piece of rubber or small piece of leather is suitable also.

Fig. 6-14 Using a rib to smooth the exterior of a thrown form.

A tool with a round head held against the piece will make a groove, while a stick with a depression in the end will produce a raised bead, as shown in Figure 6-15. It is easy to make such a tool by notching the end of a thin, flat piece of wood with a round file. A tongue depressor is excellent for this purpose.

106

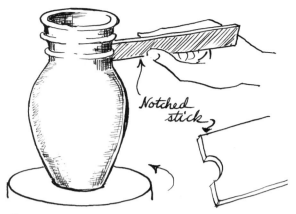

Fig. 6-15   A notched stick can be used to form a
raised bead for decoration.

Turning

Before a thrown piece is fired, it may need to be trimmed slightly. Extra-thick portions of the wall may need to be thinned. If a rimmed foot is desired, this must be cut as shown in Photo Series 13 step 10.

A turning stick like the one shown in Figure 6-16 is a help in turning. You can make one out of a broomstick about 3 feet long. Put a spike in one end and a flat piece of wood about 3 by 5 inches on the other. In use the spike is driven into a wooden board erected for that purpose in back of the wheel, and the other end is braced against the chest. The hand can then rest on the stick.

A piece is ready for turning when shavings can be cut off in long curls. If the piece is still sticky, it is too wet. If the clay cut off by the cutting tool is a powder, it is too dry. If you leave a

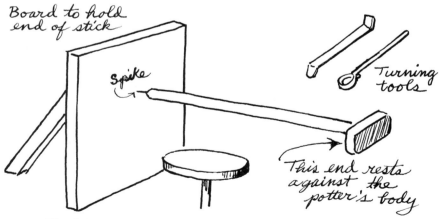

Fig. 6-16   A turning stick to use in trimming can be made by
the potter.

piece covered with a plastic bag for a day after it has been thrown, it will be just right for turning.

It is difficult to fasten a piece to the wheel upside down if it has a delicate top edge. A vase with a narrow neck will need a cradle of soft clay to support it. A sheet of thin plastic between the piece and the cradle will keep them from sticking together. A vase with a long thin neck can be set into a plaster cylinder that serves as a chuck while the base is trimmed and a foot is cut.

Flat bases

A majority of potters today leave their thrown pieces with flat bottoms so that all the trimming of the foot can be done with a wooden rib or a scraper while the piece is still on the wheel. This not only saves the work of cutting a foot rim but simplifies stacking in the kiln.

Often, thrown pieces need no turning at all. On those that require it, don't do too much. Rely upon your fingers to form your pieces, rather than cutting tools, thus you will be better able to preserve the beautiful plastic quality so vital in thrown ware.

Fig. 6-17   Bob Sharpe joins two thrown pots.

108

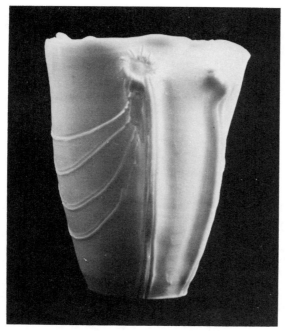

Fig. 6-18   Vase of translucent porcelain, thrown
and incised, 9 " x 5", Rudy Staffel.

A Different Approach

When you have mastered the techniques of throwing you can
adopt a freer approach to the wheel, using it to create forms of
imagination or whimsy, completely outside of the classic tradition. Thrown shapes can be combined in many ways (the teapot
was an example of this); two large pots can be combined to
make one twice as tall (Fig. 6-17); thrown pieces can be joined
in clusters.

Norman Smith (see Ch. 16), a craftsman who throws several
hundred pots of similar shape in a day, varies his routine now
and then to make a few piggy banks out of jugs just for the fun of

Fig. 6-19   Pig Bank, Norman Smith.

109

Fig. 6-20 Covered Jar by Lee Shank, 18″ diameter, stoneware with mishima decoration; photo by John Charles Hutchins.

it (Fig. 6-19). Other potters with a sense of humor use their wheels to create amusing animals, birds, turtles (Fig. 6-21).

Wheel-thrown pots can be paddled into rectangular forms; they can be textured.

All the methods described in Chapter 2 for embellishing slab ware can be used on thrown ware as well. Pieces can be incised,

Fig. 6-21 Tortoise by Dorothy Shank, 6½″, stoneware with mishima decoration; photo by John Charles Hutchins.

110

Fired samples of glazes with various coloring oxides. (Numbers refer to recipes in Ch. 15.)

Top row, left to right:
    Glaze No. 1 with manganese carbonate.
    Glaze No. 11, mirror black.
    Mottled effect obtained by putting glaze No. 2 over brown luster glaze No. 12.
    Glaze No. 1 with chromium oxide.
    Glaze No. 3 with red iron oxide.

Middle row, left to right:
    Glaze No. 1 with cobalt oxide over a red clay body.
    Glaze No. 1 with cobalt oxide over a white clay body.
    Glaze No. 2 with cobalt oxide over a red clay body.
    Glaze No. 4 over a red clay body.
    Glaze No. 2 with antimony oxide.

Bottom row, left to right:
    Glaze No. 1 with pink oxide over a white clay body.
    Glaze No. 1 with copper oxide over a red clay body.
    Glaze No. 17, rutile with copper oxide over a red clay body.
    Glaze No. 15, borosilicate with copper oxide.
    Glaze No. 14, alkaline with copper oxide.

Opposite page, top:
>Sunfaces #1. All cone 8, reduction fire.

Top row, left to right:
>Local clay slip on brown body, glazed with No. 24 + CuO.
>White body, glaze No. 22 + Fe_2O_3 and CuO.
>Effect of high reduction fire on a low fire red clay (no glaze).

Bottom row, left to right:
>Brown body, glaze No. 22 + TiO_2 and Ni_2O_3.
>White body, glaze No. 22 + Co_3O_4 and Cr_2O_3.
>Brown body, glaze No. 22 + Fe_2O_3 and CuO.

Opposite page, bottom:
>Sunfaces #2. All fired to cone O2 oxidation except #1.

Top row, left to right:
>Brown body, glaze No. 22 + Co_3O_4 and Cr_2O_3, cone 8 reduction.
>Red body, glaze No. 10 + Fe_2O_3.
>Buff clay, glaze No. 10 + MnO_2 and Co_3O_4.

Bottom row, left to right:
>Buff clay, glaze No. 10 + Fe_2O_3.
>Brown body, glaze No. 10 + Cr_2O_3.
>White body, glaze No. 10 + Cr_2O_3 and SnO_2.

Cups #1. All cone 8 oxidation.

Top row, left to right:
>Red body, glaze No. 25 + CuO.
>Brown body, glaze No. 25 + SnO_2.
>Buff body, glaze No. 23 oversprayed with glaze No. 24 + CuO.
>Buff body, ash glaze No. 32.

Bottom row, left to right:
>Buff body, three coats of glaze No. 30 + red iron.
>Brown body, glaze No. 23 + red iron with overspray of glaze No. 24.
>Brown body, three coats of glaze No. 30 + red iron with overspray of glaze No. 25 + CuO.
>Buff body, covered with local clay slip, glazed with ash glaze No. 33.

Cups #2. All fired cone 10 reduction.

Top row, left to right:

Buff body with brush strokes of Co_3O_4 engobe, salt glazed.

Buff body, three coats of glaze No. 30, trailed with glaze No. 26, overspray with glaze #27.

Buff body covered with local clay slip + CuO, oversprayed with glaze No. 25.

Brown body, three coats of glaze No. 30 + red iron, trailed with glaze No. 26, oversprayed with glaze No. 25.

Bottom row, left to right:

Brown body, three coats of glaze No. 30 + CuO, overspray with glaze No. 28.

Brown body, four coats of glaze No. 26, overspray two coats of glaze No. 29.

Brown body, glaze No. 30 + red iron, trailed with glaze No. 26, overspray glaze No. 29.

Brown body, glaze No. 30 + CuO, overspray glaze No. 25.

Below: Slab built lamp and thrown bowl, majolica decoration.

Above: Four thrown pitchers. Front row left, underglaze decoration on white body; right, slip decoration on stoneware. Back row left, slip decoration on stoneware, salt glazed; right, brown luster glaze on buff clay.

Below: Four square plates made in a solid casting mold, majolica decoration.

Above: Three porcelain vases, sang-de-boeuf and celadon glazes.

Right: A luncheon set of native clay made in drain molds. One surface shows the natural color of the clay under a transparent glaze; the other surface is covered with an opaque glaze containing copper, tin, and zinc.

A display of raku in Charlie Brown's studio.

Above: Majolica.

Above: Underglaze decoration on white engobe.

Above: Stoneware with slip trailed decoration, salt glazed.

Above: Majolica.

Right: Sgraffito decoration in copper engobe over buff body.

Trojan Horse, relief wall plaque, 18" x 27", by Charlene deJori

Fig. 6-22   Candle Lamp, pierced, 12″, Lee
Magdanz.

Fig. 6-23   Lantern in two pieces
for standing or hanging, 24″,
Irene Batt.

111

Fig. 6-24 Three-faced planter on
stilts, 32″, Celeste Simon.

Fig. 6-25   Fountain, 36″, Celeste Simon.

Fig. 6-26   People Pot, 12″ x 20″,
Lewis D. Snyder; photo by Peter J.
Meadows.

Fig. 6-27   Flower Girl, 6″, Jacqueline
Lerat.

113

Fig. 6-28 Seated Bolivian Woman,
wheel-thrown sculpture by Marguerite
Wildenhain; photo by Fran Ortiz.

carved, pierced. Ornaments can be modeled on; ribbons can be applied; features can be added to make faces.

Interesting and original sculpture, fountains, etc., can be created through combinations of thrown shapes. Most interesting of all are sculptures thrown on the wheel, then modeled, like the remarkable pieces by Marguerite Wildenhain with which we close this chapter (Figs. 6-28 and 6-29).

Fig. 6-29   Boys' Friendship, wheel-thrown sculpture by Marguerite
Wildenhain; photo by Fran Ortiz.

115

Chapter 7

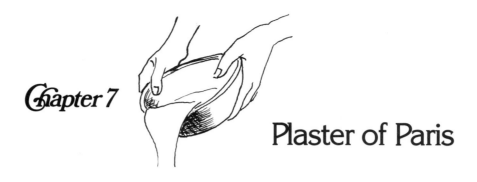

Plaster of Paris

Plaster of paris is useful to the potter because it will absorb moisture from clay either in the liquid or the plastic state. If a lump of clay is left on a slab of dry plaster for only a few minutes, the portion touching the plaster will become dryer and harder than the rest, while a drop of slip falling on the same slab will turn into a dry, hard button almost immediately. Any scratches in the slab will be faithfully reproduced as ridges on the underside of the button.

Let us try an experiment. Suppose we gouge a depression in a plaster slab, making it roughly the shape of a small cup, and then pour clay slip into it. The plaster will begin immediately to draw water out of the slip, and the surface of the liquid will be lowered. If we turn over the plaster slab at the end of 5 minutes and empty out all the slip which will still pour, we will note that a thin layer of clay remains, lining the inside of the depression and taking on its shape. In a few minutes, as the plaster continues to absorb moisture, this clay layer will begin to harden; in an hour it will have shrunk and pulled away from the plaster, so that we can lift it out. In a few hours more it will be hard enough to pick up and, behold, we have a clay cup. In a day or two it will be dry enough to put into a kiln and fire.

This is the property which makes plaster of paris essential to the pottery industry—makes it, in fact, the basis of practically all commercial ceramics. Don't think, however, that its use is restricted to the factory. Not at all; it is a valuable aid to the individual craft potter as well; and when used with appreciation and understanding of what it can do, it will help him to produce highly individual ware which has no suggestion whatsoever of commercialism.

116

What is Plaster of Paris?

Briefly, plaster of paris is gypsum rock which has been heated. When mined, the rock is hard. The heating process drives off chemically combined water and reduces the rock to a soft material that is easily crushed into a fine white powder. Unlike clay—which, once it has lost its chemically combined water, will never take it back—this powder has an affinity for water. When mixed with water, it sets or crystallizes once more into a hard, white solid just about like the original rock. And there's the whole secret of plaster of paris.

Buying Pottery Plaster

Many different kinds and brands of plaster are sold. The best type for the potter is the U.S. Gypsum Company's pottery plaster. This comes in 100-pound bags or 250-pound barrels, but smaller amounts are sold by ceramic supply dealers.

Don't buy more plaster than you can use within a few weeks. Unless you are able to store it in an absolutely airtight container, it won't keep.

How to Use Plaster

Mixing

Best results in plaster work are obtained when both plaster and water are accurately measured. The correct proportion for mold work is 2¾ pounds of plaster to 1 quart of water. A greater proportion of plaster produces a mix which is hard and dense, not absorbent enough for molds. A smaller proportion of plaster makes a weak substance which crumbles easily and is not strong enough for use.

When mixing, measure the water first and put it in a plastic pail or a bowl, then weigh the plaster and sprinkle it into the water. *Sprinkle* it in—don't dump it; otherwise you'll have a lumpy mess on your hands that will be hard to stir. When all the plaster has been sprinkled in, allow it to slake for two minutes. This slaking period is important, for if you stir too soon the plaster will form lumps. After the slaking, stir.

If you don't have a scale, add plaster to the water until a mound of plaster projects above the surface. After the plaster has slaked, pour off any free water which remains on top. This will give a mix approximately right.

The stirring should be done by hand in such a way that the whole mass is agitated and air bubbles are driven out. Don't whip the mixture, for that will get more air bubbles in. If a pail is used, a good method of stirring is to put the hand, palm upward, on the bottom of the pail and wiggle the fingers vigor-

117

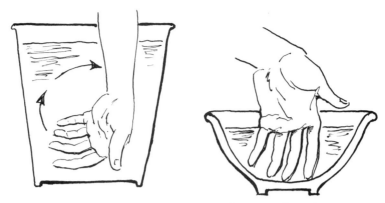

Fig. 7-1   Using fingers to stir plaster up from the bottom.

ously so that the plaster is constantly forced up to the top as shown in Figure 7-1. For a smaller batch, stir so that the fingers rub the bottom of the bowl or, if you prefer, use a large spoon.

Stirring should continue for another 2 or 3 minutes. By that time the plaster will begin to thicken. When the mixture is thick enough so that a finger drawn over the surface leaves a slight trace, it is ready to pour.

You will soon be able to recognize the feel of plaster and be able to judge the proper pouring time. You will also be able to tell when you start the stirring if the proportions are right. Any lumps in the mix should be broken with the fingers. Incidentally, such lumps indicate that the plaster was put into the water too rapidly or that not enough time was allowed for slaking; perhaps, too, the plaster itself was lumpy. Examine your plaster supply; if you find lumps in it, screen it through a sieve before you use it.

Pouring

Plaster must be poured smoothly without any splashing. The trick is to pour it so that no air bubbles are trapped and so that no vacant spaces are left next to the model. It is good to work on a table which can be jarred right after the plaster has been poured, forcing air bubbles to the surface. The plaster can be stirred with a small stick immediately after it has been poured, provided you are careful not to touch the model.

Adding new to old

When making plaster models, you will sometimes want to add new plaster to old. Whenever you add plaster this way, be sure to soak the old plaster thoroughly and scratch the surface where the new plaster is to be attached. Unless the old plaster is saturated it will draw water out of the new batch causing it to

118

"short," that is, set extremely hard like a mix with too much plaster and not enough water. When this happens, the new plaster won't hold on.

Disposing of waste

Let's not ruin the plumbing. If you clean a bowl in which plaster has been mixed by rinsing it in the sink, you will almost certainly have an expensive repair job on your hands. Don't let a bit of plaster get into the drain!

For small amounts of plaster work, the disposal problem can be solved by wiping the mixing bowl with old newspapers as soon as the plaster is poured and before it begins to harden. Another method is to allow what remains in the mixing bowl to set completely hard, then fill the bowl with cold water. If the surface of the bowl is perfectly smooth, the water will cause the plaster to crack off in chunks which can be disposed of as ordinary refuse.

If much plaster work is to be done, the studio should have a special sink trap like the one shown in Figure 7-2. When plaster accumulates in the large container, it can be removed and emptied. A simpler arrangement is to rinse all plaster bowls in a large pail of water, disposing of the accumulated plaster the same way as above.

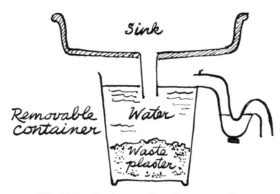

Fig. 7-2 Sink trap for plaster studio.

Plaster which gets on the clothes should be allowed to dry, and then be rubbed off. If necessary, the material may be soaked in cold water, but don't use soap—that makes plaster stick to the fabric.

Making Plaster Slabs

In your pottery work you will always have use for a number of flat, rectangular plaster slabs and for round plaster bats. Let's learn how to mix and pour plaster by making some of these. Prepare four strips of wood ¾ inch thick, 1 inch wide, and 12

119

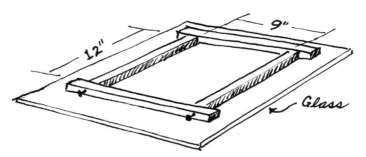

Fig. 7-3 Frame for casting a plaster slab.

inches long. Fasten them together so that they make a frame enclosing a 9 by 12 inch area, and lay it on a sheet of glass as shown in Figure 7-3. This will act as a retaining wall for the plaster. The wood should be coated with oil or Vaseline. If the glass is clean it need not be oiled. When the plaster is poured, it will lift up the frame and flow out underneath unless the wooden strips are fastened down with clay or held in place by some heavy objects, such as a pair of bricks, placed on top.

Now put a quart of water in a large bowl, weigh out 2¾ pounds of plaster, and mix as directed above. When it is ready, pour the plaster into the frame. The sheet of glass should be on a table with an absolutely level surface, so that when the plaster flows it will make a layer of even thickness. Jar the table vigorously immediately after pouring so that the plaster will flow into all corners. If air bubbles come to the surface, blow on them to break them.

In a few minutes the plaster will begin to set and the surface will lose its shine. If you were to stick your finger into it now, you would find it to be the consistency of cream cheese. It is passing through its period of plasticity, which potters call the cheese state. Later we shall learn how to use this period of plasticity to model in plaster or to run forms with a template; but for the present, leave the plaster undisturbed. In a few more minutes it will harden and then begin to get warm. This is the period of crystallization. Let it stand until it begins to cool. When it is once more cold to the touch, crystallization is completed and it is safe to remove the wooden frame and lift up the slab.

Computing amount of plaster

You will note when you have completed the slab that the quantity of water and plaster you mixed was just enough to fill the frame. The slab is 9 by 12 inches and ¾ inches thick, or 81 cubic inches. Remember this figure—one quart of water plus 2¾ pounds of plaster equals 81 cubic inches. This will help you compute the amount of plaster to mix for other mold jobs.

120

Making Plaster Bats

Round plaster bats are useful for wheel work and coil building. To make them, use a pie tin about 6 or 8 inches in diameter. Use oil or Vaseline on the pan but wipe off all the excess before pouring plaster. Bats of even thickness can be made if the table is absolutely level and the plaster is poured soon enough so that it can flow. Another way of making sure the bats are even in thickness is to pour just a little too much plaster into the pan; then when it begins to set, draw a straight edge or a ruler across the top as shown in Figure 7-4.

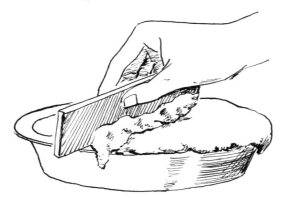

Fig. 7-4   Leveling the top of a plaster bat.

Drying plaster

Freshly made plaster will need to dry for five or six days before it is ready for use. The drying process can be hastened if the plaster is placed near a warm radiator. Don't let it get hot—that weakens it and causes it to crumble. A good way to dry plaster molds (clay, too, for that matter) is by using infrared lamps. The rays from such lamps penetrate solid objects, causing them to dry on the inside as well as on the surface. You will find a pair of these lamps useful in your studio. Set them up so that they shine on the object to be dried from a height of 3 feet, and arrange shades so that the rays do not reach any other part of the room.

Sizing

Plaster can be poured over moist clay or onto a clean sheet of glass, and when it hardens, it will come away without sticking. If it is poured onto another piece of plaster, however, it will stick fast unless we use size as a parting.

Soap

Size is soap. A good grade of soft soap is suitable for this purpose, available from ceramic supply dealers. When you buy

121

it, it has the consistency of axle grease. Don't use it in that form. Size should be as thin as water for the first application, slightly thicker for those that follow.

To prepare it, boil about a pound of soft soap in 2 quarts of water and then thin the resultant syrup by adding 2 more quarts of water when it is cool. An easier way of preparing size is to put a lump of soap as big as your fist in the bottom of a gallon jar, then fill the jar with hot water, cover it, and shake violently. Let it stand overnight. The next day there will be some thick size at the bottom of the jar, while at the top will be a clear honey-colored liquid just right to use. When most of this has been used up, add more hot water and repeat the process. Any size which gets on the working surface of a mold will spoil it because the absorption of the plaster will be killed at that spot. If this happens, remove the size by wiping the mold several times with a cloth soaked in vinegar.

Stearine

Mold makers sometimes prefer to shellac plaster and then use stearine as a parting compound. This works a little better than soap size, but it must not be used on surfaces from which drain molds are to be cast, for any stearine which gets on the mold kills the absorption at that point and hence spoils it for use.

Stearine is made from stearic acid. Put about 2 tablespoons in a can and heat it until the stearic acid melts, then remove the can from the fire and add 8 tablespoons of kerosene. Be sure to extinguish the fire before you add the kerosene. Stir for 15 minutes, then put the mixture aside to cool. When you are ready to use it, whip it up with a brush until it forms a creamy mass just right for applying. Add a little more kerosene if necessary.

Shellac the plaster before you use stearine, applying three or four coats in succession and allowing each to dry before the next is put on. Use the shellac thin. When the last coat of shellac is dry, brush a coat of stearine of the surface, then wipe off all the excess.

Plaster can be cast against a dry clay shape if the clay is given several coats of shellac and then coated with size or stearine.

Applying size

Much of the craftsmanship of the mold maker depends upon proper sizing. Size must be put on in several successive applications, each of which is thoroughly wiped off. It may be put on with a soft brush and wiped off with a sponge, although some potters prefer to use the sponge for both operations.

In the first application, the size should be very thin. Apply it quickly and wipe it off at once. This reduces the absorption of

122

the plaster surface. The second application may be made with size which is slightly thicker. Rub it in well with the sponge, then squeeze the sponge dry and wipe it all off. Repeat this process at least five times. At the end of the last application, squeeze the sponge as dry as you can and wipe off every bit of size. *Don't* rinse the sponge in water. Don't even rinse your hands. Keep a clean cloth handy, and when you are ready to take off the last coat, roll the sponge in the cloth to get all the size out.

Is it really necessary to be so fussy? Yes—the smallest trace of size left on a plaster model will spoil the surface of the mold which is cast from it. When you have finished sizing, the model should look like a piece of old ivory. Flick a drop of water against it. If the size job is good, the water will skip as it would on a hot stove.

Don't size a model and then leave it for an hour before pouring plaster—by that time the size will no longer be effective. Sizing must be done just before plaster is poured.

Plaster Tools

You will need a few special tools for working in plaster—a steel scraper with a saw-toothed edge, two flexible steel kidney-shaped scrapers (one with a saw-toothed edge and one plain), a spatula, a chisel, and half a dozen steel plaster carving tools as shown in Figure 7-5. If you plan to do any plaster work on the wheel, you will need two turning tools: one with straight sides and one curved. The toothed edge of the scraper is valuable for smoothing surfaces. The best way to get a perfectly level surface is with such a tool. After the saw-toothed edge has

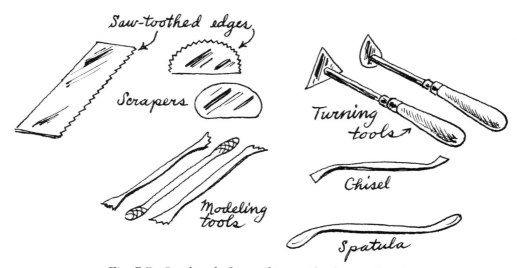

Fig. 7-5 Steel tools for working with plaster of paris.

123

been used to take down any bumps and make the surface level, the straight edge can be used to take off the scratches.

When plaster is wet it is comparatively soft and easy to cut. When it is dry it can be worked on with sandpaper. For final finishing of plaster surfaces, use the finest grade of sandpaper you can buy. Number 6-0 garnet paper is best.

Some Points on Plaster

1. When mixing, sprinkle the plaster into the water slowly. Never pour water into plaster.
2. Store plaster in an airtight container; otherwise it will absorb moisture from the atmosphere.
3. If your plaster contains lumps, sift before using it.
4. Old plaster won't work. A dirty scum on the surface of the water when you are mixing indicates that the plaster is no good.
5. Plaster can be cast against moist clay or glass without the use of a parting compound. Wood and metal surfaces should be oiled or greased before plaster is cast against them, and plaster surfaces should be sized.
6. Be thorough when you apply size.
7. Plaster tools deserve good treatment. Clean them each time they are used and oil them occasionally.
8. Take pride in your work. Even though the things you make of plaster are for temporary use, make them with care and accuracy.

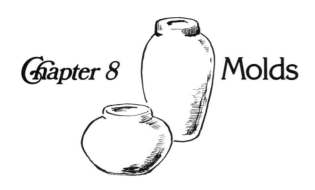

Chapter 8   Molds

Plaster molds can be made in many different ways. They may be cast from clay shapes or plaster models, or even natural objects. In fact, a plaster mold can be made of practically anything at all.

Potters as a rule prefer to make their molds from plaster models because better surfaces are possible that way. In making a mold of a small figure or of a rectangular plate, the potter would first model the shape in clay, then make a waste mold and cast the shape again in plaster. This plaster shape would then be carefully finished with plaster tools and sandpaper, and the final mold cast from it.

Plaster models can be turned directly on the wheel, or on a lathe, or they may be carved by hand. Models are sometimes made by running templates over plaster while it is setting.

One-Piece Drain Molds from Clay Forms

Some molds use liquid clay, while others require clay in plastic form. The simplest molds are *drain molds.* In these, clay slip is poured into the mold and allowed to stand until a clay wall of the proper thickness is built up on the inner surface of the mold, after which all the slip which is still liquid is poured out. The clay wall remaining in the mold is then allowed to dry, after which it is removed from the mold, finished, and fired.

A mold for a bowl

A bowl or a cup can be cast in a one-piece drain mold, provided the shape is widest at the top and diminishes steadily from top to bottom (Fig. 8-1). Such a shape is said to have "draft." It can be easily lifted out of a mold.

125

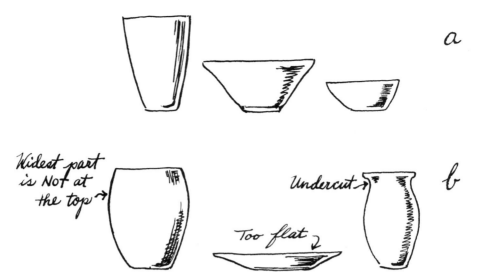

Fig. 8-1 (a) Shapes that can be made in one-piece molds;
(b) shapes that cannot be made in one-piece molds.

The model for such a mold may be shaped on a potter's wheel out of a solid lump of clay. Wedge the clay well to remove all air bubbles and use a plaster bat about 3 inches greater in diameter than the shape you are making. After fastening the bat to the wheel head, throw the ball of clay and center it just as if you were going to make a vase. However, instead of opening the ball of clay, mold it to the shape of the outside of your bowl, upside down. Remember to allow for shrinkage. The shape must be at least one-sixth larger than the finished bowl.

A mold works best when it contains a waste rim, that is, a small collar on the form which can be trimmed off and discarded. In making the shape, allow an additional piece about ½ inch high and ½ inch wide for this purpose, as shown in Figure 8-2. This can be easily formed with a wooden modeling tool. Use the wooden tool, also, to finish the foot, and smooth the sides with a rubber rib.

When the shape is finished, the mold may be poured. This can be done without removing the work from the wheel head. Size the plaster bat thoroughly but don't get any size on the clay. It will now be necessary to erect some type of retaining wall or cottle to hold the plaster. For this purpose, a piece of heavy roofing paper works well. The paper should be cut slightly wider than the height of the mold and long enough to wrap around the plaster bat three or four times. Roofing paper used this way is called a cottle. The cottle may be tied with a length of twine or fastened with a snap-on clothespin. A roll of clay pressed firmly around the base of the cottle will prevent plaster from leaking out (Fig. 8-2).

126

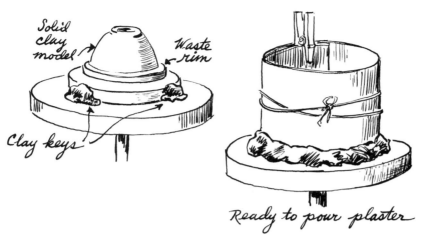

Fig. 8-2 Making a mold from a solid clay model.

When the cottle is in place, mix the plaster and pour. Immediately after pouring the plaster, jar the wheel head by striking it sharply with your fist several times. This will get rid of any air bubbles adhering to the clay form. When the plaster has reached the consistency of cream cheese, remove the cottle and smooth the outside surface of the mold by holding a scraper against it as the wheel is turned. This must be done before the plaster gets hard, otherwise the work will come loose from the wheel head. After the outside of the mold is reasonably smooth, allow the plaster to set, then remove the mold from the clay model. It is finished. Set the mold aside to dry for five or six days. We shall learn in Chapter 9 how it is used.

A plaster drying bat

In Chapter 1 mention was made of plaster drying bats into which liquid clay could be poured and allowed to harden for reuse. The method of making such a bat is the same as that described for the bowl above, except that you may work directly on the wheel head and the clay model should be wider and shallower as shown in Figure 8-3.

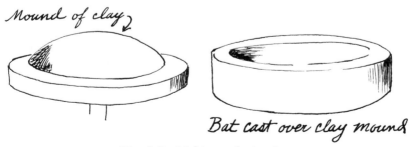

Fig. 8-3 Making a drying bat.

127

A mold for a box

Rectangular shapes can be made in one-piece drain molds just as easily as round ones, provided we allow draft. In designing a rectangular box, we should remember that we are potters, not carpenters. We work with clay, and so our box must not look like wood—corners should be rounded rather than square and surfaces should not be too flat (Fig. 8-4). There is a sound structural reason for this. Sharp corners do not cast easily nor take glaze well, and absolutely flat surfaces tend to sag and become concave during the firing.

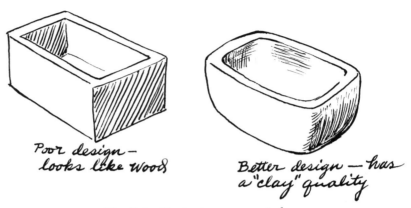

Poor design—
looks like wood

Better design — has
a "clay" quality

Fig. 8-4   Designing a ceramic box.

For a mold of a box we shall need a flat plaster slab which is perfectly smooth, preferably one cast against glass. Cut the slab into a rectangular shape 3 inches longer and 3 inches wider than the box. Take care in cutting the slab to have the corners square and the sides true. Accuracy here will help in making the mold later on.

Draw a line with indelible pencil through the center of the slab, dividing it in half the long way, then draw another line through the center of the first one at right angles to it (Fig. 8-5).

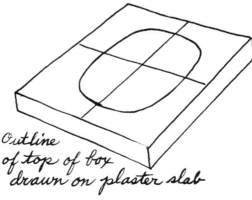

Outline
of top of box
drawn on plaster slab

Fig. 8-5   Outline centered on plaster slab.

128

It is important that these two lines be perpendicular to each other; our box will be lopsided if they are not.

The next step is to draw an outline of the top of the box on the plaster slab. Remember to allow for shrinkage when you plan the size. You will find it helpful to fold a piece of paper in quarters and cut out a pattern for the top. In this way you can be certain that the shape is symmetrical. Keep trimming the paper pattern until the shape pleases you. When the pattern is right, lay it on the plaster slab so that the folds in the paper are on the lines previously drawn, then trace the outline with indelible pencil.

Now comes the job of building a solid clay form shaped like the box upside down. This clay form must fit the outline you have drawn and must slope up evenly on all sides to a height equal to the depth of the box. There are no shortcuts here—patience and a lot of careful modeling are needed.

Use a piece of wood about 2 by 2 by 4 inches to block out the form, then finish it with modeling tools (Fig. 8-6). Draw a flexible steel scraper up the sides to make them smooth and uniform. Use a cardboard template as a guide (Fig. 8-7). The top of the form must be flat or else slightly concave, otherwise the box will not stand level. Lay a ruler on the clay to make sure that the top is not convex. You can, if you wish, model a raised rim for the box to stand on, or else make four feet, one in each corner. Feet of this type must be small and must taper sharply to avoid trouble in the casting.

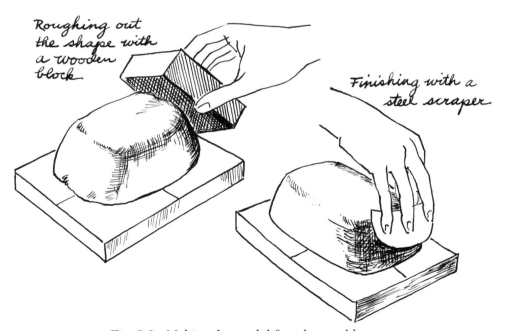

Fig. 8-6   Making the model for a box mold.

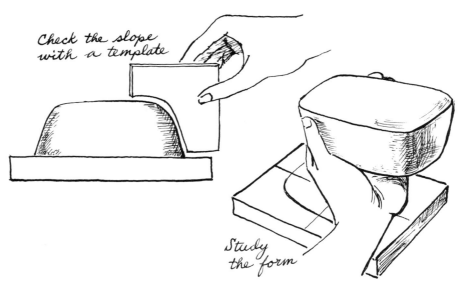

Fig. 8-7   Completing the clay model for the box.

Study the shape as you work by looking at it from all angles. Compare opposite sides for symmetry. Look straight down on it. Study it by feeling as well, for your fingers will often tell you more about form than your eyes.

For a final check, lift the clay model off the plaster slab and look at it right side up. Is the shape pleasing? Does it feel right in the hand? Does it stand well on the table? If so, you are ready to pour the mold. Size the slab, and put the clay form back in place, then set the retaining wall at the edge of the slab and pour the plaster for the mold.

The retaining wall may be made out of four pieces of wood. When you pour plaster to a depth of several inches, the pressure on the retaining wall is greater than you may think, so fasten the pieces of wood securely, either by tying or nailing them together. Put clay at the joints to keep the plaster from seeping out.

A casting box

This is a good place to describe a casting box, a simple device for casting rectangular shapes. This consists of four pieces of wood about 6 by 15 inches and ¾ inch thick, each with a piece of strap iron fastened to the end. These four pieces fit together to make a box of any size up to 15 inches square. Four wedges, used as shown in Figure 8-8, hold them tightly together while the plaster is poured. Remember to size the inner surfaces of the box.

When the retaining wall is in place, mix plaster and pour. Allow the plaster to set, then remove the casting box and take

130

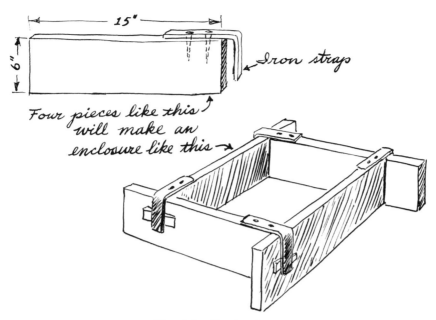

15"

6"

Iron strap

Four pieces like this
will make an
enclosure like this

Fig. 8-8   Casting box.

out the clay model. Try to remove the clay form without destroying it. This may not be easy. If you have to break it to get it out, patch the pieces together again, for you will need the model to help you in the next job, which is designing a lid.

A mold for a lid

A lid for the box we have just designed must have a flange or collar to fit into the box. Hence, we cannot make it in a one-piece mold. We can, however, make a simple two-piece mold which will work.

Start as before with a flat plaster slab. In fact, the same slab that was used for the box may be used again. This time draw an outline about ⅛ inch larger all around than the outline of the box. This is to allow the lid to overhang slightly. Now build up a clay form for the lid, forgetting the flange for the time being. The lid should not be entirely flat, but slightly domed in the center. The thickness may be about ¾ inch at the midpoint, tapering to ⅛ inch at the edge. Model this just as you did the box, using a steel scraper for the final smoothing. When you have it as you think it should be, take it off the slab and try it on the clay model of the box to see if the two go well together and if the lid is pleasing when in place. If it is, size the slab, put the lid back in position, set the casting box or the retaining wall, mix plaster, and pour (Fig. 8-9).

This is only half of the job. When the plaster has set, turn the mold upside down and remove the original slab, allowing the

131

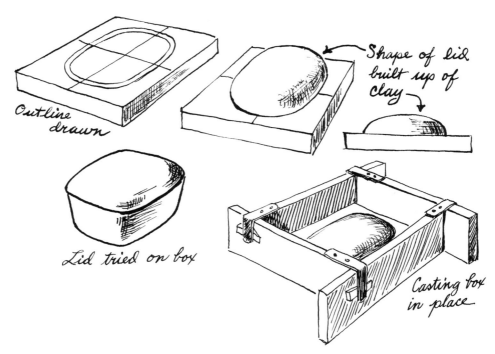

Fig. 8-9   Making a mold for a lid.

Outline drawn

Shape of lid built up of clay

Lid tried on box

Casting box in place

clay shape of the lid to remain embedded in the mold. Make a shape for the flange. The flange can be cut out of a layer of clay rolled flat, ½ inch thick. It should be the same shape as the box itself, but ½ inch smaller all around. This may make the flange a trifle too small, but it will be possible to enlarge the opening in the mold later if the finished lid fits too loosely. The sides of this piece should be almost vertical, tapering slightly toward the top. Lay this piece in place on the underside of the clay lid which is still embedded in the plaster mold.

Before pouring the second half of the mold, cut some notches in the first half so that the two will fit together (Fig. 8-10). A knife with the end of the blade bent into hook shape is a good tool for this purpose. Such knives can be bought from ceramic supply houses. (*Note:* Don't cut the same number of notches on each side. If you do, you will always be annoyed when putting the two halves together, for somehow or other, you will be sure to try them the wrong way first. Put two notches on one end and one on the other. That way it will be quite evident which way the halves fit.)

When the notches are cut, size the exposed portion of the first half of the mold, set the casting box and pour the second half. This half will be quite thin, since it should not extend higher than the piece of clay which forms the collar.

When the molds of both the box and the lid are dry, pour trial

132

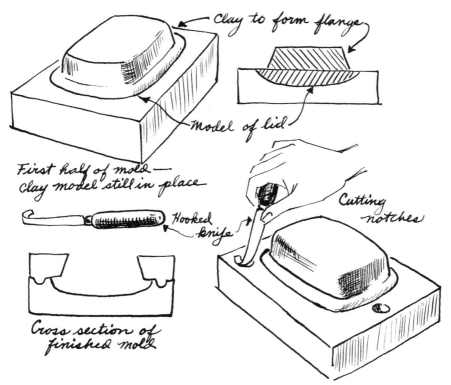

Fig. 8-10   Completing the lid mold.

pieces. As we mentioned above, the lid may fit too loosely. If it
does, the portion of the mold making the flange may be enlarged by scraping or rubbing with sandpaper until a good fit is
obtained (Fig. 8-11). Remember that the finished box will have
a coating of glaze; so the lid must not fit too tightly in the raw
state.

Fig. 8-11   Trying the lid for fit.

One-Piece Drain Molds from Plaster Forms

The drain molds described so far, the bowl, the box, and the lid, were made directly from clay models. Each of these would have been a better mold had the model been made in plaster first, for plastic clay does not permit the finish which is possible with plaster.

A mold for a box

To make a plaster model of box, start as described above, first making the shape as carefully as possible out of clay; then instead of casting a mold from the clay, make a waste mold. As the name suggests, this is a mold which will be thrown away after one use, so it is not necessary to take too much care in making it. A ¾ inch shell will suffice. When this has hardened, remove the clay, smooth the inside of the waste mold with sandpaper, size it, and pour in plaster. When this plaster has set, remove the waste mold (break it away if necessary), and the model of the box is ready for finishing with plaster tools and sandpaper.

In describing the method of making a mold for the box directly from a clay form, no mention was made of a waste rim. This was not overlooked; it was left out to make the job less complicated. The mold can be used without a waste rim, but it is better to have one. Before pouring plaster over the model, make a layer of clay ½ inch thick, place the box upside down on it, and cut the layer so that it forms a band ½ inch wide all the way around. Put this on the plaster slab with the model on top of it, then size the slab and the model, set the casting box, and pour the mold.

A mold for a lid

To make a model of the lid, proceed as before, shaping the lid in clay without a flange; then make a waste mold and cast the lid, still without flange, in plaster. The models of the box and lid may then be studied together, and any changes needed to improve appearance can be made. In making the mold for the lid, the first half is cast over the plaster model, then the second half is made as before. A layer of clay is cut to form the flange and notches are cut so that the two halves will fit together. The mold for the lid will not need a waste rim.

Wheel-Made Molds from Plaster Forms

Molds for round objects can be made from plaster models cast and turned on a wheel, but it is quite difficult to operate a foot-power wheel and cut plaster at the same time. A motor-driven wheel is a necessity for this kind of work, because a speed of 200 revolutions per minute is required.

Plaster work on the wheel requires a working surface of plaster; it is, therefore, essential to have some means of fastening a large plaster bat firmly on the wheel head. For a wheel with the drop type of head, cast a bat to fit according to the method described in Chapter 6, but make the bat larger and thicker. If your wheel has a flat head, it will be necessary to fasten some lugs of metal or wood to the surface so that a large plaster bat cast on the wheel head will be held in place.

Tools

You will need a turning stick, like the one shown in Figure 6-16, for this work and a board to hold it. You will need some turning tools (one with a straight edge and one with a curved edge), a flexible steel scraper, a knife, and a chisel, as illustrated in Figure 7-5.

Making a chuck

The first step in making a mold on the plaster wheel is to make a chuck. This is merely a projection on the wheel head, over which a cylinder of plaster can be cast and held while it is worked on. The chuck must be shaped so that the form cast over it can be easily lifted off and replaced. A truncated cone with a slot cut in it serves well. The base of the chuck can be used to fasten the cottle when the mold is poured.

To make a chuck, place the plaster bat on the wheel head and start the wheel. Then brace the turning stick in the board and hold a pencil against it so that it draws a circle on the plaster bat about 7 inches in diameter (Fig. 8-12). Next, size the plaster bat and set a cottle on the circle just drawn, fastening it firmly with clay. Mix enough plaster to fill the cottle to a depth of 3 inches (a quart and a half water plus 4 pounds and 2 ounces of plaster will do the trick) and pour it in. As soon as the plaster is firm enough to stand by itself, remove the cottle and start cutting the chuck.

Don't let the plaster get hard. Remember, you have sized the bat; therefore, as soon as the plaster hardens, it will come loose. As long as it is soft you can work on it safely.

Hold the triangular cutting tool as shown in Figure 8-12, the left hand grasping the handle of the tool against the turning stick and the right hand squeezing the shaft of the tool and the turning stick together. A firm grip like this will give you perfect control of the tool. Keep the point of the stick tight in the board and brace the other end firmly against your body. By moving your body slightly you will be able to move the stick and the tool without loosening your hand grip.

135

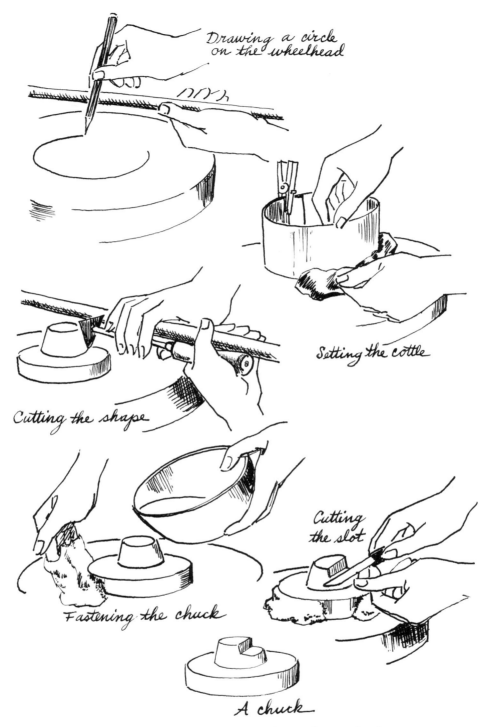

Drawing a circle on the wheelhead

Setting the cottle

Cutting the shape

Fastening the chuck

Cutting the slot

A chuck

Fig. 8-12   The steps involved in making a chuck.

While the plaster is still soft, cut the cylinder into shape: cut straight up for half its height, then cut in to make a small truncated cone about 3 inches in diameter at the base and 2 inches at the top. (The size of the cone will vary according to the size and shape of the piece you plan to make.) As soon as you have this shape roughed out, stop cutting and fasten the chuck to the bat by mixing a small quantity of extra-thick plaster and using it to make wads or keys to hold the edge of the chuck to the bat in three places. These plaster keys will stick firmly against the chuck; but in order to have them hold on the bat, it will be necessary to scrape through the coating of size and wet the plaster bat at each point where a key is to be placed.

It may seem odd that we took the trouble to size the plaster bat before pouring the plaster for the chuck, and that we then mixed fresh plaster to hold the chuck in place, but there is a reason for doing so. We want the chuck held firmly while we work; but when we are finished, we want to be able to chip away the keys and lift it off the wheel.

When the keys have set, work on the chuck some more. It will be hard by now, and you will be able to cut a perfectly smooth surface. Be careful to remove any little ridges. When this is done, stop the wheel and cut a slot in the top of the cone. Now the chuck is finished and you are ready to make some shapes.

A mold for a simple vase

To make a vase, size the chuck thoroughly, then set a cottle around its base and pour enough plaster to make a cylinder slightly wider and taller than the vase will be (Fig. 8-13). Take away the cottle as soon as the plaster is firm enough to stand and

Pouring plaster over the chuck

Blocking out the shape while plaster is still soft—

Fig. 8-13 Making a model of a vase.

137

start roughing out the shape before it gets hard. Finish the shaping after the plaster hardens.

Here is where the chuck comes in handy. When you have the shape just as you think it should be, lift it off the chuck and study it right side up. You will be surprised to see how different it looks and how defects which you did not notice before are now glaringly evident. Put the model back on the chuck and correct the mistakes, then take it off for further study. The flexible steel scraper is a good tool for final shaping because it can be bent in the fingers and adapted to almost any curve. It gives a good surface, too. The chisel will be useful in shaping the foot.

Before the mold is poured, cut a step on the chuck as shown in Figure 8-14, to serve as a waste rim in the mold. Size the model, place the cottle around the base of the chuck, and pour plaster for the mold. As soon as this starts to stiffen, remove the cottle and use the turning tools to trim up the outside surface. Make the bottom of the mold slightly concave so that it will stand level on a table without rocking. When that is done, the mold is finished—put it aside to dry.

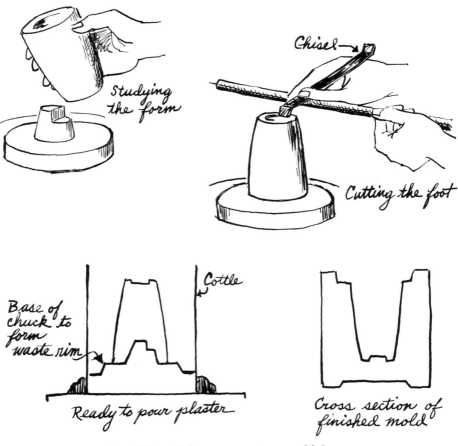

Fig. 8-14 Making a one-piece mold for a vase.

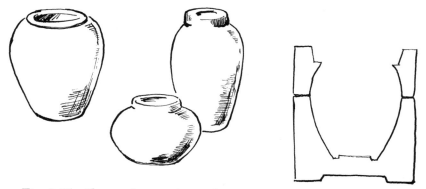

Fig. 8-15 Shapes that can be made in two-piece horizontal molds.

A two-piece mold

Shapes similar to those in Figure 8-15, which have their widest diameters somewhere between the top and the bottom, and whose profiles do not have undercuts, can be made in two-piece molds divided horizontally. The model for such a mold is made in the same manner as the model for the one-piece vase mold. Prepare a chuck, size it, cast a cylinder of plaster over it, then cut the shape upside down. Take it off the chuck to study the form. When it is just right, finish the foot, and polish the surface.

Before you cast the mold, it will be necessary to determine accurately the position of the widest part of the model. Use a try square as shown in Figure 8-16 to mark the spot where it touches the side. (If you haven't a try square, cut a right angle out of cardboard and use that.) Rotate the wheel and hold an indelible pencil at the point just marked so that a line is drawn

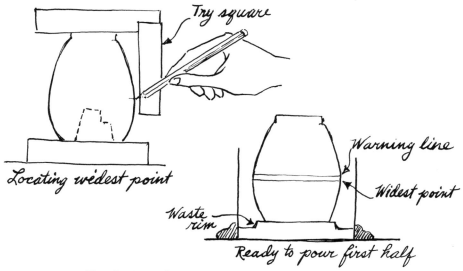

Fig. 8-16 Making a two-piece horizontal mold.

139

completely around the model. Then make another line ¼ inch above the first to serve as a warning line.

Now you are ready to cast one-half of the mold. Cut a step in the base of the chuck to form the waste rim, size the model and the base of the chuck, and then set the cottle in place. Mix plaster and pour enough into the cottle so that it just covers the two lines you have drawn on the model. Pour the plaster a minute or two sooner than you would ordinarily, while it is still fairly liquid, and jar the wheel head vigorously after you pour, for bubbles tend to collect on the underside of curved surfaces like this one.

The next step is to cut the top surface of this half of the mold until it is exactly level with the line drawn at the widest point. As soon as the plaster is firm enough, remove the cottle and start cutting the mold. It is important not to cut into the model, so for the first part of the cutting, use a wooden tool. This will cut the fresh plaster, which is still soft, without marring the model. Lower the surface of the mold until your warning line is visible. This tells you that you must go exactly ¼ inch farther. Use the steel tool now and continue cutting until the second line is just visible. Stop! You can trim up the side of the mold, but don't take any more off the top edge.

Before the second half is poured, cut notches in the first part, as shown in Figure 8-17, so that the two halves will fit together. Now you are ready to pour the second half. Size the

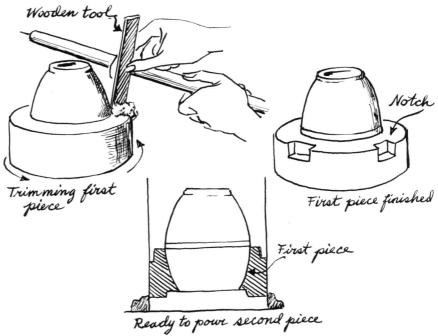

Fig. 8-17 Completing a two-piece horizontal mold.

model again (the first size coat is no longer any good), set the cottle in place, mix the plaster and pour. When the plaster has set, remove the cottle and trim up the outside surface of the mold. The job is done.

A two-piece lateral mold

A shape with undercuts or returns, like the vase shown in Figure 8-18, cannot be made in the type of mold just described. Such a shape requires a mold which separates laterally. If the form has an indentation in the base it needs a mold of three pieces, but if you are willing to accept a vase with a flat bottom, you can use a simple two-piece mold, easy to make.

Make the model by casting a cylinder of plaster over a chuck and cutting the shape, upside down, in the same manner as that described for the simple vase. When the form is finished, remove it from the chuck and cut a template to fit its profile. In order to get the correct profile, you will need to draw center lines on opposite sides of the model, dividing it exactly in half. This can be done with a try square (Fig. 8-16).

The template may be cut out of a thin sheet of plaster or out of heavy cardboard. Cardboard is easier to handle because it is less apt to break. If it is given three coats of shellac and then sized, a cardboard template will work very well.

Lay the template on a bed of soft clay and put the model in place so that it is embedded exactly to the centerline. Any space between the model and the template should be filled with clay so that a perfect fit is secured. Make a plug of clay to form the opening in the mold and put it at the top of the model. This plug will form the waste rim, also. Make it carefully and see that it projects a half-inch beyond the top rim of the model.

When the plug is in place, size the model and the template, set the casting box and pour the first half of the mold. When this has set, turn it over; remove the clay backing and the template, but leave the model embedded in the mold.

Put another plug of clay at the top of the model, cut notches in the first half of the mold, size the mold and the model, set the casting box again, and pour the second half. The mold is finished.

Drain Molds for Small Sculpture

In Chapter 3, we saw how to hollow out a little figure so that it could be safely fired. A better method would be to make a plaster mold of the figure and then cast it in slip. This way we would be sure that all parts were hollow and all walls even in thickness. Let us see how a mold for an animal with four legs can be made.

141

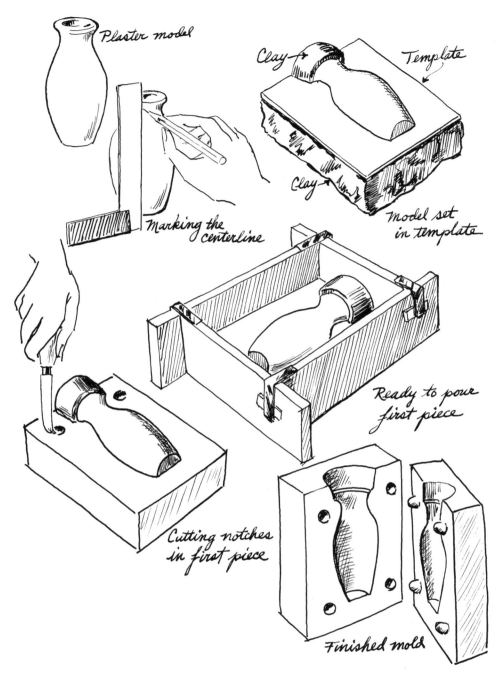

Plaster model

Clay

Template

Clay

Model set in template

Marking the centerline

Ready to pour first piece

Cutting notches in first piece

Finished mold

Fig. 8-18   Making a two-piece lateral mold for a shape
with an undercut.

142

She and the Serpent, by Irene Batt, slab and coil built, lustered with silver nitrate and gold chloride, raku, 21″.

Nun, by David F. Silverman.

Sweetmeat Stand, by Bruce Brecken-
ridge.

Monument, 8'6",
by Ted Randall

Making a Five-Piece Mold for an Elephant Figurine

1. The figure has been modeled and allowed to become leather hard. The potter studies it to decide how many pieces will be needed for the mold. This takes imagination, for the pieces must be planned so that they will "draw," that is, come apart without marring the delicate figure inside.

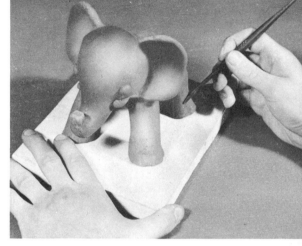

2. A line has been drawn along the center of the back, over the head, and down through the trunk; the mold must separate along this line. Another line of separation is drawn along the edge of the ear.

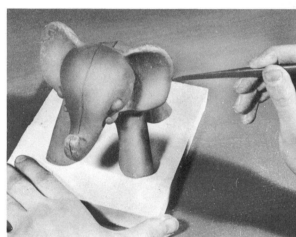

3. One piece of the mold will have to be contained within the four legs and the portion under the trunk. The potter builds a wall of clay to block off this area.

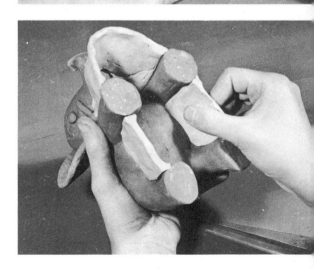

143

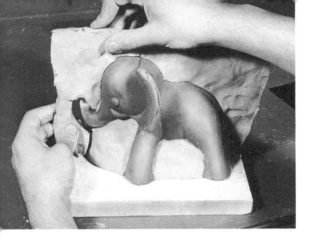

4. The elephant stands on a plaster slab while the potter sets another wall of clay along the centerline.

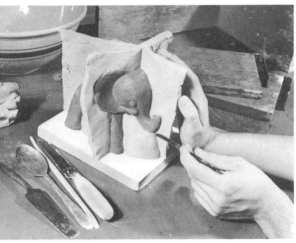

5. A clay wall has been set on each side, along the line of separation which follows the edge of the ear and passes down the center of the front leg. The separating walls are now all in place. Layers of clay were rolled with a rolling pin and cut to shape to make these walls.

6. The casting box is set in place so that it comes tight against the edge of the plaster slab on which the elephant stands. The clay separating walls will be pressed tightly against the sides of the casting box. To save time, two pieces of the mold will be poured at once in the next operation: the right front and the left rear.

7. Pouring the plaster. The sides of the casting box and the plaster slab were sized beforehand.

144

8. The plaster has set, the casting box and the clay separating walls have been removed. The clay wall blocking off the portion under the trunk and between the legs remains. The potter cuts notches in the two portions of the mold just poured, so that the next pieces to be poured will fit securely.

9. The notches have been completed. The potter sizes the sides of the two finished pieces of the mold and the plaster slab preparatory to pouring two more parts.

10. Setting the casting box again.

11. Pouring the right rear and the left front portions of the mold.

145

12. Four pieces of the mold have been poured. The plaster has set, the casting box has been removed, and the mold has been turned upside down. The potter has removed the clay which blocked off the portion under the trunk and between the legs.

He now cuts notches so that the last piece of the mold will be held in place. When this operation is finished, he will size the exposed portions of the mold and pour plaster into the opening, making the surface *level* with the other four parts of the mold: the bottoms of the elephant's feet are not covered with plaster. This will form the last piece of the mold.

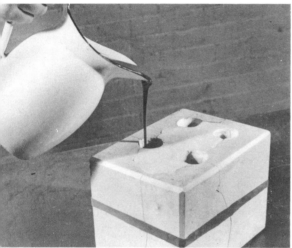

13. Several days later. The mold has been completed, the pieces have been taken apart, the figure of the elephant removed, and the separate parts of the mold allowed to dry.

Now the five pieces of the mold are together again, fastened with a heavy rubber band cut from an inner tube, and the potter pours slip into one of the openings left by the legs.

This is a drain mold. The slip will be allowed to stand until a wall of proper thickness is built up, then poured out again. This means that the bottoms of the feet will be open. The potter can close these openings by rolling little balls of clay and using them as plugs, pressing them into place after the slip has set, but before it becomes hard. Thus, no opening at all will be left in the figure.

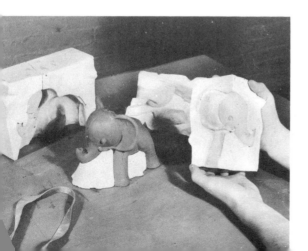

14. The slip has dried sufficiently to allow the potter to take off the rubber band and separate the pieces of the mold. The little elephant is now ready for trimming and firing.

146

15. There he is in the kiln.

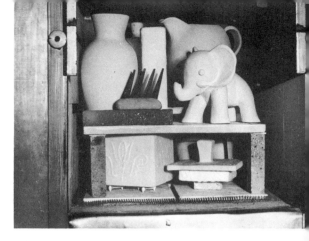

16. The finished product.

Note: In high-fired work, porcelain or stoneware, a hollow figure like this would need an opening; otherwise, as the clay matured during the firing and became vitreous the air inside the figure would be trapped. Continuing to expand as the temperature of the kiln rose, this trapped air would cause the figure to bloat or even blow up. For low temperature work, however, the body is porous enough to allow air to get through; so it is not essential to leave an opening in the surface of the piece.

A difficulty sometimes encountered in molds of this type is that during the pouring, air is trapped in some portion, such as the bottom of the trunk or the lobe of the ear, and slip is not able to fill all parts of the mold. If you have this trouble, make a vent to allow the air to escape.

Thread separation

Silk threads can be used to separate the pieces of a mold which must be made in several parts. This method is not as good as that just described but it is much quicker. The threads are placed on the clay model along the lines of separation of the mold as shown in Figure 8-19. The retaining walls are placed so

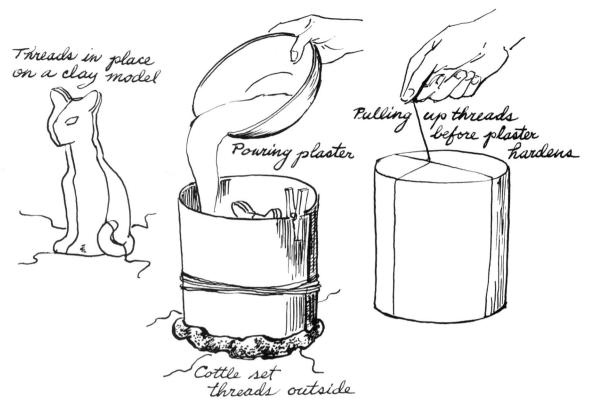

Fig. 8-19 Using threads to separate the pieces of a mold.

that the ends of the threads remain outside. Plaster is then poured over the entire model.

When the plaster has started to set, but before it becomes hard, the threads are pulled upward and out so that they divide the plaster into the separate parts of the mold. Such molds will not fit together as well as those made according to the steps in Photo Series 18, but they can be tied and made to work.

Some points on plaster and molds

Plaster work demands good craftsmanship. Carelessness is sure to cause trouble. Here are some things to watch out for:

1. Measure the water and weigh the plaster. If you rely upon guesswork, some of your guesses will be wrong.
2. Be sure to mix enough plaster for each operation. When in doubt, compute the volume in cubic inches and divide by 81. That will tell you how many quarts of water you will need.
3. Do a good job when sizing. Apply at least five coats and wipe each one off, thoroughly.
4. Stir the plaster well.

148

5. If the cottle gives way, you'll have quite a mess! Be sure it is secure before you pour.
6. Immediately after pouring, jar the work by rapping the wheel or the table with your fist to loosen air bubbles.
7. Look out for undercuts. The merest scratch, almost invisible to the eye, will be enough to lock the model firmly in the mold.
8. If there is trouble getting the model and the mold apart, try putting the model back on the chuck and twisting the mold. When this doesn't work, hold a piece of wood against the outside edge of the mold and strike it sharply with a hammer or, if you have a spray gun, disconnect the hose and shoot a stream of air at the crack between the model and the mold. This should get them apart. Next time do a better job of sizing and don't have any undercuts.

149

Chapter 9

Slip Casting

Clay mixed with water makes slip, but this is not the best material for casting. The water content of the mixture is high: usually 100 percent of the dry weight of the clay, since equal parts of clay and water are required to make slip which will pour. Consequently, there is a large amount of shrinkage. This is not so bad in simple drain molds; but in more complicated molds, casting with ordinary slip is extremely difficult. Some way must be sought to make a casting slip with less water. The answer is *deflocculation*.

Making Casting Slip

Deflocculation

We are not certain what makes clay plastic. It is believed that the very minute particles of clay substance have a static electrical charge which makes them flock together, just as bits of paper stick to a rod when it is rubbed. Ordinary water is a nonconductor of electricity, but if a small amount of alkaline substance is introduced, it becomes a conductor. When this is done to a clay slip, the static electricity of the clay particles is discharged, they lose their attraction for each other, and they no longer flock together. The slip is then said to be deflocculated. Alkaline substances used in deflocculation are called electrolytes.

This phenomenon can be illustrated dramatically with certain types of clay. When 1000 grams of dry clay are mixed with 400 grams of water, the result is a thick, sticky mass. If a few drops of sodium silicate or water glass (the alkaline substance or electrolyte) are added, the mixture will suddenly change into a smooth, creamy liquid easy to pour: it has become a *defloccu-lated slip*, suitable for casting.

Unfortunately, this does not work the same way for all clays. Some are temperamental and require a mixture of two or more electrolytes, while others cannot be deflocculated at all. If you have a natural clay or a clay body which you want to use for casting, the only thing to do is run a series of experiments.

A well-deflocculated casting slip should have about the same percentage of water as plastic clay, 35 to 45 percent. There are several substances which may be used as electrolytes. The best are sodium silicate and soda ash, which work well in combination. The percentage of electrolyte needed is extremely small, ranging from 1/10 of 1 percent to 3/10 of 1 percent (percentages are based on the weight of dry clay). It is important not to add too much, for a slight excess of electrolyte reverses the process and, instead of making the slip more liquid, causes it to jell into a semi solid mass.

Here is one way to conduct your experiment. Take 1000 grams of dry clay and 400 grams of water and mix them together. Put 25 cc. of water in a glass graduate and add 3 grams of soda ash and 3 grams of sodium silicate. Soda ash is a powder, but sodium silicate is a liquid. To weigh it, put the graduate containing the water on the scale and note its weight, then drop sodium silicate into the water until three grams have been added. After both electrolytes are dissolved in the graduate, add enough water to bring the quantity up to 30 cc. Now you know that 1 cc. of this solution contains 0.1 gram each of sodium silicate and soda ash. Add the solution, drop by drop, to the mixture of clay and water, stirring it constantly as you do so. If the clay suddenly turns liquid, your experiment has been a success. By consulting the graduate, you can tell how much electrolyte you have used. In preparing future batches of casting slip you can put that amount into the water before you add the clay.

If the mixture starts to become liquid, then thickens and starts to jell, you have added too much electrolyte. Prepare another batch of clay and begin again. If the electrolytes make the mixture partly liquid but not thin enough to pour, try adding another 50 grams of water and, if necessary, 50 grams more. This will bring your total water content to 500 grams or 50 percent—don't go higher than that. If you still don't have any luck, try adding a few drops of sodium tannate. Sodium tannate can be made by boiling 100 cc. of distilled·water and adding 10 grams of soda ash and 10 grams of tannic acid. Next try Calgon (a commercial water softener). If none of these work, you may have a clay which cannot be deflocculated at all; however, as we said before, some clays are temperamental in this respect, so keep on trying. You may hit the right combination.

151

Another way to conduct a deflocculation experiment is to put 40 grams of water into each of several containers (glass tumblers will do) and then add various quantities of different electrolytes. To one container, add 0.2 gram of sodium silicate, to another 0.3 gram of sodium silicate, to a third 0.1 gram of sodium silicate and 0.1 gram of soda ash, and so on, keeping a record of what goes into each container. Then add 100 grams of dry clay to each solution and stir it thoroughly. The resultant mixture which is thinnest and pours most easily is nearest to correct deflocculation.

Aging

Casting slip works better when it is allowed to age slightly; so wait three or four days after preparing a batch before you use it. Keep it in a covered container meanwhile, and stir it often. Screen it through a 40 or 60-mesh sieve every time you cast with it. If you have trouble with air bubbles, use two pitchers and pour the slip back and forth from one to the other several times until the bubbles are all driven to the surface and broken.

Sometimes natural clays contain sulfur, which causes trouble by making blisters in the glaze. If you have this difficulty, add a small percentage of barium carbonate to the slip (1 percent will be enough). This will not affect the working properties of the slip but will prevent the sulfur from bubbling out under the glaze during the firing.

Adding grog to slip

If you plan to cast large pieces with thick walls, you can add grog to casting slip just as you would to clay. When slip is properly deflocculated, grog will not settle to the bottom but will remain suspended almost indefinitely. A piece cast this way will have a smooth surface, as though the slip contained no grog at all. If you want the grog to show in the texture of the finished piece, sponge the surface after it has dried.

Prepared Casting Slips

In Chapter 11, recipes are given for clay bodies for various firing temperatures. Some of these make excellent casting slips. Instructions for deflocculating them are given along with the recipes.

Many ceramic dealers offer prepared casting slip for sale, with the deflocculating agents already added. It can be bought as a dry powder or in liquid form.

Now let's see how molds are used with casting slip. We'll watch the pouring of two molds, a one-piece mold for a cup and a two-piece mold for a bowl with bulging sides.

Pouring Molds

1. Slip has been poured into the one-piece mold shown on the right. Now it is being poured into the two-piece mold on the left. The slip must be poured exactly level with the top of the mold without slopping over. As the mold starts to absorb moisture from the slip, the level of the surface will fall. More slip must be added from time to time to keep the mold full.

The longer the slip stands in the mold, the thicker the wall of the cast piece will be. It is not possible to tell you how long the slip must remain in the mold in order to build a wall of the proper thickness; it may be five minutes, it may be thirty, depending upon the consistency of the slip, the density of the mold, and the thickness of wall desired. You can judge the progress of the casting by scraping away the slip with a knife and cutting into the waste rim. That's one reason why a waste rim is provided.

2. When the proper thickness has been built up, pour out the excess slip. The smoothness of the inside surface of the piece depends to a large extent upon the skill with which this is done. Take the mold in two hands. Now, holding it over a bowl or a pitcher, rotate it with a slow steady motion until it is almost, but not quite, upside down. Hold it in that position until all the excess slip has run out, but *don't shake it.*

Then rest it on two sticks laid across a bowl until the slip starts to harden. One of the sticks should be higher than the other so that the mold tips slightly. This prevents drops of slip from collecting on the inside bottom and forming lumps.

153

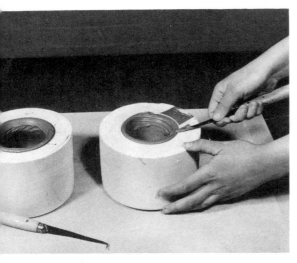

3. When the slip starts to dry, the shine will disappear from the surface; now the mold may be turned right side up and the edges cleaned with a knife.

As the casting continues to dry, it will shrink away from the mold. It is important that the shrinkage be even all the way around; otherwise the piece will warp. Watch the casting as it shrinks and carefully loosen it at any point where it tends to stick.

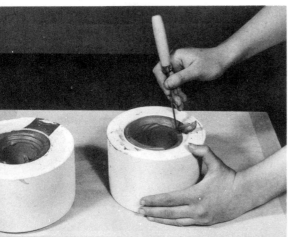

4. Allow the piece to dry for an hour or so, then trim off the waste rim, using a bent knife. (This is a handy tool. To make one, bend the end of a potter's knife at a right angle.) Run the knife around the edge of the waste rim and lift out the ribbon of clay trimmed off. Now the casting is complete. In another hour the piece should be hard enough to remove from the mold.

5. To remove a casting from a one-piece mold, place a flat slab of plaster on top of the mold and reverse the two together; then lift the mold. The piece will remain upside down on the plaster slab, where it may be left to dry. In the two-piece mold, the top half of the mold has been lifted off and the piece left to dry in the bottom half.

A simple two-piece mold of the type illustrated does not have to be tied together before it is poured. More complicated molds, however, must be held together with heavy twine made tight by wedges, or fastened with strong rubber bands.

Finishing the top edge

After the waste rim is trimmed off, the top edge of a cast piece will need smoothing. Do this by grinding it on a piece of glass in the manner shown in Figure 2-8.

Fettling

Pieces cast in molds of two or more parts will have ridges at the seams where the mold parts join. These ridges are called *fettles* and the process of removing them is called *fettling*. Trim the ridges off with a knife and remove any remaining traces with a sponge.

These ridges are a good measure of your craftsmanship. If they are hardly noticeable, you are a good mold maker. If, however, they are quite prominent, better take more care with the next mold you make.

Some points on slip casting

1. Mold pouring must be done with care; otherwise pieces will be warped, lumpy, or marred by air pockets.
2. Stay with your casting. Don't pour a mold and then go away and forget it.
3. Casting slip must be screened just before it is used to eliminate lumps.
4. Air bubbles in slip cause trouble. Get rid of them by pouring the slip back and forth in two pitchers.
5. Pour excess slip out of the mold with a steady, even motion. Shaking the mold will spoil the inner surface of the piece.
6. Time yourself when you pour a new mold so that you know about how long it takes to cast a piece.
7. As a mold is used, it absorbs moisture; therefore, each successive casting requires more time. After six castings, a mold will be too damp for further use. Set it aside to dry overnight.
8. A one-piece mold must be turned right side up as soon as the slip starts to harden to keep the piece from falling out when it shrinks.
9. Clean the top edge of the mold immediately after the slip has started to harden.
10. Release the edge of the casting so that it can shrink away

from the mold evenly. If it sticks in one spot, the piece will be warped.

11. An infrared lamp can be used to hasten the drying of cast pieces.

12. Keep casting scraps separate from other clay. These scraps can be mixed in with the dry ingredients when a fresh batch of casting slip is prepared.

13. Deflocculation is a tricky business. Don't be discouraged by lack of success at first—keep on trying.

Chapter 10

More About Plaster Molds

All the molds described so far have been for drain casting. Now it is time to learn about some other ways of using molds—solid casting with slip, pressing with plastic clay, and a special method of forming plates called *jiggering*. Also, let us study some different ways of working with plaster—the mold maker's method of "running" it under templates while it is setting, and the sculptor's method of building up molds over clay models by applying plaster directly without the use of retaining walls.

Solid casting is different from drain casting in that the mold shapes both the inside and the outside of the cast piece (Fig. 10-1). This method has many advantages, among them the fact that both surfaces of the piece can be controlled, as can the thickness of the wall. In drain casting, the inside of a cup always shows a ring at the foot, while in solid casting the inside is perfectly smooth. In drain casting, two pieces poured in the

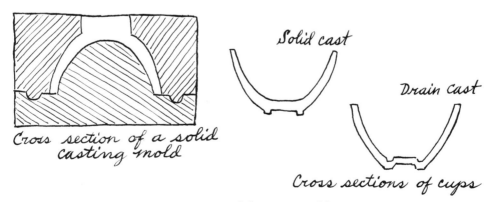

Cross section of a solid casting mold

Solid cast

Drain cast

Cross sections of cups

Fig. 10-1 Solid casting mold.

157

same mold may have walls of different thickness, depending upon how long the slip was left in the mold; but in solid casting, every piece is identical. In solid casting, the thickness of the walls may be made greater at the base. Plates and shallow bowls which cannot be made in drain molds can be solid cast. Obviously, a solid casting mold must be in two or more parts.

Photo Series 20

Making a Solid Casting Mold for a Rectangular Dish

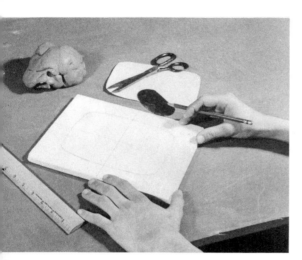

1. Start by drawing the shape of the inside edge of the dish with indelible pencil on a slab of plaster; use perpendicular axes and paper templates to help you, as you did in making the mold of the box. Use a plaster slab about 3 inches longer and wider than your dish will be.

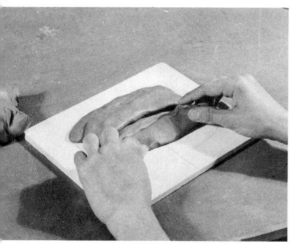

2. Next build up a clay mound on the slab, shaped like the inside of the dish in reverse. Make this as smooth and as symmetrical as you can.

3. A small steel scraper with a toothed edge will be helpful in forming the mound. Drawing the toothed portion over the clay in different directions will take down any irregularities and help pull the form together. The scraper can be bent in the hand to conform to the

158

curve of the corners and can be drawn upward over them.

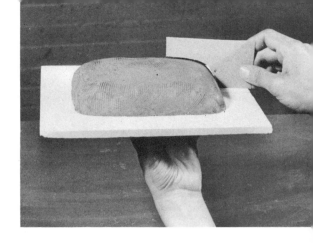

4. It is an easy matter to smooth the scratches when the proper shape is obtained. Cut a cardboard template with which to judge the slope of the sides.

In making a mold of this type, there is a temptation to make it too flat. Since the final dish will become flatter during drying and firing, make the mound higher than you think it should be—and don't forget shrinkage when you plan the size.

5. When the mound is finished, size the plaster slab, size the casting box and put it in place around the edges of the slab. Then pour a layer of plaster about ¾ inch thick to make a waste mold.

6. When the plaster has set, remove it and take out the clay.

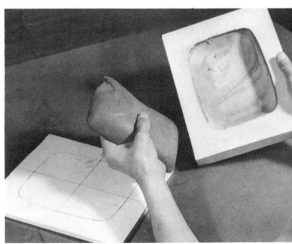

159

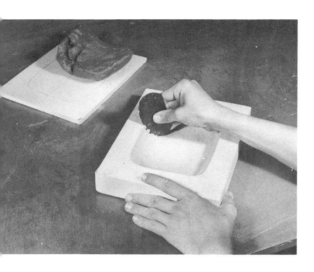

7. Finish the inside surface as well as you can with a scraper.

For an extra-fine surface, use sandpaper. Ordinary sandpaper won't work on wet plaster; so if you have plenty of time, let the waste mold dry thoroughly before finishing it. If you can't afford to wait, use 6-0 garnet paper (sometimes called wet-and-dry sandpaper) which will work pretty well on the wet plaster. The inside of the waste mold is the shape of the inside of your final plate. Study it carefully and make any alterations needed to improve the design.

8. When the waste mold is as good as you can make it, size it, place it in the casting box again, and pour plaster to a depth of about 1½ inch. This will be one-half of the final mold. When this has set, remove the waste mold. (If you have trouble getting the waste mold off, try prying the two apart with the straight edge of your steel scraper. If this does not work, break the waste mold.)

The mold is similar to the clay mound on a slab with which you started, except that now the mound is of plaster. Here you have still another opportunity to smooth the form.

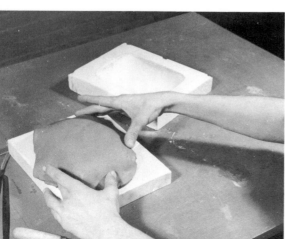

9. The next step is to roll a layer of clay and put it over the mound to form a dish. Use a rolling pin and two strips of wood 3/16 inch thick as guides in making the layer. Draw an outline with in-

160

delible pencil around the edge of the mound, ¼ inch away from it, then work the layer of clay carefully against the plaster and trim it to conform to the outline you have just drawn.

10. The shape you make out of this layer of clay will be the shape of your final dish. Taper it toward the edge so that it is slightly thinner at that point. It will be good to let the clay harden a bit on the plaster so that you may take it off and study its thickness, its weight and its general contour.

You may even cut the clay plate in half to study the cross section. The two halves can be put together again easily on the plaster mound.

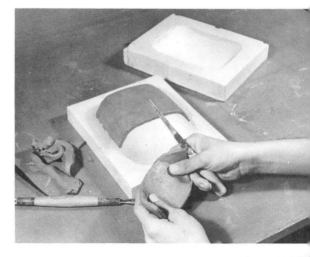

11. The second half of the mold must have an opening or *gate* through which to pour the clay slip. This opening usually coincides with the foot of the piece. When the clay slab is shaped, put it on the mound and build a column of clay to make the gate. Since this will form the foot of the dish, it should start at the point where the curve of the plate changes from horizontal to vertical—in other words, where the bottom joins the sides. The column should taper toward the top and should be high enough to project beyond the plaster which will be poured for the second half of the mold.

12. Now for the final step. Cut notches in the plaster slab. Remember not to put one notch in each corner; cut two at one end and one at the other so that it will be easy to see which way the halves fit together. Size the plaster, set the casting box, and pour the second half of the mold.

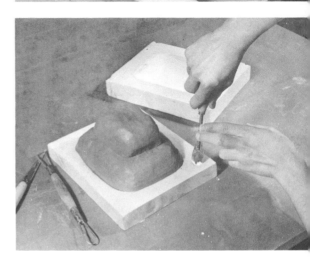

161

13. When the plaster has set, remove the clay. The two pieces of the mold are finished.

14. The mold you have just made requires a deflocculated slip—clay and water won't work. Tie the two halves of the mold together and pour in slip until the mold is half full. Tip the mold from side to side so that no air pockets are trapped, then stand it on a level surface and fill it to the top. As the slip settles, keep adding more so that the mold is always full.

You will have to pour the mold a few times before you know just how long the slip must stand in it. Watch the thickness of the wall which builds up at the edge of the gate. When this is as thick as the wall of your dish or a little thicker, pour out the slip and let the mold dry upside down on two blocks of wood.

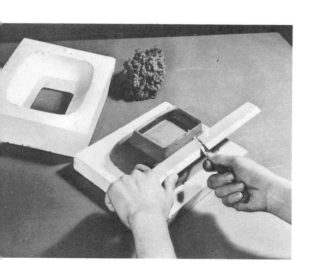

15. When the slip has hardened, remove the top half of the mold, leaving the cast dish in position on the bottom half. The foot will be over 1 inch high and must be cut down to a height of about ¼ inch. Use a ruler as a guide to trim off the excess with a knife. The height of this foot is a matter of taste. You may want it a little higher, or you may prefer no foot at all, in which case, trim the bottom level.

16. When the foot is trimmed, the cast dish is finished. Put it aside to dry.

Loosening a cast piece

Sometimes a solid cast plate sticks to the bottom half of the mold. This is bad because, unless the cast piece is able to loosen and rise off the mold, it will split as it shrinks. If you have this trouble, study the mold to see if there are any undercuts which grip the piece—if there are, remove them with fine sandpaper.

Dusting the surface of the mold with flint before you pour in the slip will help to prevent sticking. Sometimes you can loosen the plate by holding the mold in one hand and rapping it sharply with the other fist. Strike downward and avoid hitting the clay piece. You may use the hose of your spray gun to shoot a stream of air under the piece and lift it free. Be careful, however, that the piece is not blown off entirely and destroyed.

Press Molds

A small figurine of fairly simple design can be made in a two-piece mold, provided its widest part is along the centerline. For example, the little squirrel shown in Figure 10-2 could not be made in a press mold because his ears stick up above the top of his head and his legs project beyond his body; but if we can get him to pull in his ears and his legs a bit, a press mold will work.

Making a press mold

To make a press mold, model the figurine in clay and let it get leather hard. Then mark the centerline and cut a template which will have the profile of the figure at that point. The template must be cut large enough to extend at least 2 inches beyond the figurine.

When the template is cut, place the figure in it so that the top of the template is even with the centerline and lay them both on a bed of clay, as shown (Fig. 10-2). You are now ready to size the template, set the casting box, and pour one half of the mold. When this has hardened, turn it over, leaving the figure embed-

163

This figure can not be made in a press mold — but this one can

Template

Ready to pour first half of mold

Second half of mold — clay model in place

Soft Clay

Trough for excess clay

Cross section of mold

As the two halves are pressed together excess clay is forced into the trough

Fig. 10-2 Making a press mold and pressing a figurine.

ded in the plaster; remove the clay backing and the template, cut the notches, set the casting box, and pour the second half.

The job is not yet finished. When the mold is used for pressing, it must have a trough in each half, completely around the figure, into which the surplus clay will be squeezed when the two halves are pressed together. This trough will have to be cut by hand. Bring it right up *to* the figure, but be careful not to break the edge. If the edge is left sharp, the surplus clay will be cut off when the mold is pressed and the figure will come out clean.

Using a press mold

To use a press mold, take a lump of soft clay the right size (experience will help you to judge), and lay it in the depression of one-half of the mold; then put the other half in place and press. In about a minute, you should be able to open the mold and take out the little figure. If there is any trouble with sticking, dust the mold with flint before pressing.

A press mold gets a lot of rough treatment, so make it extra-thick and make the notch holes large enough so that the projecting lugs don't break off.

Sprig Molds

The English potter, Josiah Wedgwood, devised a method of decorating ware by applying raised figures or ornaments of white clay to colored backgrounds. These ornaments were made in *sprig molds*. As you may imagine, a sprig mold is a block of plaster with a depression shaped like the ornament in reverse (Fig. 10-3). Let's look at a sprig mold in use.

Fig. 10-3   Sprig mold for pressing ornaments.

Photo Series 21

Pressing an Ornament

1. A ball of clay is flattened out.

165

2. The clay is then pressed into the depression in the sprig mold.

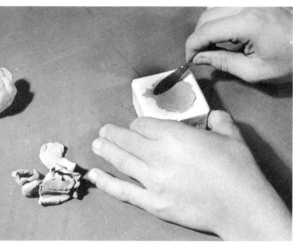

3. The back is smoothed with a spatula.

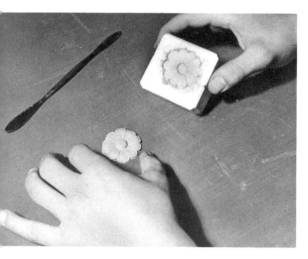

4. The pressing is carefully lifted out. The ornament can then be fastened to the side of a piece with slip.

Some of Wedgwood's sprig molds were made by the outstanding sculptors of his day. If you examine his Jasper ware, you will marvel at the dexterity of the craftsmen who were able to press these delicate figures and attach them without marring them.

A sprig mold is really a one-piece press mold which may be used for small pieces of jewelry, as well as decorations for ware. It is not difficult to make. Model the form in clay, making sure there are no undercuts, then put it on a glass slab. Moisten the clay and press it firmly against the glass before pouring the plaster; otherwise there is danger that your little ornament may float up into the plaster and be lost. Cast a block of plaster over the clay. When the plaster is dry, any slight irregularities may be removed by tooling. (The sun faces shown in the color section, demonstrating glaze samples, were pressed in a mold of a sun with rays but no features. Eyes, noses, hair, and other details were added freehand for the sake of variety.)

A sprig mold may be made, without preliminary modeling, by cutting a hollow design in a plaster block with a gouge similar to that used for cutting linoleum block prints. This method gives a different quality to the ornament produced. It is especially suited to abstract decorations and plant forms.

Jiggering

We now come to a highly mechanical method of making tableware, called *jiggering*. In this process, a lump of clay is placed on a convex plaster bat and turned while a template is held against it. The bat shapes the inside of a plate and the template cuts the outside. When bowls are jiggered, the bat is concave, forming the outside surface, while the template cuts the inside. Jiggering is the most efficient method there is of making bowls and plates. Practically all commercial dinnerware is manufactured this way.

Factory equipment for jiggering is heavy and expensive; comparatively simple jiggering devices can be bought from manufacturers of studio equipment (Fig. 10-4).

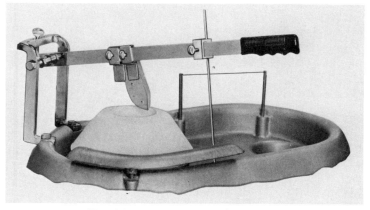

Fig. 10-4   Jiggering outfit, Amaco.

167

Using a Jigger

1. The potter has a bat which fits into the recessed head of his wheel and a template which will form the outside of the saucer.

2. The template is set in place so that it is the right height above the bat. A little piece of wood is used as a thickness gauge.

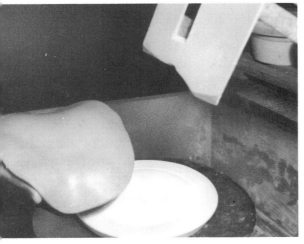

3. A ball of clay the right size is flattened on a board until it is a clay pancake big enough to cover the jigger bat.

4. The top surface of the clay has been smoothed with a steel spatula. The potter puts the clay on the jigger bat so that the smooth surface is next to the bat.

168

5. He rotates the wheel and presses the clay down firmly. Using a sponge, he wets the top surface of the clay and slowly lowers the template, keeping the wheel in motion all the time. The sponge is kept handy to wet the surface of the clay if it starts to get dry.

6. When the jigger arm is down all the way, he holds it there for several seconds to get a smooth surface, then raises it. The saucer is formed. He cuts off the excess clay at the rim.

7. Excess clay is removed. The bat can now be lifted out of the wheel and put aside to dry.

Drape Molds

A very simple type of mold can be used to make flat shapes such as plates and platters. This mold is a convex block of plaster shaped like the inside of the plate in reverse. It can be made in the same way as the bottom piece of the mold for the rectan-

169

gular dish described in *Photo Series 20*. Or, if the plate is round, it can be cut on the wheel. For ease in trimming, the outside edge of the mold is shaped like the plate itself.

When a drape mold is used, a thick layer of clay is rolled out, laid over the mold, and pressed into shape (Fig. 10-5). The edges are then trimmed and the clay is allowed to dry on the mold. When dry, it has the form of the plate.

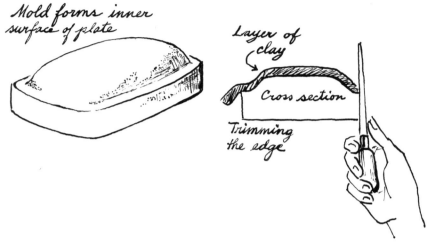

Fig. 10-5   Using a drape mold to make flat shapes.

This is an easy type of mold to use but it has one bad feature—the plates produced are perfectly flat on the bottom. If a foot is desired, it must be modeled and attached while the clay is still on the mold and before it has dried.

"Running" Plaster

Here is an entirely different method of making plaster models. The method makes use of the period of plasticity which plaster goes through before it sets hard; objects are shaped by running a template over the soft plaster—hence the name *running* (plaster workers call this "screeding").

Let's see how we can take advantage of this period of plasticity to shape a model for a bowl. Our first problem will be to rig up some device for running a template over the plaster while it is soft.

A turning rig

To run a model for a bowl, we can borrow a trick from the patternmakers and construct what they call a turning sled. We shall need a perfectly smooth slab of plaster, about 14 by 14 inches and 1 inch thick, with a ¾ inch wooden dowel set in the center as a pivot post, as shown in Figure 10-6. The dowel must be slightly higher than the model will be and must be firmly

170

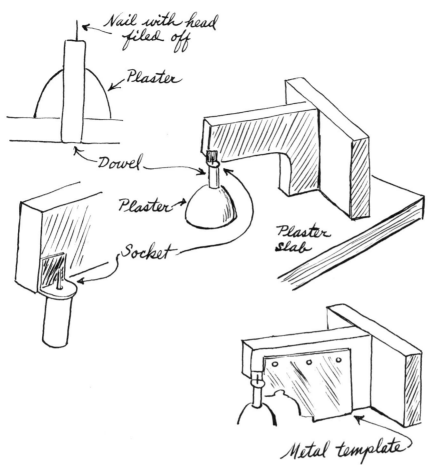

Fig. 10-6   Setting up a turning rig.

held in place. Make a hole for it first, then cast a cone of plaster around it. A small nail driven into the end of the dowel will serve as a pivot for the sled. The sled is made of two pieces of wood nailed together, with a small piece of zinc or tin fastened on the end to serve as a socket for the pivot. The pieces of wood may be any convenient size, but the metal socket must rest on the top of the dowel when the sled stands flat on the plaster slab.

The next step is cutting the template for the shape. This should be drawn on paper first, then scribed on metal. A thin sheet of zinc may be used, or a flattened piece of ordinary tin can. The template is cut out with a pair of tin snips and the edge carefully filed until it is perfectly smooth. If the model is to be any good, the template must be really smooth. In drawing the pattern for the template, remember to allow a waste rim. When the template is finished, nail it to the sled so that one end will just touch the dowel and the other the plaster slab. Now you are ready to begin turning.

171

Sizing

The plaster slab must be either sized or shellacked and coated with stearine. Since the sled must slide freely on the slab, stearine is preferable because it makes a more slippery surface than size. Give the slab three coats of shellac, allowing about 20 minutes for each coat to dry; then brush stearine over the surface and wipe off the excess. The method of preparing stearine is described in Chapter 7. Put a protective layer of clay around the dowel and the plaster cone which holds it, so that the model will come off easily.

Tools

You will need a spoon, a flat steel scraper, a kidney-shaped scraper, a spatula, and two bowls. Have a pail of water handy in which to wash your hands, and a towel for drying.

Mixing

Put water in one of the bowls and add the plaster; allow it to slake in the usual fashion. When it has slaked, stir it once or twice, then dip out a cupful into the second bowl. The plaster in this second bowl will remain undisturbed while you stir the first bowlful. Plaster which is left alone does not set as rapidly as plaster which is stirred; so the cupful you dipped out will remain soft longer and be available for a finish coat after the other has set.

Photo Series 23

Using a Turning Rig

1. Stir the plaster in the first bowl until it starts to thicken. When it is thick enough so that one spoonful will stand on another, dip out some using the spoon (or your fingers if you prefer), and pile it on the clay which you have pressed around the pivot post. Build up a shape which is roughly that of the model, then swing the sled around.

172

2. The first cut of the template will leave several voids in the model where the plaster was not built up high enough; so using the spoon, add more plaster at those points and run the template around again. Repeat the operation until no hollows are left. Lift the sled off the pivot occasionally to clean off the excess plaster, and scrape the plaster slab. It is important that the sled run freely·on the slab; keep both as clean as you can.

3. By this time the first bowlful of plaster will probably start to harden; set it aside and use the plaster in the second bowl to make a "splash coat" for a finishing run. This plaster will still be fairly liquid and you can cover the whole model with it quickly.

4. Then spin the template around for two or three turns to give the final surface. Now carefully lift off the sled without marking the model. In a few minutes the model will be ready to lift off the pivot post—the operation is finished. The model will have a hole in the bottom where the pivot projected through, but this can be plugged with clay and a mold made of the bowl in the usual way.

The turning sled should be cleaned and set aside until you are ready to run another shape. You will be able to use the same rig over and over to make circular plates, bowls, and cups by merely changing the template.

It is a simple matter to run plaster for vase shapes if you construct a turning box. The box has two bearings to hold a

173

metal rod, one end of which is bent into a crank and a handle so that it can be turned. A removable piece of wood holds the metal template. As the plaster is piled up on the rod and the rod is turned, the template cuts the plaster to the desired shape. Let us see how the turning box is used.

Using a Turning Box

1. The potter has assembled his tools and the bowls for mixing plaster. A template to form a vase shape has been cut out of a piece of tin and fastened to the template board. The potter turns the rod and wraps a piece of heavy twine around it. This will give the plaster something to hold to.

2. The potter has mixed his plaster in the large bowl and dipped out a smaller bowlful to work with. The plaster in the larger bowl will be left undisturbed, to be used for the finishing coat. Using a spoon he piles plaster on top of the cord tied around the rod.

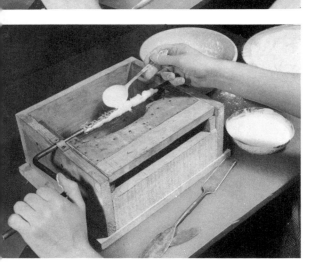

3. Continuing to pile plaster on the rod.

174

4. More plaster is piled on the rod. It is almost time for the first turn.

5. The potter has started to turn the rod, cutting the plaster with the template. A rough vase shape begins to appear.

6. More plaster has been piled on and the rod turned until the complete vase shape is formed. The potter has taken the template board out and is scraping plaster off the template.

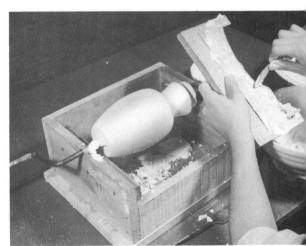

7. Putting on the finishing coat.

175

8. The turning is finished—the potter removes the turning board.

9. The model completed. The potter has unfastened one of the metal strips which hold the rod in place and has pulled the rod out of the model.

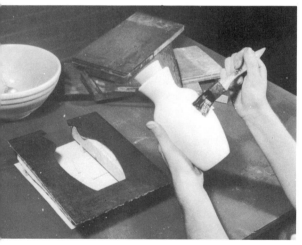

10. Making the mold. A template has been cut out of heavy cardboard, shellacked and sized. The potter is now sizing the model.

11. Setting the model in the template. A thin coil of clay seals the joint.

176

12. Putting the casting box in place. (The inside of the casting box was sized.)

13. Pouring the first half of the mold.

14. Removing the casting box after the first half of the mold has set.

15. Cutting notches in the first half of the mold.

16. Casting box in place, ready to pour the second half of the mold. (The model, the first half of the mold, and the inside of the casting box have been sized.)

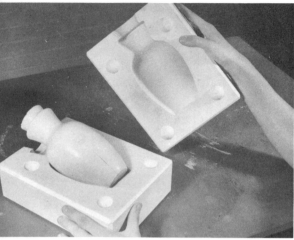

17. The finished mold. The plaster model ready to be removed.

18. Pouring slip into the mold. This picture was taken after the mold had been allowed to dry for several days. Note heavy rubber bands holding the two halves of the mold together.

19. Pouring out the excess slip.

20. Removing the cast piece from the mold. The portion on top is a waste rim and will be trimmed off.

21. The finished vase.

Molds for Ceramic Sculpture

Large pieces of terra cotta—that is, clay sculpture intended for firing—are usually pressed inside of molds. When sculptors make such molds they handle the plaster in a way quite different from any we have described so far. Instead of building a retaining wall and pouring plaster around the clay model, they throw plaster against the model, or paint it on with a soft brush. When the mix is fairly liquid, the model is completely covered with a thin plaster coating. As the plaster starts to set, more is piled on, until a layer an inch thick is built up over the entire model. To make the mold stronger, strips of burlap or heavy twine are sometimes pressed into the plaster while it is still soft, to serve as reinforcement. The places where the mold must separate are marked off first and thin strips of brass, called *shims*, are pressed into the clay along those lines. In this way a mold of several parts can be made in one operation.

179

Pressing terra cotta

Pressing clay in a mold like the one just described is easy if the mold has an opening at the base large enough for the hand. It is merely necessary to tie the pieces of the mold together and brace them firmly; then press a layer of clay over the entire inner surface. The thickness of the layer will depend, of course, on the size of the piece. Unless the sculpture is more than 3 or 4 feet tall, a ¾ inch layer of clay should suffice.

Take care to make the layer uniform, and look out for folds or cracks. When you add clay to some which already has been pressed in the mold, do not put the new clay alongside of the old because you are almost certain to leave a little space where the two pieces join. Instead, put the new clay on top of that already in place, and press the two together so that they form a single mass. This will avoid creases in the surface of the piece. Make sure also that the clay is forced into every corner of the mold.

If, when the pieces of the mold are fastened together, the opening which remains is not big enough to get your hand into, you will have to press a layer of clay in each separate part of the mold, then tie them together and weld the joints on the inside with a long-handled tool. A piece made this way will show cracks at the seams when it comes out of the mold. These will have to be worked over with modeling tools.

The clay used for terra cotta should contain a high percentage of grog. One part of 40–60 mesh grog to two of clay is about right. For large pieces use a coarser mesh.

As soon as the clay has hardened enough to hold its shape, take the mold apart and remove the piece. Trim off the ridges at the seams and do any necessary finishing.

The surface of terra cotta may have a rough texture or may be smooth. Rubbing with a wooden tool or a small steel spatula will give a polished surface with no sign of grog showing. For the opposite effect, use a damp sponge. This will bring the grog into sharp relief and give as rough a texture as you wish.

Photo Series 25

Making a Mold for a Terra-Cotta Sculpture

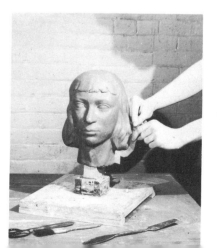

1. The sculptor is setting the shims in place on the model.

180

2. A thin layer of plaster is brushed over the entire model.

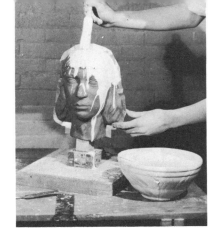

3. Building the mold up to proper thickness, the potter presses the plaster against the model.

4. Reinforcing the plaster with heavy twine to make a stronger mold.

5. Separating the two halves of the mold where the shims were added.

181

6. Removing the front half of the mold from the model.

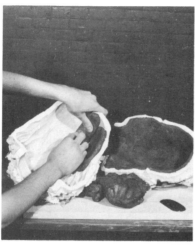

7. A layer of clay is pressed into each half of the plaster mold.

8. The two halves of the mold are tied together. The sculptor must now reach inside and weld the two layers of clay firmly together with his fingers or a wooden tool.

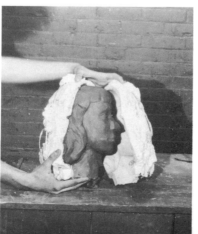

9. Removing the pressed clay sculpture from the mold.

182

Garden Sculpture

Terra-cotta figures can add much to the beauty of a house and its grounds.

The little fountain shown in the color section stands against the rear wall of our own garden, and for a number of years it has splashed merrily away, giving us a lot of pleasure. It was made by a combination of methods. The girl and the fish were built with coils. The bowl was modeled in clay, a plaster mold was cast from the model, and the bowl was pressed in the mold. Holes were cut in the back so that the fountain could be bolted to a wall (Fig. 10-7).

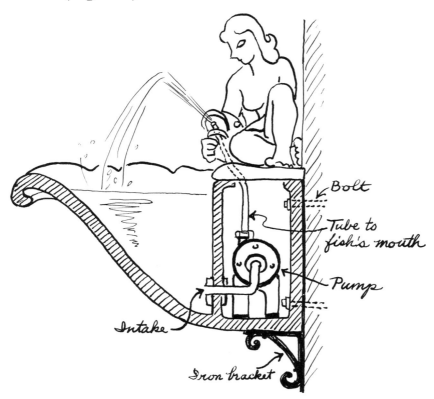

Fig. 10-7   Diagram of a fountain; different methods were
used to build parts of the sculpture.

The fountain contains a small electric pump which circulates water up from the bowl through the fish's mouth, from which it splashes back into the bowl again. A wall at the back of the bowl, built by the slab method, conceals the pump from view.

Some Principles of Design

Pottery made in molds is different from pottery built by hand or thrown on a wheel. It has its own style of beauty; it can be made thinner, lighter in weight (without molds we could never

183

have the pleasure of drinking from paper-thin, translucent tea cups).

Everyone who works with clay should have some knowledge of plaster of paris. For those who plan to make porcelain tableware, skill in the techniques of plaster is essential.

Plaster is well suited to the clean, streamlined surfaces of modern design. One reason for the preeminence of the Scandinavian countries in the field of contemporary ceramics is that the artist-potters of those countries are thoroughly familiar with plaster of paris and its relationship to commercial production. Hence, they are able to lend their talents to the industry.

A mold can be made of any shape, but unless one is interested in figurines it is best to avoid over-elaborate forms.

A mold-made piece should look like what it is, not like something made by hand. However, a discreet use of molds combined with handwork can produce a line of ware with each piece bearing the stamp of the potter's originality.

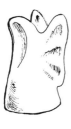

Working with plaster develops craftsmanship and that is good. Sloppy workmanship is inexcusable. Except for waste molds, every mold should be made with as much care as if it were intended for an exhibition.

Finally, the possibility of combining handcraft pottery production with designing for industry should not be overlooked. Cooperation between artists and manufacturers will benefit both.

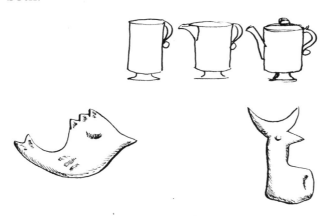

Chapter 11   Clay and Clay Bodies

What is clay? A number of different answers could be given to this question. The chemist would call it a hydrous silicate of alumina; the little boy, nice sticky mud; and they would both be right. But only in part. Clay is not a single substance but a mixture of several substances; while aluminum silicate is the chief ingredient, impurities are always present. These impurities affect the working properties; hence no two clays dug from the ground are exactly alike. All clay, however, has two essential properties: when moist it is plastic, when heated it becomes hard.

A Little Chemistry

An exhaustive knowledge of chemistry is not necessary for ceramic work, but you should be familiar enough with a few chemical elements to recognize their symbols and know something about their behavior. You should also know the chemical composition of a dozen or so minerals indispensable to the potter.

The earth's crust contains over one hundred known elements, each of which has a letter or two as its symbol. When atoms of two or more elements combine to form a molecule of a new substance, the chemical formula of the new substance is made by grouping the symbols of the combining elements with numbers written below the line to indicate how many atoms of each element are in the molecule of the new substance. Thus, two atoms of hydrogen (H) combine with one atom of oxygen (O) to

185

form a molecule of water. The chemical formula of water is therefore H_2O.

Only a few chemical elements are important to us here. Surprisingly, one of these elements is present in such great quantities that it makes up more than one-half of the entire earth's rocky crust—about 58 percent. That element is silicon (Si). The next most plentiful element constituting about 15 percent, is aluminum (Al). These elements are usually found in combination with oxygen, in which case we call them silica (SiO_2) and alumina (Al_2O_3).

Pure clay is composed of one part alumina and two parts silica, plus chemically combined water. Its formula is $Al_2O_3 \cdot 2SiO_2 \cdot 2H_2O$. That is why the chemist calls it a hydrous aluminum silicate. Note that the chemically combined water is not the water which gives clay its plasticity. If you allow clay to become bone dry, the chemically combined water will still be there.

Feldspar

Feldspar is the parent of clay. There was no clay on our globe in the beginning, for all our clay is a product of change, formed by the decomposition of feldspathic rock weathered by air and water during many thousands of years. Feldspar is an important material to the potter because it is used in most glazes and almost all clay bodies. It is the chief ingredient of granite and many other rocks. There are several different kinds of feldspar, but all of them contain alumina and silica plus something else. In the case of orthoclaze, the purest of feldspars, the something else is potash (K_2O) and its formula is $K_2O \cdot Al_2O_3 \cdot 6SiO_2$. Other feldspars contain soda (Na_2O) in addition to potash, some contain lime (CaO), and some contain several ingredients. During the weathering process, these substances are dissolved out of the feldspar, while alumina and silica remain to form clay.

A potter who uses feldspar in a clay body needs to know its chemical formula (or at least whether is a *potash spar*—one containing more potash than soda—or a *soda spar*—one containing more soda).

Close relatives of the feldspars include *Cornwall stone,* a feldspar-like material found in England and used extensively in that country for porcelain-type bodies, and *nepheline syenite,* a feldspathic rock with an unusually high amount of soda and potash in relation to the amount of silica.

Residual clay

Pure clay is composed of alumina, silica, and chemically combined water; but absolutely pure clay is almost nonexistent.

186

The clay most nearly pure is that which has remained in the same spot where it was formed. This is called *residual clay*. *Kaolin*, or china clay, is of this type. It is coarse in texture, difficult to work with (nonplastic), and highly refractory. (A refractory substance is one which resists heat and will not melt readily.) When kaolin is used in a clay body, feldspar or some other flux must be used with it, otherwise the kaolin would not mature in any ordinary kiln. It is white both before and after firing. Kaolin is the principal ingredient in china and porcelain.

Sedimentary clay

Most clay has not remained where it was formed, but has moved great distances, carried by streams, by winds, by glaciers. Such clay is called *sedimentary clay*. As a result of its transportation, it has been ground finer in grain and contains many impurities, hence it is more plastic and less refractory than residual clay. Its color in the natural state may be almost anything—blue, green, yellow, red, brown, gray, or even black. When fired it is usually some shade of red or buff.

Here are some different kinds of sedimentary clay you will have occasion to use.

Plastic kaolin   *Plastic kaolin* is almost a contradiction, for actually no kaolin is really plastic. The term refers to clays which have been transported without becoming contaminated, and so burn white. Because of their finer grain size, they are a little more workable than regular kaolins and are therefore valuable as body ingredients.

Florida lake kaolin or Edgar plastic kaolin (EPK) is of this type. Grolleg, a white clay imported from England, is a plastic kaolin. Grolleg has a lower shrinkage from wet to dry than any other kaolin. This makes it especially well suited for slip casting and extruding.

Ball clay   *Ball clay* is a sedimentary clay which, in most cases, has been carried in a stream and deposited on the bottom of some body of water. It is extremely fine in grain and usually has carbonaceous material mixed with it. As a result, it is highly plastic. When mined it is often dark in color, but it fires almost white. It is used in porcelain and white ware bodies to provide workability.

Fire clay   *Fire clay* is a rough-textured clay, usually dark in color, which will stand high temperatures. It is an important ingredient in stoneware bodies. Fire clays are used commercially in the manufacture of refractory brick.

Stoneware clay   Like fire clays, *stoneware clays* will stand high temperatures, but they are smoother and more plastic and usually fire to a light buff color. In a reducing fire they become

187

dark gray or brown. Monmouth and Jordon (or Gordon) are stoneware clays.

Common clay *Common clay* is the material used to make bricks. It is abundant throughout the country, usually fires dark red or brown, and hardens at low temperatures. Common clays vary widely in their characteristics, but they have much to offer the potter who will take the trouble to learn their secrets.

Digging your own

There is no thrill in pottery quite equal to that of digging your own clay, preparing it for use, and making something from it. Common clay is abundant, and the chances are that you are closer to a clay bed than you imagine.

No two common clays are alike. They differ in color, they react differently to the fire, they have different degrees of plasticity. Some can be cast and some cannot.

You may find clay at the side of a stream or where a road has been cut through. It is often about 5 feet below the surface of the ground. You can recognize it by the fact that it will be plastic when wet and can be modeled into shapes. Dig some and prepare it for use, then test its properties.

Preparing clay

Clay, after being dug, must be spread out to dry, preferably on wooden boards in the bright sun. When it is thoroughly dry, large lumps may be pounded with a mallet or a block of wood and broken up. Then the clay can be made into slip by sifting it into a pail of water and allowing it to slake for several hours. It is advisable to use twice as much water as clay so that the resultant slip will be quite liquid and easier to screen. After the clay has slaked, stir it thoroughly and then pour it through a 40-mesh sieve. The clay would be better screened through a sieve of finer mesh than this, say 80 or 100, but it would be difficult to get it through. If trouble is experienced in screening through a 40-mesh sieve, you may have to pour the clay through a coarser sieve first.

After screening, allow the liquid slip to settle for three or four hours, then pour the excess water off the top. The remaining clay slip can then be poured into plaster drying bats and allowed to harden until it is the right consistency for wedging. *Note*: Three or four layers of cheesecloth laid in the drying bat before the slip is poured in will make it easier to lift the clay out and will keep the drying bat cleaner.

The next step is to try out the clay to see how it works. Make a pinch pot or two; throw a bowl. Let them dry, fire them, and examine the results. You may be in luck and find that your clay is good for the kind of work you plan to do. If not, you will have to make some tests to find out what must be done to improve it.

Testing Physical Properties of Clay

A great deal can be learned about a clay by feeling it when it is moist. Plasticity and working quality can be judged that way, but until you try it out, you will not be sure at what temperature your clay matures. There are other things which you should measure—density, porosity, and degree of shrinkage.

Plasticity

Plasticity is the property which makes clay workable. If a small piece can be rolled into a thin cylinder about the size of a lead pencil and then formed into a bracelet, the clay is plastic or "long." If it refuses to take such a shape, but breaks and crumbles instead, the clay is nonplastic, or "short."

Adding from 10 to 20 percent of ball clay will improve plasticity; so will the addition of a small percentage of bentonite.

Bentonite Bentonite is a clay of volcanic origin, about the most plastic substance known. When it is wet, it swells and becomes a colloidal or jelly-like substance. From 0.5 to 2.0 percent added to a clay increases plasticity considerably. It must always be mixed dry with dry clay in powder form. Too much bentonite will make a clay sticky and impossible to wedge.

Aging It is not known for sure what makes clay plastic. Fineness of grain has something to do with it. Organic matter and bacterial action have a lot to do with it, also. It is said that the old Chinese potters used to throw the carcasses of dead animals into their clay pits so that the products of decomposition would improve the clay.

Aging clay by keeping it moist in a covered container for several weeks improves its working properties. Sometimes, inoculating a fresh batch of clay with some from an old batch promotes the growth of bacteria and so increases plasticity.

Water of plasticity You may wish to measure the percentage of water needed to make your clay plastic. To do this, weigh out 100 grams of dry clay powder and put it on a glass slab. Then put 50 grams of water into a graduate from which you can pour it, drop by drop onto the clay, meanwhile working the clay with a spatula until just the right amount of water has been added to make the clay plastic. The reading on the graduate will show the number of grams of water you have used. Since you started with 100 grams of clay, this number of grams is the percentage of water of plasticity. In most clays the percentage is between 30 and 45. Usually the higher the percentage, the more plastic the clay.

189

Firing range

To measure the maturing temperature of your clay, make draw trials. Prepare five tiles 6 x 1½ inches and ¼ inch thick; number them. Place these in the kiln with the ends resting on two kiln props.

Make a cone pat with a series of five cones, small clay pyramids with fluxes added so they will melt at known temperatures (see Ch. 12, Pyrometric Cones). If you plan to fire your ware in the temperature range between cone 04 and cone 1, use cones 06, 04, 02, 1, and 2. For higher firing, use higher cones. Put the cone pat in the kiln where you can see it through the peep hole, then fire the kiln. When cone 06 bends, remove tile #1; at cone 04 remove tile #2; and so on. When the tiles have cooled, examine them for color and deformation.

The maturing temperature of the clay is the one at which it attains optimum hardness and density without slumping. To raise the maturing point, add some more refractory clay; for example, from 5 to 15 percent of stoneware clay or fire clay.

To lower the maturing point, add from 5 to 15 percent of fluxing materials such as nepheline syenite, talc (a ground up steatite rock), or body frit. (Frits are most useful to the potter as glaze ingredients; we shall learn more about them in Ch. 13.)

Density

When you have determined the best temperature at which to fire the clay, test its density at that point. You can judge this quality in your ware by tapping it and listening to the ring. The denser it is, the clearer the tone.

A more accurate measure, however, is the absorption test. Weigh a piece of fired clay, then let the piece stand in water overnight. After it has soaked for 12 hours, take it out of the water, remove any surface moisture, and weigh the piece again. Its percentage of absorption will be indicated by the following formula:

$$\frac{\text{weight wet minus weight dry}}{\text{weight dry}} \times 100 = \%\ \text{absorption}$$

In general, an absorption of 5 to 10 percent is all right. Above 10 percent, the ware will be too absorbent for use. Glazes will craze and liquids will be absorbed into the body, eventually seeping through.

Density can be increased and absorption reduced by using fluxes or by adding flint. Try various amounts from 5 to 20 percent, making a number of test tiles and firing them to find out which percentage gives the best results.

Porosity

A clay may be extremely plastic and easy to work with, yet be unsuitable for making ware because every piece comes out of the kiln warped or cracked. The clay is not porous enough. There is no way for the water to leave and so, in drying and during firing, distortion takes place. Something must be added to the clay to "open it up," to give it porosity. Your problem will be to do this without destroying its plasticity to the point where the clay becomes unworkable, for plasticity and porosity do not often go together. You may have to sacrifice some of one in order to increase the other.

Try adding from 10 to 20 percent of a coarser-grained clay, such as fire clay. If this does not solve your problem, try using a coarser screen in preparing the clay, for frequently a natural clay contains enough sand to make it porous. Thus a clay which warps badly when screened through a 60-mesh sieve may work satisfactorily if screened through a 20-mesh sieve. (Some potters who use native clay don't screen it at all, preferring the rougher surface obtained that way.)

In heavy pieces or where coarse texture is desirable, porosity can be obtained by the use of grog. Use a 40–60 mesh and add 20 to 30 percent grog. For large sculpture, clay can be made porous and lighter in weight by using organic materials such as sawdust or coffee grounds in place of grog. These burn out during the fire, leaving voids.

Shrinkage

Clay shrinks as it dries and it shrinks some more when it is fired. Different clays shrink different amounts.

To measure shrinkage, make a tile out of the clay, about 6 inches long, 1 inch wide, ¼ inch thick. On this, score a line with a knife and measure two points exactly 10 centimeters apart. (We use centimeters because it is easier to measure tenths that way.) Allow the tile to dry, then measure the distance between the two points. This will show you the dry shrinkage of the clay. Next fire the tile to the maturing point and measure the distance again. This will give you the fired shrinkage. This shrinkage may be expressed as a percentage as follows:

$$\frac{\text{original length minus fired length}}{\text{original length}} \times 100 = \% \text{ shrinkage}$$

For example, if the distance between the two points after the tile is fired is 8.4 centimeters, the percentage would be:

$$\frac{10\text{-}8.4}{10} \times 100 = 16\% \text{ shrinkage}$$

191

Evaluating the tests

At the conclusion of this series of tests you will have a pretty good idea of the possibilities of your clay. If you decide that it is worthwhile to make a clay body out of it, let it dry, add the ingredients you have found necessary (also in the dry state), mix them together, then pour them into a large container of water. (Adding clay to water rather than water to clay ensures that the clay can slake without balling up into a sticky mass, as sometimes happens when water is poured onto dry clay.) Stir the mixture, screen it, and pour it into drying bats. You may decide that the advantages of digging your clay are not great enough to offset the hours of labor spent in digging, screening, and mixing, and that it is preferable in the long run to buy clay already prepared. Even so, you will feel that the experience has been a good one.

Clay Bodies

Developing a clay body formula

Working out a body formula of your own is a matter of trial and error. Start with a clay body you have used, whose formula you know. Decide which of its qualities could be made better for your requirements, then try a number of experimental additions. Following the suggestions given in the last section, see if you can improve its working properties or its firing range. Keep a record of your experiments.

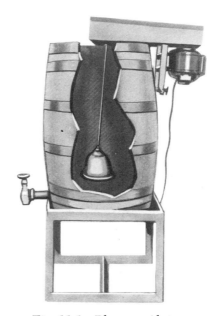

Fig. 11-1   Blunger, Alpine.

192

Equipment

Industrial Clay mixing   In industrial work, clay bodies are prepared by weighing out the ingredients dry, then putting them in water and allowing them to slake, after which the mixture is put through a *blunger*. This is a stirring machine which thoroughly mixes the slip for several hours. After this, in the case of white ware bodies, the slip is passed over magnets to remove iron particles.

The slip then goes to the *filter press*, where moisture is pressed out and it becomes layers of plastic clay. These are put into a *pug mill* for further mixing, after which the clay is ready for forming on the jigger. If the ware is to be cast, the clay which

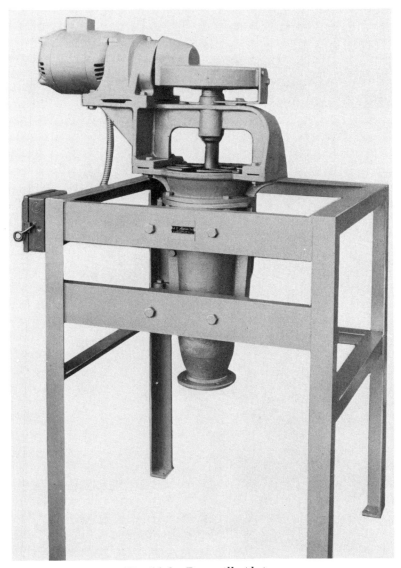

Fig. 11-2   Pug mill, Alpine.

Fig. 11-3　Pug mill, Amaco.

comes from the filter press is allowed to dry, then made into a casting slip and deflocculated.

Studio equipment　　Few studio potters are able to afford the kind of equipment common in industrial use. Some small

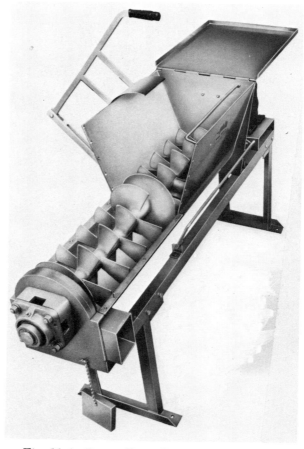

Fig. 11-4　Pug mill, Walker Jamar Company.

studios, however, have been able to make use of old concrete mixers, discarded by builders, as clay mixing machines. Ceramics classes in schools can sometimes use an old dough mixer no longer good enough for the school cafeteria.

Manufacturers aware of the growth of ceramic shops in schools and community centers have begun to manufacture smaller, less expensive blungers and pug mills.

With this kind of mixing machinery, dry ingredients can be blended with just the right amount of water to make a workable body (*see Water of plasticity*), thus eliminating the need for drying bats.

Some Clay Body Recipes

Quantities refer to parts by weight.

Low fire bodies

Most natural clays can be used for earthenware fired from cone 06 to cone 1. These usually fire some shade of red or buff.

Talc is used in white bodies prepared for studio potters and school use. Bodies with high percentages of talc mature at low temperatures and have a long firing range. They are not plastic enough for throwing unless 1–2 percent of bentonite is added.

White art ware body for cone 06
Ball clay	33.3
Talc	66.7

Low fire stoneware type body for cone 04
Ball clay	60
Nepheline syenite	5
Talc	15
Ferro frit #3293	20

White body suitable for throwing; cone 04
Florida lake clay (EPK)	50
Ball clay	10
Feldspar	10
Flint	27
Cryolite	3
Bentonite 1%	2

White talc body suitable for throwing; cone 04
China clay	15
Ball clay	30
Feldspar	8.75
Talc	25
Flint	15

195

Ferro enamel frit 3195	6.25
Bentonite 2%	2

For making a casting slip, omit the bentonite and deflocculate as follows:

Body	1000
Water	480
Sodium silicate	1.5
Soda ash	1.5
Sodium tannate	2.0

Terra-cotta body for sculpture; cone 04 to cone 2

Monmouth or Jordan clay	30
Dalton red clay	25
Grog 20–40 mesh	30
Flint	15

This body has a wide firing range. At 04 it will be pale red, at higher temperatures it becomes darker.

Medium fire bodies

Earthenware fired in the middle range from cone 1 to cone 5 is dense and durable. It can have the characteristics of stoneware and at the same time have the brilliant colors obtainable from low and medium fired glazes.

Red body for cones 1 to 5

Local red clay	25
Stoneware clay	25
Ball clay	25
Fire clay	10
Flint	15

White body for cones 1 to 5

China clay	30
Ball clay	20
Flint	10
Nepheline syenite	30
Talc	10

Parian ware

This is a type of soft-paste porcelain much used for figurines in England during the latter half of the nineteenth century. When fired but not glazed it is almost white with a surface texture resembling Parian marble from the Greek island of Paros.

Parian ware body for cone 4

Ball clay	35
Nepheline syenite	65
Bentonite 3%	3

Stoneware bodies

At stoneware temperatures, impurities in clay melt and produce specks of color and interesting textures.

Stoneware body good for throwing; cone 8

Monmouth or Jordan clay	20
XX sagger clay	55
North American fire clay	10
Nepheline syenite	5
Flint	5
Grog 40-60 mesh	5
Iron chromate	2

This body will fire a warm red. For casting, make a deflocculated slip as follows:

Clay body	1000
Water	400
Sodium silicate	1.5
Soda ash	1.0

High fire bodies

At cone 8 and above, many technical problems disappear. Clay becomes hard and vitreous and is serviceable even without a glaze. Pieces are stronger. Colors are more subtle, approaching the natural colors of rocks. The longer you look at high fired ware, the more you will like it.

A porcelain body for cone 10 to cone 15

English china clay	17
Florida lake clay	8
Ball clay	25
Feldspar	25
Flint	25

A porcelain body using Grolleg (David Silverman), cone 10 to cone 15

Grolleg	35
EPK	25
Feldspar	20
Flint	15
Ball clay	5
Bentonite	2

These two bodies can be deflocculated in the same manner as the stoneware body.

Porcelain fired to cone 18 and above can stand extreme variations in temperature. This makes it an important material in the manufacture of spark plugs, jet engines, and space rockets.

197

Flameproof and ovenware bodies

For many centuries mankind has cooked with earthenware pots. In Mexican villages today such pots are put directly on charcoal fires.

To stand the shock of alternating heating and cooling, pots must be of a coarse-grained clay, underfired.

Stoneware can be used in the oven if it is glazed with a glaze that fits it well and is fired to cone 10. Body formulas for such ware should contain as little silica as possible (no flint) and should have some feldspar.

The shapes of ovenware should be compact and rounded, without corners. Walls should have an even thickness.

Raku bodies

To withstand the shocks of raku firing and cooling, pieces must be made out of extremely coarse and porous clay bisqued at low temperatures ranging from 010 to 02.

The best methods of forming for raku are variations of the pinchpot technique. When a pot is made by combining two or more pieces of clay, the chance of its coming through the raku fire safely is greatly reduced.

Color in clay bodies

Clay bodies can be colored in the way that glazes are, by the addition of metal oxides; but if you plan to do any quantity of work with colored bodies, you will find it cheaper to use the prepared body stains. Red iron oxide and iron chromate are good, inexpensive body colorants.

Grog adds much to the beauty of clay bodies, especially when it is of a contrasting color. Buff grog looks good in red clay and, similarly, red grog gives an interesting effect in buff clay. Red grog can be made by pounding up a common brick and screening the fragments. An easier way to make colored grog is to add the desired color to some plastic clay, then let it dry, crush it with a rolling pin, and screen it to the proper size. After this, put it in an unglazed bisque dish and fire it in your kiln. When it has been fired it will need crushing and screening again, but this will be much easier than crushing hard fired clay.

A small percentage of manganese dioxide will produce interesting specks in clay when it is fired.

When you add color to a clay body, don't overdo it. Often, bright colors which attract at first soon lose their appeal. The subtle natural colors of clay are best in the long run.

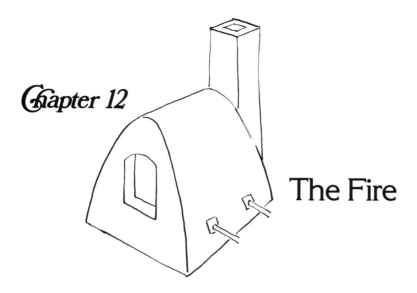

Chapter 12

The Fire

The discovery that fire hardens clay was made many thousands of years ago in widely separated parts of our earth. We can imagine how it came about—a basket, lined with clay to make it hold water, fell by accident into a fire; when the basket had burned away, a hard, somewhat waterproof pot remained. Thus, one of mankind's oldest sciences was born.

The earliest potters fired their ware in open pits on beds of burning twigs. More burning twigs were put on top of the piled up pots and the whole arrangement was covered with potshards or manure.

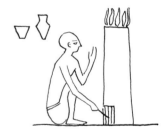

With time, improvements were made in the open pits; grates were provided to allow air to circulate under the fire so that it would burn hotter, then walls of brick were added. By the time roofs and chimneys made their appearance, the open pits had become kilns.

Kilns

Temperature and heat

Applying heat to an object raises its temperature. How much depends on the amount of heat, how it is applied, and how it is confined. A lighted match, for example, held under a teaspoon filled with water will raise the temperature of the water several degrees. The same amount of heat, however, would have practically no effect in raising the temperature of a room. In the first case the heat is confined within a small space, in the latter it is dissipated. Heat is measured in British thermal units (BTUs); temperature is measured in degrees centigrade or degrees

Fahrenheit. The potter's problem is to produce heat and keep it confined within the kiln so that the clay reaches its maturing temperature without loss of time or fuel.

Fuels

Anything that will burn can be used to fire pottery, but since time immemorial potters have relied upon wood and coal, and more recently, gas and oil. Most recent of all—a source of heat for potters is electricity. We'll consider the last of these first.

Electric kilns

For studio potters and for schools, electric kilns are the most convenient to use. They are easy to fire, inexpensive, do not require chimneys. Manufacturers of electric kilns offer a wide choice for the studio potter. Some are top loading (Fig. 12-1), others are front loading (Fig. 12-2). Some are made in sections so that the height of a kiln may be increased by adding additional rings.

Electric kilns are heated by elements which get hot when an electric current passes through them. The earliest electrical kilns used elements of nichrome wire but, because of its low temperature range, nichrome has been largely replaced by Kanthal, a metal alloy made in Sweden which can reach tem-

Fig. 12-1   Top-loading electric studio kiln, 3 cubic feet, Alpine.

200

Fig. 12-2   Front-loading electric kiln, 16 cubic feet, Alpine.

peratures high enough for stoneware and porcelain. Another type of element is Globar—a ceramic product (silicon carbide) containing no metal; this can reach still higher temperatures.

Electric kilns can be equipped with pyrometers to measure temperature within the kiln. They can have automatic cutoff devices which will turn off the kiln when the desired temperature has been reached, or even automatic timers like those in electric ovens. The heat is apt to be more uniform throughout the kiln, especially in the top-loading type which has elements on four sides of the chamber. In electric kilns the problem of unwanted reduction never occurs.

One disadvantage of electric kilns is that elements burn out. Proper care will prolong their life but in spite of all precautions, they will eventually need to be replaced. Before purchasing an electric kiln, it is wise to check on the cost of replacement elements.

Some small electric kilns can be plugged into a regular 110-volt house circuit, but medium sized kilns require 220 volts and heavy duty wiring. Information on this point should be obtained from the manufacturer before buying.

201

Fuel-burning kilns

The potter's choice of fuel is usually limited to gas or oil. Coal is used for little other than heavy industrial ceramic production, and wood is becoming hard to find.

The decision between gas and oil will depend upon the availability of natural gas. Manufactured gas does not burn with as hot a flame as the natural product so, if the latter is not available, oil would be the better choice for the potter. Oil is cheaper than gas but a bit more troublesome to fire.

Gas and oil-burning kilns require specially designed burners, usually equipped with blowers. They also require chimneys.

Despite the growing scarcity of wood, some potters are still able to use it as a fuel. This creates a lot of smoke so kilns have to be in relatively isolated areas. When stoneware is fired with wood, some of the ash almost invariably lands on the glazes; this produces an accidental mottled effect which is pleasing.

Note: In some parts of the world, primitive potters still fire their work in open pits, using wood for fuel. (I have seen a potter in Mexico use old rubber tires, much to the distress of his neighbors.)

For studio potters, some experiments with open pit firing may

Fig. 12-3   Up draft cylindrical gas kiln, extender ring available; California Kiln Company.

202

Fig. 12-4   Sun Face, local clay covered with
borax paste, fired in open fireplace while
protected by broken flowerpot.

prove rewarding. I have had some interesting results from firing
ware in an open fireplace as well as in a charcoal grill (Fig.
12-4).

Kiln types

Portable   The term portable does not mean that a kiln can
be picked up and carried around, but merely that it was manufactured in a factory and shipped in one piece. The manufacturers of such kilns have illustrated catalogs with complete
technical information about burners, blowers and other features. Anyone contemplating the purchase of a portable fuel-
burning kiln would be wise to collect and peruse a number of
such catalogs.

Up draft   One of the simplest kilns I ever saw was a
homemade box made of insulating refractory brick, with four
holes at the bottom for bunsen burners, and an opening at the
top which could be closed by laying two bricks over it. It had no
chimney. A layer of asbestos millboard fastened with iron rods
enclosed the whole kiln and held the bricks together. This was
an up draft kiln. It could fire to cone 04.

Muffle   A *muffle* is a chamber made of refractory material
into which ware is placed for firing. Between the muffle and the
outer wall of the kiln is a space through which flames circulate,
entering at the bottom, passing all around the muffle, and leaving through a flue at the top. In some muffle kilns, the wall of
the muffle contains passage for the flames; in others, the flames
travel in tubes just inside the muffle itself. The latter type pro-

203

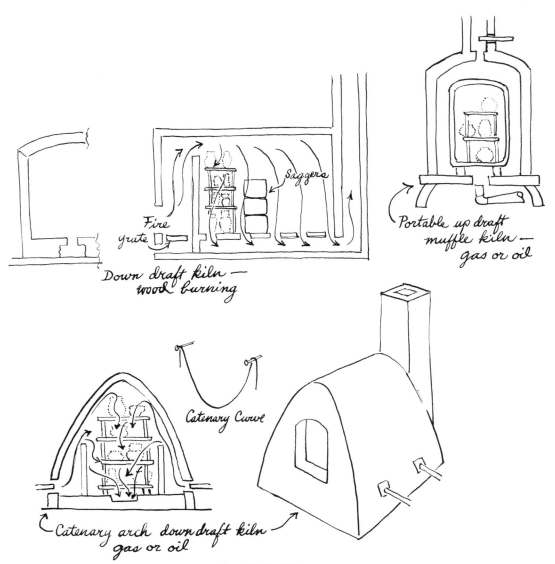

Fire grate

Saggers

Down draft kiln —
wood burning

Portable up draft
muffle kiln —
gas or oil

Catenary Curve

Catenary arch down draft kiln —
gas or oil

Fig. 12-5   Kiln types.

vides more even heat because tubes are placed at the front and
rear as well as the sides (the tubes at the front are removed
when the kiln is loaded or unloaded). Muffle kilns without a
passage for the flames inside the door are apt to be cooler at that
portion.

Muffle kilns protect the ware from contact with the flame—an
important factor in most glazed work. They do not use fuel
economically, however, as too much heat escapes up the chimney.

Down draft   A *down draft* kiln has no muffle. The flames
enter from the front or sides at the bottom of the kiln, pass over a
baffle or bag wall, and reach the ware at the top. They are then
drawn down through openings in the floor into a flue connected

204

to a chimney. In their passage through the kiln the flames come in direct contact with everything in it. This is alright for most stoneware, but for certain types of porcelain the ware must be stacked in saggers, boxes made of refractory materials which act as separate muffles.

Down draft kilns use fuel more economically than muffle kilns; for extremely high fire work a down draft kiln is essential.

Almost all down draft kilns must be built on the spot, but some manufacturers are now producing portable models (Fig. 12-6).

Fig. 12-6   Portable down draft gas kiln, 12 cubic feet, Geil Kilns.

Car kilns   As the name implies, a car kiln is one in which ware is loaded on a car and then rolled into the kiln (Fig. 12-7). This makes loading the kiln much simpler—especially for large pieces of sculpture.

Tunnel kilns   All the kilns described so far are *periodic*, that is, they must be fired, allowed to cool, unloaded, then loaded and fired again. A more efficient type for industrial use is the continuous or tunnel kiln, in which ware travels slowly on a moving platform through a tunnel where it encounters successively increasing temperatures until, at the center of the tunnel, full maturing temperature is reached. Continuing on its way, the ware cools slowly until at the end of the tunnel it is ready to be lifted off the platform and sent to the shipping room. The firing cycle takes from 70 to 90 hours.

205

Fig. 12-7   Car shuttle kiln, 60 cubic feet, Alpine.

Kiln Construction

Many potters today build their own kilns and so can you—but don't try it until you have had considerable experience in firing kilns of different types and have had an opportunity to study their construction. No attempt will be made in this book to furnish plans for kiln building. You can get such plans, however, from the manufacturers of refractory brick, along with helpful advice to suit your special needs.

Circulation and insulation

The main problems in building a kiln are providing proper circulation of heat and adequate insulation. The portions of the kiln which come in contact with the flame must be refractory, able to stand intense heat. The best insulator is dead air space. Other insulators are fuller's earth, asbestos, glass fiber, and vermiculite (bloated mica). Ordinary clay, mixed with 60 percent of coarse sawdust and burned slowly, produces a porous brick with good insulating properties.

"Fiberfrax," a product of the Carborundum Co. of Niagara Falls, N.Y., is a new insulating material made by melting alumina and silica grains in an electric furnace and then blasting by high velocity gases into light and fluffy fibers. This thermal insulation combines high heat resistance with the light weight and flexibility of fiber. It is available as a bulk fiber, as a paper, and as a felt blanket. We shall discuss some of the special uses of this material later in this chapter.

Refractory bricks

Refractory insulating bricks are made by a number of different manufacturers. These will stand high temperatures and act as nonconductors of heat at the same time. Such bricks are

206

labeled K20, K26, K28, and so on. The number indicates the hundreds of degrees Fahrenheit the brick can stand. Thus K20 is good for 2000°F, K26 for 2600°F. K26, K28, and K30 are suitable for almost any kiln work. K20 is good for low fire kilns, especially electric kilns, while bricks numbered below K20 will not stand direct contact with the fire, but must be used in back of a refractory layer.

To simplify kiln construction, manufacturers of refractory insulating brick make them in a number of different shapes and sizes adaptable to all sorts of arches and walls. You will find these fully illustrated in their catalogues. Some firms also produce high-temperature mortars suitable for casting roof slabs or floors.

Stacking a Kiln

A few simple precautions followed in stacking and firing your kiln will save heartaches when you open it. Where production is large, raw ware and glazed pieces are fired separately, but the studio potter usually fires both at the same time. There is no harm in doing this if the firing schedule is controlled so that both types of ware are matured properly.

Too often impatience leads us to put raw pieces into the kiln before they are bone dry. The result is that moisture cannot get out and the pieces blow up. One such explosion can ruin everything else in the kiln. Remember, clay needs several days to dry out: for safety's sake, allow too much time for drying rather than too little. If in doubt, hold the piece against your cheek. The least sensation of coolness means that the piece is not dry enough to put into the kiln. Don't fire a piece of pottery if any part of it is an inch thick or more, unless it contains grog.

When clay matures, the fluxes in it melt and soften. Any unequal strains on a piece at this time will cause it to warp. Be careful that pieces have level surfaces to stand on. Grind any bumps off kiln shelves to make them even and, if necessary, put a little flint under pieces to give them uniform support.

Unglazed raw ware can be stacked quite closely, one piece inside another, without ill effects; but watch distribution of weight.

Dry footing

Glazed ware will stick fast to anything it touches during the fire. This means especial attention must be paid to the foot. Most potters today *dry foot* their work by removing all the glaze from the rim on which the piece stands or by applying their glazes in such a way that the bottom of the piece is left bare. This not only prevents pieces from sticking but also provides better support. Glazes, of course, must not flow too freely.

207

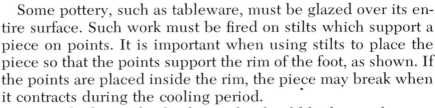

Stilts

Some pottery, such as tableware, must be glazed over its entire surface. Such work must be fired on stilts which support a piece on points. It is important when using stilts to place the piece so that the points support the rim of the foot, as shown. If the points are placed inside the rim, the piece may break when it contracts during the cooling period.

Ware which is to be fired on stilts should be bisqued two or three cones higher than the temperature of the glaze firing, otherwise there is danger that the stilts will push pieces out of shape. Raw ware to which glaze has been applied without bisque firing first should not be stood on stilts. Such pieces must be dry footed.

Some further precautions

Before putting a glazed piece in the kiln, examine it to see if the glaze is apt to cause trouble. If it is unevenly applied, thick in some places and thin in others, the piece should not be fired. Glaze which is too thin will not flow and form the desired surface.

Glazed pieces must be thoroughly dry before being placed in the kiln.

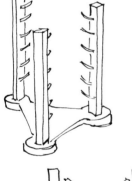

Examine the surface of the glaze. If there are cracks, the glaze will probably crawl. Try rubbing the cracks gently with your fingertip to remove them and produce a smooth, even surface. This will sometimes correct the difficulty; but if sections of the glaze flake off, the piece should be washed and reglazed.

Place glazed pieces in the kiln so that they are protected from each other. Every new batch of glaze is to be regarded with suspicion—you might have forgotten to put in the alumina or made a mistake in weighing the flux, and the glaze may be much more fluid than you suspect. Guard against this possibility by placing the ware in such a way that if the glaze should run, it will not ruin other pieces. A good potter will never use any glaze until he has fired a test sample first.

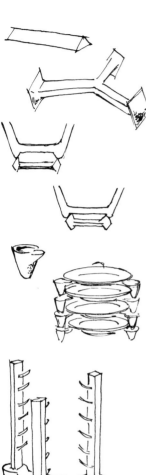
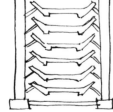

Kiln wash

To protect kiln shelves from bits of glaze which will fall on them, paint them before each firing with a coat of kiln wash made of equal parts flint and china clay, mixed with water to the consistency of cream. Brush this mixture on the shelves with a varnish brush. Kiln wash does not fuse during the firing; any glaze which falls on it can be easily chipped off.

Kiln wash should be applied to the floor of the kiln but not to the top or the sides, and it should be used only on the top surface of kiln shelves. If you put it on the underside of a shelf, it will flake off during the firing and fall into glazed pieces, making ugly blemishes almost impossible to remove.

Some glazes affect others during the fire. Chrome is a bad actor in this respect, for a glaze containing it will give a pinkish tinge to any tin glazes which stand near it. Lead will sometimes volatilize and settle on nearby pieces. With bright glazes this won't matter, but mat pieces will become glossy when you don't want them that way. You will learn by experience which glazes need to be kept to themselves and will be able to take the necessary precautions when stacking.

Potters are finding fiberfrax paper to be valuable as a substitute for kiln wash. It allows kiln shelves to remain cleaner and avoids the danger of bits of kiln wash getting into glazed pieces.

Kiln dirt

Too many pieces of pottery are marred by kiln dirt. Shelves and walls constantly shed particles, hard to notice when the kiln is stacked but big enough to ruin the beauty of a glazed bowl when they land in its center. Stack your glazed pieces with care to avoid this. Just before the final placing, take them out of the kiln and blow gently on the inside surface to remove any specks.

Placement in the kiln

Some parts of your kiln will fire hotter than others. Consider this variation when you place the ware, so that those glazes which require the highest temperature will be in the hottest part. As a rule, in a muffle kiln the hottest part is on the floor in back, and the coolest is in the top front section. In down draft kilns, the reverse is true; the hottest part is at the top. Until you know your kiln thoroughly, place cone pats in different parts of the kiln during each firing to gain an accurate picture of the temperature of each portion.

Uneven heating causes warping. Try to place large bowls in a portion of the kiln where they will receive the same degree of heat from all sides. Kilns which are heated at the front and back, as well as the sides, are a big advantage in this respect.

Kiln Temperatures

Pyrometric cones

The temperatures at which kilns are fired are much too high to be measured by ordinary thermometers; hence, pyrometric or heat measuring devices must be used. The most popular of these is the *pyrometric cone*. A cone is a little pyramid of clay

209

with fluxes added so that it will melt at a known temperature. A number, indicating its temperature, is stamped in the side. When the potter fires his kiln, he sets a series of cones in a lump of clay called a *cone pat* and places it in the kiln in such a way that he can see it through the peephole. The series always includes at least three cones, one of the temperature needed, one lower, and one higher. Thus if the kiln is to be fired to cone 4, the cone pat will hold cones 3, 4, and 5. The cones are set at a slant, as shown in Figure 12-8, tipping in the direction of the cone which will bend first. This is done to allow each cone to bend freely without falling against another. The clay out of which the cone pat is made should contain a lot of grog so that it does not crack during the firing and drop the cones.

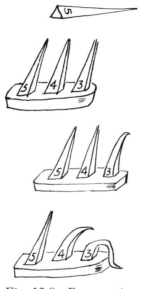

Fig. 12-8 Pyrometric
cones in a cone pat.

As the temperature of the kiln rises and approaches the desired point, cone 3 will start to bend. This is a warning signal to the potter. He continues the firing until cone 4 bends and then shuts off the kiln before cone 5 has begun to bend. This shows that the kiln has reached the temperature of cone 4 but has not gone beyond it.

In a rapid fire, a cone requires a slightly higher temperature to bend than it does when the fire is slower and the heat has more time to "soak" the ware. Thus the cone is not merely a measure of temperature; it is also an indication of the effect of the fire upon a piece of clay. This is what makes cones so valuable to the potter.

210

Table 12-1 Cone Temperatures

Cone	Centigrade	Fahrenheit	Color of Fire	What Happens to Clay	Type of Ware and Glazes
15	1435	2615			
14	1400	2552			
13	1350	2462		porcelain	porcelain
12	1335	2435		matures	
11	1325	2417			
10	1305	2381	white		china bodies
9	1285	2345		stoneware clays	stoneware
8	1260	2300		mature	salt glazes
7	1250	2282			
6	1230	2246			
5	1205	2201			
4	1190	2174		red clays melt	china glazes
3	1170	2138			
2	1165	2129			semi-vitreous ware
1	1160	2120			
01	1145	2093	yellow		
02	1125	2057		buff clays	earthenware
03	1115	2039		mature	
04	1060	1940			
05	1040	1904			
06	1015	1859		red clays mature	
07	990	1814			low fire earthenware
08	950	1742	orange		
09	930	1706			low fire lead glazes
010	905	1661			
011	895	1643	cherry red		
012	875	1607			lustre glazes
013	860	1580			
014	830	1526			
015	805	1481		organic matter in	chrome red glazes
016	795	1463		clay burns out	
017	770	1418	dull red		
018	720	1328			overglaze colors
019	660	1220			enamels
020	650	1202			
021	615	1139			
022	605	1121		dehydration begins	

Table 12-1 gives the temperatures of cones from 022 to 15. These temperatures apply only if the rate of firing is comparatively rapid (about 170° C per hour). At a slower rate, the cones would bend at slightly lower temperatures.

The color of the kiln at each point in the firing can be described only approximately and the same is true of what happens to clay. Don't interpret this table as indicating that the maturing point of all native red clays is cone 06, but rather that most red clays mature somewhere in that neighborhood.

211

Pyrometers

Another device used to measure kiln temperatures is the electric pyrometer with a thermocouple. This is a metal bead made by soldering together two different elements, usually platinum and rhodium. When such a bead is heated, a tiny electric current is generated. If the bead is attached to an ammeter, the current can be measured and translated into degrees of temperature. This type of pyrometer is especially useful with studio electric kilns.

In the operation of big furnaces, a telescope type of pyrometer is often used. This has a small wire which can be made to glow by an electric current passing through it. The wire is mounted in a tube through which the operator looks into the kiln. The wire cuts across his line of vision so that it makes a black line against the glowing background of the kiln. As current is passed through the wire, it starts to glow until, as the current increases, a point is reached at which the wire disappears because it is glowing just as brightly as the kiln itself. By reading the amount of current passing through the wire at that moment, the operator can tell the temperature of the kiln.

The firing schedule

The best word of advice here is go slowly. This applies not only to the firing process but to the cooling as well. It should take at least 8 hours for a small kiln to reach the temperature of cone 04. Larger kilns require more time. There are parts of the firing cycle where the rate may be increased, but these differ for bisque and glazed ware.

The first portion of the firing is the "water smoking" period, during which atmospheric water is driven out of the clay. This must be slow for raw ware, especially if there are any large pieces in the kiln. If, however, everything in the kiln has been fired once before, the kiln may go up more quickly.

Between 350° C and 400° C, organic matter in the clay burns out; go slowly during this period if you have any native red clays in the kiln. At 500° C, the water smoking period is ended and densification begins.

At 573° C the kiln begins to get red hot, and a physical change takes place in the silica, making it expand. Go slowly here, for big pieces are apt to break at this point. This is a critical point in the cooling period, as well as the heating period, for the silica changes back again and contracts. If a piece comes out split, you can tell if the trouble occurred during the heating or the cooling by examining the edge of the break. When the glaze has flowed over the edge of the crack, it indicates that the piece broke while being heated. If the edge of the break is hard and sharp, the piece broke while cooling.

Beyond 600° C, when the kiln is cherry red, the firing rate of bisque ware can be speeded up. Glazed pieces must be fired a little more slowly because too rapid firing of a glaze causes pin holes.

When the kiln has reached maturing temperature, shut off the fire and allow the damper to remain open for 10 minutes so that any products of combustion may escape; then close the damper and allow the kiln to cool slowly, and wait at least 24 hours before opening it.

Don't be in a hurry to take pieces out of the kiln. A good rule is never to remove ware until you can lift it with your bare hands.

The Flame

Oxidation

Combustion is the union of carbon with oxygen. Fuels are largely organic matter, combinations of carbon, oxygen, hydrogen, and nitrogen. When the flame gets all the oxygen it needs and burns with maximum efficiency, you have *oxidizing* fire. In this case, the combustion produces carbon dioxide (CO_2), water, and nitrogen, which escape up the flue. If there is not enough oxygen for the flame or too much carbon, the combustion will produce carbon monoxide (CO) plus free carbon. Carbon monoxide is hungry for oxygen and will steal it from other substances. When this happens, you have a *reducing* fire.

Reduction

There is an old Chinese legend which tells of a potter who lived many centuries ago. One day he was firing his kiln and was having a lot of trouble. It was one of those days when everything goes wrong. The fire wouldn't burn properly, the chimney wouldn't draw, the place was full of smoke and the air was filled with a horrible odor. The potter was afraid that most of the ware, which he had glazed with a lovely green copper glaze, would be ruined.

When he opened the kiln he found his fears were justified, for piece after piece came out blistered, blackened, and dull. But in the very center of the kiln, there was one vase which was a beautiful blood red. Such a color had never been seen before on any piece of pottery. The potter's neighbors and co-workers marvelled at it. It was so beautiful that it was sent to the Emperor as a gift. The Emperor in turn admired the color so much that he had the vase broken and the fragments set in rings as

213

though they were precious stones. Then he sent the potter an order for a dozen more red vases.

There the potter's troubles began. He tried again and again but he could not reproduce that red color. He checked his glaze formulas carefully and used exactly the same ingredients that he used that day, but all the pots came out green. The Emperor grew impatient. Messengers arrived from the palace, saying *produce or else!* Finally our potter was in despair. He decided to fire one last kiln and loaded it with vases covered with glazes as before. But during the height of the fire, his courage failed him. He opened the door of his kiln and jumped in.

His assistant ran up quickly. The kiln fire was smoky and there was a bad smell in the air. They shut down the flames and allowed the kiln to cool, and when they opened it, what did they find? No trace of our poor potter, but—yes, you've guessed it—the kiln was full of beautiful red pots.

And there, according to the legend, was discovered the secret of reduction. The potter's assistants reasoned that if a human body produced such results, maybe a dead pig would work and they tossed a pig into the next fire. Again they got beautiful red pieces. Then they tried substituting such things as wood and straw and still the trick worked.

Reduction, as we said before, results when the fire is over-loaded with carbon. When this happens, green oxide of copper loses some of its oxygen and becomes a red oxide. Likewise, red oxide of iron loses some of its oxygen and becomes a black oxide. Red oxide of copper produces the *sang-de-boeuf* or ox blood color, while the black oxide of iron produces the gray-green color known as celadon.

Ordinarily the use of reduction is reserved for high fire work with porcelain or stoneware (as a matter of fact, it is difficult to control a high fire without getting some reduction in spite of all precautions). At low temperatures, reduction is something the potter tries to avoid at all costs, for it ruins any glazes which have lead in them. However, there are times when you will want to produce reduction deliberately for special color effects with leadless glazes or for making lusters.

Reduction is obtained in the down draft type of kiln by closing the damper and adjusting the burners so that the flame does not get enough air and burns yellow. This sends free carbon into the kiln. There is loss of heat during this process, so in high fire work the potter has to alternate periods of oxidation and reduction. With the muffle type of kiln, it is not so easy to produce controlled reduction, for the flames do not touch the ware; and, if the muffle is tight, even though the flame releases free carbon it will not get a chance to act on the pieces. Reduction

214

can be produced, however, by putting some organic material, such as pine splinters, inside the muffle. In the case of some low fire luster glazes, organic material is actually mixed in with the glaze itself.

Local reduction   A series of experiments at Ohio State University, under the direction of the late Arthur Baggs and the late Edgar Littlefield, produced some remarkable copper red glazes and also some celadon glazes without the need for a reducing atmosphere in the kiln. Various forms of carbon were put into the glazes. After many trials it was found that small amounts of silicon carbide produced satisfactory results.

Silicon carbide, or Carborundum, is sold in hardware stores as an abrasive powder. Grade FFF, very fine, was used. Recipes for local reduction glazes are given in Chapter 14.

Raku

Now we shall proceed to contradict almost everything we said earlier in this chapter.

Raku, a method of making ceremonial tea bowls, originated in Japan in the sixteenth century. Small hand-fashioned bowls were bisque fired, then glazed by dipping or pouring. When glazes dried, the bowls were thrust into red hot kilns, allowed to

Fig. 12-9   Vase, 10″, by Jim C. Davis; raku, partially covered with sawdust during reduction.

215

remain just long enough for the glazes to melt, then removed with tongs and put into pails containing straw, leaves, or other organic material. More organic material was piled on top and the pails were tightly covered. After a few minutes in this reducing atmosphere the bowls were taken out and lowered into cold water.

American potters did not learn about raku until a couple of decades ago, but once they made its acquaintance it was literally love at first sight! The great freedom offered by raku, the elimination of many hours of firing time, the unpredictable, often startling results, were too exciting to resist, as were the opportunities to explore new paths and to break old rules.

Many potters today work exclusively in raku, and what they make is entirely different from the small Japanese tea bowls. The pieces they make are large, rarely functional, often daring and flamboyant in design.

The raku process can be accomplished with almost any existing kiln. Charlie Brown fires pots 2 feet tall and a foot wide in a top-loading electric kiln. When a pot is red hot he lifts it out with asbestos gloves, leaving the kiln turned on. Without waiting for the pot to cool, he brushes or pours on glaze which dries immediately, then puts the pot back into the kiln again.

Raku kilns

One reason for the great popularity of raku is the ease with which potters can build their own kilns. For firing out of doors, a simple kiln can be assembled by piling insulating refractory brick into a box form.

Fiberfrax makes it possible to fashion ingenious kilns out of

Fig. 12-10 Raku kiln, Peach
Valley Farm Pottery.

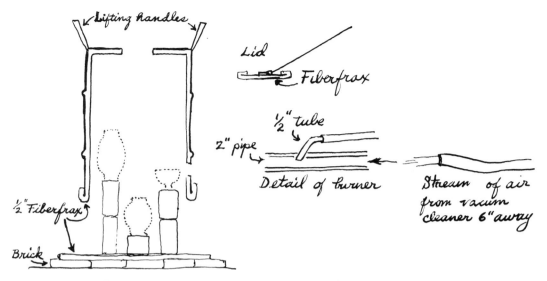

Fig. 12-11 Diagram of raku kiln built by Jerry Friedman.

galvanized garbage pails or empty oil drums. The kiln shown in
Photo Series 26 was made by Jerry Friedman out of such a
drum. One end was removed, then the inside of the drum was
cleaned with a wire brush and steamed. A hole 8 inches in
diameter was cut in the roof of the kiln (the bottom of the drum)
and a hole 2½ inches in diameter was cut in the wall of the kiln
for the burner. Two U bolts were welded to the rim of the roof
opposite each other, these serve as lifting handles.

The inside of the drum was insulated with a ½ inch thick
layer of Fiberfrax low-con felt. This comes in strips ½ inch
thick, 24 inches wide and 25 feet long. The inside of the roof
and the walls were painted with a layer of Fiberfrax coating
cement, applied thickly enough so that the whole area took on
an opaque appearance. A circle cut just the right size was gently
pressed by hand onto the inside of the roof, then two 70 inch
strips were cut. A layer of felt was pressed against the inner side
of the drum starting at the roof. Then a second strip was
cemented into place, allowing an inch overlap. This left an excess of felt projecting beyond the rim. The excess felt was cut in
6 inch intervals to the open drum rim. Coating cement was
applied to the outside lip of the drum and the pieces folded
back over the outside. A piece of baling wire was used to bind
the outside felt to the drum.

Then the kiln was turned over and the felt was trimmed away
from the opening in the side and the opening in the top (the
flue). A circle of metal 9 inches in diameter serves as a lid for the
flue. A layer of the felt was cemented to the underside of the lid
and a metal strip to serve as a handle was welded to the top.

217

The floor of the kiln is a layer of refractory brick with a layer of Fiberfrax on top of it.

The burner for the kiln was made by cutting a hole in the side of a 2 inch diameter pipe 12 inches long. The hole was the proper size to allow for the insertion of a ½ inch diameter copper tube. During firing this tube is connected by rubber tubing to a tank of propane gas.

Firing Raku Pieces

1. The potter stacks glazed pieces on refractory bricks. The kiln shown in the background will be lifted up and lowered over the ware, a two-man job.

2. The kiln has been placed over the ware. The burner (*lower left*) has been put into position and the gas has been ignited. The nozzle of a vacuum cleaner resting on the ground directs a stream of air toward the open end of the pipe.

Glazed pieces on top of the kiln are drying out to be ready for the next fire. The potter lifts the lid off the flue opening from time to time to watch the melting of the glazes.

218

3. The glazes have melted, the fire has been extinguished, the burner has been removed from the hole. The kiln is lifted up and off.

4. Fired pieces have been lifted by tongs, put into a pail filled with straw, and covered for a few minutes of reduction. Now they are plunged into water.

219

Raku firing parties are often social occasions or "happenings." Experiments are tried, accidental results are obtained.

A variation of raku

The tall vase by Richard deVore shown in Figure 12-12, was hand built, bisque fired at cone 010, then glaze fired at cone 9 (oxidation), then fired several times more at cone 04, each time with an overglaze of mat translucent glaze. The final firing was done in a trash can at about 1000 degrees F. Newspapers and oil were put into the can. The pot was put in cold, then the fuel was ignited. After one minute, when the fire was burning furiously, the can was covered until a heavy yellow smoke appeared. The lid was then removed and there was an explosion of blue flame. The artist calls this method *carbon impregnation* since it does not draw oxygen out of the glaze, but drives carbon in. (In the artist's words, "... it also cracks many pieces.")

Experiments are being made to find clay bodies and kiln designs that will make it possible to fire wet clay pieces, thus eliminating the many hours of waiting for pots to dry. If this becomes feasible, raku may be called "instant ceramics."

Actually, raku in Japanese means enjoyment. Potters delighted by the spontaneity of the method will agree that the name is well chosen.

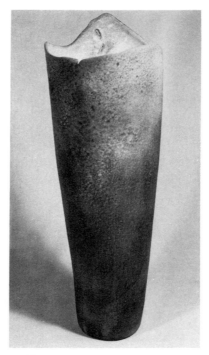

Fig. 12-12   Vase, 18″ by 6″,
Richard DeVore; carbon
impregnation.

Some safety precautions

1. Fire can hurt people—so take care. Most of the safety rules for working with fire are merely common sense.
2. Gas or oil-burning kilns, if not out of doors, should be built where there is adequate space all around. The chimney must have proper flashing at the point where it goes through the roof. Kiln rooms should be well ventilated to avoid the dangers of breathing carbon monoxide gas.
3. When firing a kiln, guard against loose clothing—this is especially important in raku. Long hair should be bound up and covered with a scarf.
4. Avoid injury to the eyes when peering through the spyhole of a kiln by wearing dark glasses. Wearers of contact lenses should guard against their damage.
5. Don't get burned. Use asbestos gloves and tongs for raku work.
6. Keep burn lotion handy!

Pottery is a product of earth and fire—two elements which the potter must treat with equal respect.

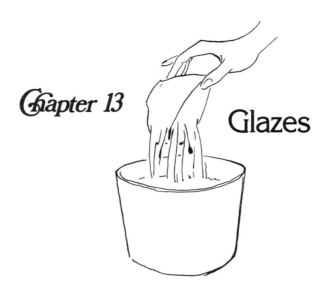

Chapter 13   Glazes

One could write a dozen lengthy books on glazes and still not cover the subject fully. There is so much to know! This chapter will give the rudiments of glaze theory—technical information about chemistry of glazes and glaze calculation. Chapter 14 will tell how to mix and apply glazes and will give a number of recipes for glazes of various types.

It is thrilling to open your kiln and take out a piece covered with a beautiful glaze which you have made yourself out of ingredients combined according to your own formula. Then you really taste the joy of creating. There are failures along the way, it is true, but the successes make up for the disappointments.

Prepared glazes can be bought from dealers, but you will probably prefer to make your own. Not only will you have the pleasure of creating, but you will find it less expensive. A knowledge of chemistry will help, but it is not absolutely necessary. As long as you know something about the three main ingredients of glazes and are willing to do some experimenting, you should have no difficulty.

What Is a Glaze?

Basic components and behavior

We know that clay contains glass-forming oxides which liquefy when subjected to extreme heat. We know also that some clays have a greater proportion of these than others and, hence, vitrify at lower temperatures. Let us suppose that we have two different clays, one a stoneware clay which needs to be fired to cone 9 or 10 in order to mature, and the other a common red clay which matures at cone 04. Let us suppose further that we made two bowls, one out of each clay, and put them in the kiln together. As the temperature of the kiln rose, the red clay bowl would mature first while the other would still be much underfired; but as the temperature continued to rise, the red bowl would start to soften and would finally melt. When the temperature of the kiln reached cone 10, our stoneware bowl would be fully matured and the other just a pool of liquid. When the kiln cooled, the pool which started out as a red bowl would harden into something looking like dark brown glass.

This suggests something. Suppose we were to make a slip out of the red clay and paint it on the stoneware bowl, then fire the bowl again to cone 10. This time, instead of being on the floor of the kiln, the melted red clay will have formed a glossy dark coating on the bowl itself—will be, in fact, a glaze. Not a very good glaze, for it might be rough in spots, but a glaze nonetheless.

Can we make this method work at lower temperatures? We know that adding a flux (a melting agent) to clay will lower its maturing point. If enough flux is added, the clay will melt at the temperature where it would ordinarily mature. Lead is the most active low-temperature flux we know of; so let us mix equal parts of white lead and red clay into a slip and paint it on a small test tile. Then let's try two parts of lead and one of clay on another tile. If we now fire both tiles to cone 04 and examine the results, we will probably find that the first tile has a dull rough surface (not enough flux), while the second is bright and glossy. We have made a glaze.

A glaze, then is glass—that is, something which has melted into a liquid and upon cooling has hardened into a glossy coating on a piece of ceramic ware. It serves to make the ware waterproof and to give it a more pleasing appearance. It is always produced on the ware itself by the action of heat.

Glass is mainly sand or silica, but silica will not melt at the temperatures reached in an ordinary kiln, so fluxes must be added. For pottery glazes, a third ingredient is necessary: silica and flux alone would make a glaze but it would be so liquid during the firing that it would drain completely off the ware. Something must be added to slow up this running action, to give the glaze viscosity. That is alumina.

And there we have the three essential ingredients of all glazes: *flux, alumina,* and *silica*.

Clay itself contains these three ingredients and so does feldspar. Either would make a glaze all by itself if we could get it hot enough; but since most of our work will be done at lower

223

temperatures, we will have to compound our glazes and use fluxes which melt within our temperature range.

The alumina and silica in glazes are obtained from feldspar, clay, and flint. The fluxes, however, come from many different sources. According to the kind of flux used, glazes may be classified as lead, alkaline, borosilicate, leadless, or feldspathic. Glazes may also be classified as raw or fritted, high fire or low fire. In addition to these, there are a number of special types of glazes such as slip glazes, salt glazes, and lusters.

Low fire lead glazes

The most widely used flux in low temperature glazes is lead, which the potter obtains by using either red lead or white lead. Red lead is cheaper but it is harder to handle. Otherwise there is not much difference, except that it is necessary to use a trifle more white lead. Red lead alone will make a glaze; some of the native potters of North Carolina used to mix it with molasses to hold it on the ware. This seems to contradict what we said about the three essential ingredients of glazes, but actually it does not. During the fire the lead dissolves some of the clay of the pot it is on and the glaze gets its alumina and silica that way.

Lead glazes are soft, brilliant, slightly yellow in color. This yellow tinge affects other colors which are added to lead glazes, sometimes spoiling their effects. Aside from this, lead is a quite satisfactory flux, easy to handle, with a temperature range from cone 04 to about cone 5. At the lowest temperature, lead could be the only flux used in a glaze; but from cone 07 upward, other fluxes such as calcium, zinc, or magnesium must be used along with it.

There is one serious drawback to lead—it is a *poison*. During the nineteenth century in the English pottery town of Bristol, so many potters died of lead poisoning that laws were passed banning the use of lead. (Hence the development of Bristol glaze.)

Care must be taken when working with lead that no particles of it get into food or on the ends of cigarettes or into open cuts in the skin. Dust must be controlled, and for the same reason lead glazes should not be sprayed. In classroom work with children *raw lead glazes should be avoided entirely.*

Lead release Another problem with lead is that some lead glazes, after they have been fired on ware, may be soluble in weak acids. This would make the ware hazardous for use with fruit juices, soft drinks, salads, stewed tomatoes, and similar foods.

The United States Food and Drug Administration has set standards for all glazed ceramic food utensils made in the United States.

224

The FDA test for glazed ware involves subjecting it to a leaching solution of organic acid similar to vinegar under rigid test conditions. The amount of lead released must be less than seven parts in one million parts of solution. Lead glazes can pass this test if they are compounded with a high enough ratio of silica to lead and contain sufficient alumina.

Raw lead glazed tableware must be fired at least to cone 04 but not above cone 7.

Copper must not be used as a colorant in lead glazes for tableware because copper oxide makes such glazes more soluble in food acids.

Potters making objects not intended for use with food may be less concerned about lead release; those who make bowls and drinking mugs might find it simpler to use lead in fritted form.

Low fire alkaline glazes

The three alkaline metals—sodium, potassium, and lithium—are good low temperature fluxes which produce bright colors. However, since they are ordinarily soluble in water, they are difficult to use. Both soda and potash are found in insoluble form in feldspar, but feldspar contains large proportions of alumina and silica, so only small amounts of it may be added to a glaze.

The potter who wishes to use more soda and potash must add them to the glaze as borax, sal soda, soda ash, sodium bicarbonate, pearl ash, or potassium bichromate. All of these substances are water soluble. A glaze which contains them must be ground by hand in a small amount of water and applied immediately. Results are never certain. The ware to which the glaze is applied absorbs some of the soluble ingredients; it is best, therefore, to use a hard fired bisque, although even then it is almost impossible to avoid crazing. The Egyptians, who were the first to use this type of glaze, often applied it to bowls which had been carved out of steatite rock (talc).

Alkaline glazes are brilliant in color. When copper is added they produce a beautiful turquoise which cannot be obtained in any other way. Potters who seek the colors made by soda, potash, and lithium—without the disadvantages of solubility— find a solution to their problem by using frits.

Fritted glazes

A *frit* is a glaze which has been fired in a crucible to form a glass and upon cooling has been ground into a powder. This material may be used alone as a glaze or may be combined with other ingredients. The advantages of using a frit are many. Soluble materials become insoluble in fritted form. Furthermore,

225

fritting gets rid of things we don't need. Many of the raw materials used in glazes contain organic matter, carbon dioxide, nitrates, and other things which must be burned out during the firing process. When these leave as gases they must bubble through the glaze; this often causes blisters. When a glaze has been fritted, all of this is done before the glaze is applied to ware; hence a fritted glaze is less apt to crawl.

Formerly, studio potters had to make their own frits—a long, tedious process that required a special frit kiln. The raw ingredients were mixed together dry and placed in a crucible with an opening at the bottom. Flames directed against the sides of the crucible melted the mixture, which ran in molten form out of the bottom and dropped into a pail of water. The sudden change in temperature shattered the drops of liquid glass into tiny fragments which then had to be pulverized for use in glazes.

Dependable frits, some containing lead, others leadless, are produced on a large scale by such companies as Ferro-Enamel, Hommel, Pemco, and others. These frits can be bought from local dealers.

Ground glass

Ground glass or glass cullet is really a frit, but since the chemical ingredients of the scrap are usually unknown, its use is a matter of trial and error. With enough clay added to slow down its running, glass can make a highly satisfactory glaze and you may wish to do some experimenting with it. Don't attempt to grind your own bottles, however: it's not only hard work, but extremely dangerous. Buy your glass already ground from a ceramic dealer.

Borosilicate glazes

Borosilicate glazes contain boric oxide (B_2O_3), which unites with silica during the fire. Lead may or may not be present. Boric oxide can be obtained from boric acid or borax, which are water soluble and so give all the troubles of alkaline glazes. Fortunately for the potter, however, boric oxide is also found in insoluble form in calcium borate (called colemanite or Gerstly borate). This is a by-product in the manufacture of borax. Colemanite is a highly satisfactory material for the studio potter. It can be used as the only flux in low fire glazes or it may be combined with lead. Copper in a colemanite glaze produces a rich greenish blue, not quite turquoise but close to it.

Leadless glazes

Leadless glazes are used at cone 4 and above. At cone 7, lead volatilizes and leaves the glaze. The following are higher temperature fluxes.

226

Fig. 13-1 Wedge Pot, 42″, Steven Kemenyffy, salt glaze.

Calcium oxide, CaO or whiting: a valuable glaze ingredient. Wallastonite, a calcium silicate, is sometimes used by potters.

Barium oxide, BaO, a flux in high fire glazes often used for mat glazes; potters use it as barium carbonate. (Barium is toxic—take care in handling it.)

Magnesium oxide, MgO, a high temperature flux, gives lovely

227

surfaces in reduction fire. Dolomite and talc are sources of MgO.

Zinc oxide, ZnO, is used in Bristol glazes.

Strontium oxide, SrO, acts a bit like CaO but costs more; it is seldom used.

Lithium oxide, Li_2O, an active alkaline flux, soluble, Lepidolite and spodumene are natural sources of Li_2O in insoluble form.

Cryolite, sodium aluminum fluoride, is a natural source of sodium in insoluble form.

Stoneware glazes

Glazes for ware fired from cone 8 to cone 10 can use feldspar and calcium as the principle fluxes. High fire glazes are simpler to make than low fire glazes. Combinations of feldspar, whiting, and flint make satisfactory glazes.

Porcelain glazes

At cone 10 or 11, feldspar alone could be used as a glaze, although percentages of calcium and flint are usually mixed with it.

Salt glazes

Salt glazing is done by throwing salt into the chamber of a kiln when the temperature has reached its highest point. The salt volatilizes and forms a mist which settles on all surfaces of the ware. The soda in the salt combines with the clay to form an extremely hard glaze. Salt glazing is best suited to stoneware, for it requires temperatures from cone 4 to cone 9. It is good for carved or embossed surfaces. On flat surfaces it produces an "orange peel" texture.

Photo Series 27

Salt Glazing

1. The pitcher made in Photo Series 17 has been put into the kiln, ready for salt glazing.

2. Bricking up the kiln.

3. Putting salt into the kiln through one of the openings for the burners.

4. The firing completed.

5. The finished pitcher with typical salt glaze finish.

229

Salt glazing has some disadvantages. It requires a special kiln reserved for that purpose, and such kilns and the chimneys leading from them deteriorate rapidly. The most important disadvantage is the pollution of the air caused by poisonous chlorine vapors. Experiments are underway to find other sources of sodium that can be used in place of sodium chloride. If it becomes possible to use sodium bicarbonate most of the drawbacks of salt glazing will be eliminated. At the time of writing, this problem has not been fully solved.

Slip glazes

Slip glazing, as described earlier in this chapter, is done by painting a slip made of a low fire clay on an unfired piece made of stoneware clay, then firing to cone 8 or above. Albany slip is excellent for this purpose. Some potters have found through experimentation that other low-firing clays available to them locally can be used for slip glazing.

Almost all low-firing clays contain iron and other mineral impurities, hence the coloring of slip glazes is limited to tan, brown, and black. However, the addition of 2 percent of manganese dioxide produces a pleasing plum color. Slip glazes are widely used on stoneware crocks and porcelain insulators.

Ash glazes

Wood and vegetable ashes contain percentages of alumina, silica, potash and lime. These oxides are all used in making glazes and potash is a good flux. At cone 10, ashes alone will form a glaze.

Ashes may be prepared for use in glazes by mixing them with water and screening through an 80-mesh screen. The water and ash mixture is then allowed to settle and the water is poured off. The trouble with that method is that some of the soluble potash is washed away. For that reason many potters who work with ash glazes prefer to sift the ash dry and use the material without washing.

While ashes alone form a glaze, better results are obtained through combinations of ash, feldspar, and clay.

Glaze Calculation

You don't need to read this section if you don't want to. Many potters develop their glazes by experimenting, varying the ingredients until they arrive at satisfactory results through a method of trial and error. So skip to the next chapter if you wish. But if you are good at mathematics and have a scientific desire to know the why as well as the how, this is the way molecular glaze formulas are developed.

The molecular formula

The materials which go into glazes are all inorganic substances which combine in some manner with oxygen. It is as oxides, therefore, that they are of value to the potter although they may or may not be oxides before firing. White lead, for example, is a carbonate, but after it is fired it becomes lead oxide (PbO). Some materials used in glazes provide several oxides. Feldspar, for example, adds oxides of potassium (K_2O), sodium (Na_2O), aluminum (Al_2O_3), and silicon (SiO_2).

In order to see at a glance what the active ingredients of a glaze are and in what proportion they are present, the molecular glaze formula was devised. This lists molecules of all glaze oxides in three different columns. In the first column are placed those elements which combine with oxygen in a one-to-one ratio (example PbO) and those which combine with oxygen in a two-to-one ratio (Na_2O). This column is called the RO or R_2O column. In the second column are placed those elements which combine with oxygen in a two-to-three ratio (Al_2O_3), and in the last column, those which combine with oxygen in a one-to-two ratio (SiO_2). These last two columns are called the R_2O_3 and RO_2 columns, respectively. Here is a tabulation which shows most of the oxides ordinarily used in glazes arranged in these three columns.

RO or R_2O		R_2O_3		RO_2	
Lead Oxide	PbO	Alumina	Al_2O_3	Silica	SiO_2
Zinc Oxide	ZnO	Boric Oxide	B_2O_3	Rutile (Titanium Oxide)	TiO_2
Potash	K_2O			Tin Oxide	SnO_2
Soda	Na_2O			Zirconium Oxide	ZrO_2
Lime	CaO				
Barium Oxide	BaO				
Magnesia	MgO				
Strontia	SrO				

All the substances in the first column are fluxes. The other two essential ingredients of glazes, alumina and silica, come in columns 2 and 3, respectively. Boric oxide, which acts as a flux, is an exception, for it comes in column 2. In column 3, in addition to silica, we find titanium, tin, and zirconium. These do not affect a glaze formula, but they change the appearance of a glaze considerably. Titanium oxide forms crystals which produce interesting effects, and both tin and zirconium make glazes white and opaque.

Remember that the quantities in molecular formulas show relationships of molecules. By changing the proportions of flux to alumina and silica and by using different substances as fluxes, we are able to suit glazes to different purposes, making some fire at low temperatures, others at high, making some glossy, others mat, and so on. Slight changes in the ratio of silica

231

will change the expansion of a glaze, making it fit on different bodies.

Quantities are always chosen so that the first column adds up to one (this makes comparison of different formulas possible). The alumina is always less than one, ranging from .05 for low temperature glazes to .6 for high fire glazes, and the silica is usually three times the alumina plus one. This is not a hard and fast rule, however—the proportions are frequently changed to secure a better fit on the body used.

You will have to experiment to work out glaze formulas suited to your clay and your kiln. Here are some general directions for glazes at different temperatures.

Limit formulas

At the lowest temperatures (from cone 015 to cone 012), lead can be used all alone as a flux. The formula for a cone 015 lead glaze might read:

$$PbO\ 1.0\} \ Al_2O_3\ .05\ \{SiO_2\ 1.15$$

Here PbO is the only ingredient in column 1, the alumina content is at its lowest limit, .05, and the silica is three times .05 plus 1, or 1.15.

For temperatures from cone 010 to cone 07, small quantities of whiting and feldspar can be added as fluxes and the alumina and silica can be increased slightly. In this temperature range the formula for a lead glaze would come within these limits:

$$\left.\begin{array}{l} PbO\ -.7\ to\ 1.0 \\ CaO\ -.0\ to\ \ .3 \\ K_2O\ -.0\ to\ \ .2 \\ Na_2O\ -.0\ to\ \ .2 \end{array}\right\} Al_2O_3 - .05\ to\ .2 \left\{ SiO_2 - 1.0\ to\ 1.6 \right.$$

NOTE. The K_2O or NA_2O in this formula would be obtained from feldspar.

Most commercial spars contain both potassium and sodium; hence, in formulas these are often computed as a single ingredient, written KNaO.

Here are two cone 07 lead glazes:

$$\left.\begin{array}{l} PbO\ -.7 \\ CaO\ -.3 \end{array}\right\} Al_2O_3 - .08 \left\{ SiO_2 - 1.25 \right.$$

$$\left.\begin{array}{l} PbO\ -.6 \\ CaO\ -.25 \\ KNaO-.15 \end{array}\right\} Al_2O_3 - \ .1 \left\{ SiO_2 - 1.5 \right.$$

Observe that as quantities in column 1 change, they still add up to one.

232

For the same temperature range, cone 010 to cone 07, we might prepare an alkaline glaze, either raw or fritted, in which potassium and sodium are used as fluxes. In this case they will be obtained not from feldspar but from borax, soda ash, or other soluble substances. The formula of such an alkaline glaze would come within these limits:

$$\left.\begin{array}{l} KNaO -.5 \text{ to } .7 \\ CaO \;\;\; -.3 \text{ to } .5 \end{array}\right\} \left.\begin{array}{l} Al_2O_3 -.05 \text{ to } .15 \\ B_2O_3 \; - \;\; .0 \text{ to } 1.0 \end{array}\right\} SiO_2 - 1.5 \text{ to } 2.5$$

Here is a formula for an alkaline glaze for cone 08:

$$\left.\begin{array}{l} K_2O \;\;\; -.2 \\ Na_2O -.6 \\ CaO \;\;\; -.2 \end{array}\right\} \left.\begin{array}{l} Al_2O_3 -.15 \\ B_2O_3 \;\; -.5 \end{array}\right\} SiO_2 - 1.6$$

For temperatures from cone 04 to cone 1 or 2, zinc and magnesium may be added to the list of fluxes. Here are the formula limits for this range:

$$\left.\begin{array}{l} PbO \;\;\; -.1 \text{ to } .7 \\ CaO \;\;\; -.1 \text{ to } .4 \\ KNaO -.1 \text{ to } .3 \\ ZnO \;\;\; -.0 \text{ to } .1 \\ MgO \;\;\; -.0 \text{ to } .1 \end{array}\right\} \left.\begin{array}{l} Al_2O_3 -.15 \text{ to } .35 \\ B_2O_3 \;\; -.0 \;\; \text{to } .3 \end{array}\right\} SiO_2 - 1.5 \text{ to } 2.5$$

Here is a cone 04 lead glaze:

$$\left.\begin{array}{l} PbO \;\;\; -.55 \\ CaO \;\;\; -.35 \\ KNaO -.1 \end{array}\right\} Al_2O_3 - .2 \left\{ SiO_2 - 1.6 \right.$$

All the glazes listed so far have been bright or glossy. A mat surface can be achieved by introducing barium to the fluxes, along with some zinc, or by increasing the alumina. The cone 04 lead glaze above can be made mat by reducing the lead and the calcium, replacing the quantities taken out with barium and zinc. The formula would now read:

$$\left.\begin{array}{l} PbO \;\;\; -.45 \\ CaO \;\;\; -.15 \\ KNaO -.1 \\ BaO \;\;\; -.2 \\ ZnO \;\;\; -.1 \end{array}\right\} Al_2O_3 - .2 \left\{ SiO_2 - 1.6 \right.$$

To alter the same glaze to an alumina mat, leave the first column unchanged, but increase the second and slightly reduce the third. The formula would now read:

$$\left.\begin{array}{l} PbO \;\;\; -.55 \\ CaO \;\;\; -.35 \\ KNaO -.1 \end{array}\right\} Al_2O_3 - .3 \left\{ SiO_2 - 1.4 \right.$$

233

Table 13-1. Ceramic Raw Materials

Substance	Formula	Molecular Weight	Equivalent Weight	Fired Formula	Fired Weight
Barium carbonate	$BaCO_3$	197	197	BaO	153
Bone ash	$Ca_3(PO_4)_2$	310	103	CaO	56
Borax	$Na_2O \cdot 2B_2O_3 \cdot 10H_2O$	382	382	$Na_2O \cdot 2B_2O_3$	202
Boric acid	$B_2O_3 \cdot 3H_2O$	124	124	B_2O_3	70
Calcium borate (Colemanite)	$2CaO \cdot 3B_2O_3 \cdot 5H_2O$	412	206	$CaO \cdot 1.5B_2O_3$	161
China clay (kaolin)	$Al_2O_3 \cdot 2SiO_2 \cdot 2H_2O$	258	258	$Al_2O_3 \cdot 2SiO_2$	222
Cryolite	Na_3AlF_6	210	420	$3Na_2O \cdot Al_2O_3$	288
Dolomite	$CaCO_3 \cdot MgCO_3$	184	184	$CaO \cdot MgO$	96
Feldspars					
Potash feldspar (theoretical)	$K_2O \cdot Al_2O_3 \cdot 6SiO_2$	556	556	Unchanged	556
Soda feldspar (theoretical)	$Na_2O \cdot Al_2O_3 \cdot 6SiO_2$	524	524	Unchanged	524
Anorthite	$CaO \cdot Al_2O_3 \cdot 2SiO_2$	278	278	Unchanged	278
Buckingham spar	$K_2O \cdot 1.13Al_2O_3 \cdot 6.45SiO_2$	596	596	Unchanged	596
Cornwall stone	$\begin{array}{l}CaO\ .304 \\ Na_2O\ .340 \\ K_2O\ .356\end{array}\Big\}\ Al_2O_3\ 1.075\ \big\{\ SiO_2\ 8.10$	667	667	Unchanged	667
Godfrey spar	$\begin{array}{l}K_2O\ .36 \\ Na_2O\ .64\end{array}\Big\}\ Al_2O_3\ 1.18\ \big\{\ SiO_2\ 8.80$	722	722	Unchanged	722
Nepheline syenite	$\begin{array}{l}K_2O\ .25 \\ Na_2O\ .75\end{array}\Big\}\ Al_2O_3\ 1.11\ \big\{\ SiO_2\ 4.65$	462	462	Unchanged	462
Orthoclase	$K_2O \cdot Al_2O_3 \cdot 6SiO_2$	556	556	Unchanged	556
Oxford spar	$\begin{array}{l}CaO\ .028 \\ Na_2O\ .256 \\ K_2O\ .716\end{array}\Big\}\ Al_2O_3\ 1.105\ \big\{\ SiO_2\ 6.38$	581	581	Unchanged	581
Plastic vitrox	$\begin{array}{l}CaO\ .053 \\ Na_2O\ .334 \\ K_2O\ .613\end{array}\Big\}\ Al_2O_3\ 1.33\ \big\{\ SiO_2\ 13.9$	1051	1051	Unchanged	1051
Flint (silica)	SiO_2	60	60	Unchanged	60

White ware and china glazes for temperatures from cone 1 to cone 5 would come within the following limits:

$$\left.\begin{array}{ll}PbO & -.2 \text{ to } .35 \\ CaO & -.35 \text{ to } .50 \\ KNaO & -.2 \text{ to } .35 \\ ZnO & -.0 \text{ to } .10\end{array}\right\} \left.\begin{array}{l}Al_2O_3 -.2 \text{ to } .35 \\ B_2O_3 -.3 \text{ to } .7\end{array}\right\} SiO_2 - 2.0 \text{ to } 3.5$$

In these glazes, the KNaO is obtained from borax and soda ash, hence the glazes are usually fritted.

Bristol (leadless) glazes for cone 4 to cone 8 have these limits:

$$\left.\begin{array}{ll}KNaO & -.25 \text{ to } .5 \\ CaO & -.10 \text{ to } .3 \\ ZnO & -.15 \text{ to } .4 \\ MgO & -.0 \text{ to } .2\end{array}\right\} Al_2O_3 -.35 \text{ to } .6 \left\{ SiO_2 - 2.5 \text{ to } 4.0 \right.$$

Table 13-1. Ceramic Raw Materials (Continued)

Substance	Formula	Molecular Weight	Equivalent Weight	Fired Formula	Fired Weight
Fluorspar	CaF_2	78	78	CaO	56
Gypsum	$CaSO_4 \cdot 2H_2O$	188	188	CaO	56
Lead, red	Pb_3O_4	684	228	PbO	223
Lead, white	$2PbCO_3 \cdot Pb(OH)_2$	775	258	PbO	223
Lead, yellow (litharge)	PbO	223	223	Unchanged	223
Lithium carbonate	Li_2CO_3	74	74	Li_2O	30
Magnesium carbonate (magnesite)	$MgCO_3$	84	84	MgO	40
Manganese carbonate	$MnCO_3$	115	115	MnO	71
Manganese dioxide	MnO_2	87	87	MnO	71
Niter	KNO_3	101	202	K_2O	94
Pearl ash	K_2CO_3	138	138	K_2O	94
Potassium bichromate	$K_2Cr_2O_7$	294	294	$K_2O \cdot Cr_2O_3$	294
Sal soda	$Na_2CO_3 \cdot 10H_2O$	286	286	Na_2O	62
Salt	NaCl	58	116	Na_2O	62
Silica	SiO_2	60	60	Unchanged	60
Soda ash	Na_2CO_3	106	106	Na_2O	62
Sodium antimonate	$Na_2O \cdot Sb_2O_5$	386	386	$Na_2O \cdot Sb_2O_3$	354
Sodium bicarbonate	$NaHCO_3$	84	168	Na_2O	62
Sodium nitrate	$NaNO_3$	85	170	Na_2O	62
Spodumene	$Li_2O \cdot Al_2O_3 \cdot 4SiO_2$	372	372	Unchanged	372
Talc (steatite)	$3MgO \cdot 4SiO_2 \cdot H_2O$	378	378	$3MgO \cdot 4SiO_2$	360
Tin oxide	SnO_2	151	151	Unchanged	151
Titanium oxide (rutile)	TiO_2	80	80	Unchanged	80
Whiting	$CaCO_3$	100	100	CaO	56
Zinc oxide	ZnO	81	81	Unchanged	81
Zircon (zircopax)	$ZrO_2 \cdot SiO_2$	183	183	Unchanged	183
Zirconium oxide	ZrO_2	123	123	Unchanged	123
Zirconium silicate	$ZrO_2 \cdot SiO_2$	183	183	Unchanged	183

In Bristol glazes the KNaO is obtained from feldspar.

Feldspathic glazes for stoneware and porcelain for temperatures from cone 8 to cone 15 fall within the following limits:

$$
\left.
\begin{array}{l}
KNaO - .2 \text{ to } .4 \\
CaO \quad - .4 \text{ to } .7 \\
MgO \quad - .0 \text{ to } .3 \\
ZnO \quad - .0 \text{ to } .2 \\
BaO \quad - .0 \text{ to } .2
\end{array}
\right\}
Al_2O_3 - .4 \text{ to } .6
\left\{
SiO_2 - 3.0 \text{ to } 5.0
\right.
$$

K_2O and Na_2O in the above glazes are obtained from feldspar.

Formula into Recipe

Given a glaze formula, how do we go about weighing out the ingredients for the glaze? Before we can do this, we must turn

235

the formula into a recipe, that is, we must find out what materials and how much of each will give us the molecular relationships called for in the formula. We shall need a table of molecular weights like the one in Table 13-1.

The molecular weight of a substance is the total of the weights of all the atoms which go to make up one molecule of that substance. The hydrogen atom is the lightest one known, so its atomic weight is called one. An atom of oxygen, which is sixteen times as heavy as a hydrogen atom, has, therefore, an atomic weight of sixteen; water (H_2O), one molecule of which contains two hydrogen atoms and one oxygen atom, has a molecular weight of two plus sixteen, or eighteen.

If you study the table you will note that one column is labeled molecular weight and another, equivalent weight. In most cases the quantities listed in these two columns are identical but in some cases they differ. We can explain why this is if we examine white lead. The formula of white lead is $2PbCO_3 \cdot Pb(OH)_2$ but when it is fired it becomes PbO. One molecule of white lead which contains three atoms of Pb would produce three molecules of lead oxide, each of which contains only one atom of Pb. Therefore, we need only one-third as much white lead to produce the equivalent of one molecule of lead oxide and so, while the molecular weight of white lead is listed as 775, its equivalent weight is only one-third as much or 258.

Let's work out the recipe for the cone 04 glaze whose formula was given above as:

$$\left.\begin{array}{l} PbO \ -.55 \\ CaO \ -.35 \\ KNaO \ -.1 \end{array}\right\} Al_2O_3 - .2 \left\{ SiO_2 - 1.6 \right.$$

We must select materials which will provide all these oxides in the proper molecular relationships. Prepare a diagram like this:

	This is the recipe			This is the molecular formula
Material	Amount of oxide in formula	$\times$ Equivalent weight	$=$ Quantity of material in recipe	$PbO.55$ $CaO.35$ $K_2O.1$ $Al_2O_3.2$ $SiO_2 1.6$
				In these columns keep track of the oxides going into the recipe.

When we list an ingredient in the column labeled material, we will multiply the number of molecules required by its equivalent molecular weight. The product of this multiplication will be the quantity of the material needed in the glaze recipe. At the same time we will enter the amount of each oxide supplied by the material in its proper column at the right. In that way we shall keep track of what is going into the glaze.

236

The first ingredient, lead, we shall obtain from white lead. Our formula calls for .55 PbO, so at the left of the diagram enter the following:

$$\text{White lead } .55 \times 258 = 141.9$$

Then in the PbO column, enter .55. This indicates that 141.9 parts of white lead will be needed to supply all the PbO called for by the formula.

The next ingredient, CaO, we shall get from whiting, whose molecular weight and equivalent weight are the same, namely 100, so the second line will be:

$$\text{Whiting } .35 \times 100 = 35$$

We have now satisfied the entire glaze requirement for both PbO and CaO. Our diagram looks like this:

Material	Amount of oxide in formula	×	Equiv- alent weight	=	Quantity of material in recipe	$PbO.55$	$CaO.35$	$K_2O.1$	$Al_2O_3.2$	$SiO_2 1.6$
White lead	.55	×	258	=	141.9	.55←This shows that we have supplied all				
						.00 the PbO called for by the formula				
Whiting	.35	×	100	=	35		.35			
							.00			

The third ingredient, K_2O, we shall get from the feldspar. If we select Buckingham feldspar, we note that its formula is: $K_2O \cdot 1.13\ Al_2O_3 \cdot 6.45\ SiO_2$. Its molecular weight is 596; so the next line will be:

$$\text{Buckingham feldspar } .1 \times 596 = 59.6$$

But feldspar contains other things besides potash. When we add .1 of K_2O, we also add .1 x 1.13, or .113 of Al_2O_3; and .1 x 6.45, or .645 of SiO_2. These must be added in the proper columns; the diagram now looks like this:

Material	Amount of oxide in formula	×	Equiv- alent weight	=	Quantity of material in recipe	$PbO.55$	$CaO.35$	$K_2O.1$	$Al_2O_3.2$	$SiO_2 1.6$
White lead	.55	×	258	=	141.9	.55				
						.00				
Whiting	.35	×	100	=	35		.35			
							.00			
Bucking- ham feld- spar	.1	×	596	=	59.6			.1	.113	.645
								.0	.087	.955

This shows that we have satisfied the entire requirements for PbO, CaO, and K_2O and part of the requirements for Al_2O_3 and SiO_2. We still need .087 of alumina which we shall get from china clay whose weight is 258, so the next line will be:

$$\text{China clay } .087 \times 258 = 22.4$$

237

But clay contains two parts of SiO_2 for every one of Al_2O_3; thus when we add .087 of china clay we ad .087 x 2 or .174 of SiO_2. This reduces the SiO_2 requirement still further, leaving only .781 to be added. We shall obtain this from flint whose molecular weight is 60: the last line is:

$$\text{Flint } .781 \times 60 = 46.9$$

The diagram now looks like this:

Material	Amount of oxide in formula	×	Equiv-alent weight	=	Quantity of material in recipe	PbO.55	CaO.35	K₂O.1	Al₂O₃.2	SiO₂1.6
White lead	.55	×	258	=	141.9	.55 / .00				
Whiting	.35	×	100	=	35		.35 / .00			
Bucking-ham feld-spar	.1	×	596	=	59.6			.1 / .0	.113 / .087 / .087 / .000	.645 / .955 / .174 / .781
China clay	.087	×	258	=	22.4					.781 / .000
Flint	.781	×	60	=	46.9					

We have satisfied all the requirements of the molecular formula; our recipe is complete. Remember that the numbers refer to parts. The quantities could be weighed out as ounces, pounds, or even tons; but for our purposes, the gram is the best unit of weight. If you weigh these quantities in grams, the formula will produce a batch of 305.8 grams, enough for a pint of glaze.

Recipes in percentages

To change the quantities in a recipe to percentages, divide each quantity by the total and multiply by 100. The above recipe would then become:

White lead	46.4
Whiting	11.4
Buckingham feldspar	19.5
China clay	7.3
Flint	15.4

Color in Glazes

The potter's prime source of color is in the clay itself; his secondary source is in various metals which he uses as oxides, or carbonates, or soluble salts—sulphates and nitrates. The form is not important; what counts is the metal. We might say that a third source of color for the potter lies in all the prepared pigments sold by dealers, the underglaze colors, the overglaze col-

238

ors, and the various ceramic stains, but these also are merely oxides and carbonates of metals.

The color of the clay will affect the color of the finished glazed piece unless the glaze is so opaque that the body is completely hidden. Think well before you make a glaze like that. Even in majolica work, the beauty of the ware is enhanced if the warm tone of the clay shows through the glaze. It is a mistake not to use the decorative possibilities of the material out of which the piece is made. Look at some of the pottery made in other generations and see how often, in those pieces which have stood the test of time, the color of the clay adds its part.

The colors which metals produce in glazes are affected not only by the clay underneath, but by the amount of metal introduced, the way the glaze is applied, the ingredients with which the metal is associated in the glaze, the temperature to which it is fired, the rate of firing, and the atmosphere of the kiln. In general, colors are more brilliant in alkaline glazes and at lower temperatures. Some metals change color completely when high temperatures are reached, and others change when the kiln is reduced. Here is a list of the principal metals used by potters, with a description of the colors they produce.

Copper

Copper is usually used as black copper oxide (CuO) or copper carbonate ($CuCO_3$). The former is stronger in coloring power. In a lead glaze, from 1 percent to 6 percent of copper will produce various shades of apple or grass green. In an alkaline glaze with high soda content and low alumina, with no lead or zinc present, copper produces a beautiful turquoise at cone 07.

In a reducing fire, black oxide of copper reduces to a lower oxide form which is red. This gives the rich scarlet of *sang-de-boeuf*. Copper has a fluxing action; if more than 6 percent is used in a glaze, it will increase the flow; hence the amount of lead should be reduced. An over-charge of copper in a glaze makes the surface dull and metallic, somewhat like gun metal.

Cobalt

Cobalt is the strongest of all the ceramic colorants. It is used by the potter as black cobalt oxide (Co_3O_4) or as cobalt carbonate ($CoCO_3$). The former is the stronger. A little bit of cobalt goes a long way, usually ½ percent is enough to produce its characteristic blue color in a glaze. Never use more than 3 percent. In the presence of zinc, the blue of cobalt becomes more intense. With rutile at high temperatures it becomes green.

239

Iron

Iron is a good ceramic colorant, usually present in the clay anyway. It is what gives native clays their warm red tones or, when calcium is also present, their shades of buff and yellow. It is almost always used as red iron oxide (Fe_2O_3); the black oxide (FeO) is rarely used. In glazes, iron produces colors ranging from amber through tan to deep red brown, depending on the quantity. Between 5 percent and 10 percent should be used (below 5 percent the color is pale and uninteresting). In a high lead glaze, 8 percent iron produces a rich dark red.

An overload of iron will sometimes produce a "gold stone" or "aventurine" glaze, a beautiful purple-red with gold flecks, but this effect is hard to get. In a reduction fire, iron produces the lovely pale green of celadon.

Manganese

Manganese is used as a dioxide (MnO_2) or as a carbonate ($MnCO_3$). The latter is the better form to use. In quantities from 5 percent to 10 percent, it produces shades of purplish brown. In an alkaline glaze, it verges toward violet and will give a beautiful aubergine or eggplant color. With copper or cobalt, manganese makes black metallic surfaces, with iron it produces luster. Its color fades above cone 4. Glazes containing manganese are apt to blister.

Chromium

Chromium is a queer character with strange behavior. At very low temperatures it is red, at high temperatures, green. It turns brown in the presence of zinc and makes tin pink. The potter usually uses 2 percent to 5 percent of green oxide of chromium (Cr_2O_3). Other forms occasionally used are potassium bichromate ($K_2Cr_2O_7$), lead chromate ($PbCrO_4$), and iron chromate ($FeCrO_4$). The latter gives a good gray in engobes (1 to 3 percent).

Chromium is not much used in low temperature glazes but it is good up to porcelain temperature. At very low temperatures (cone 012 to cone 010) in a high-lead glaze with low alumina and low silica, chromium produces a strong vermilion red. This same glaze heated higher turns brown at cone 06 and green at cone 02. Sometimes if you can stop the fire just as it is changing, the effect is pleasing. Chromium is the base of many underglaze colors and stains. Calcined with tin, it produces the red colors, pink oxide, maroon base, etc.; and with zinc, it makes many of the brown stains. Chromium won't stand reduction. Because it affects so many other substances, it can cause trouble in the kiln. Care must be taken not to place a chrome glaze near any other susceptible to its action.

Nickel

Nickel is used by the potter as green nickel oxide (NiO), black oxide of nickel (Ni_2O_3), or nickel carbonate ($NiCO_3$). When used in quantities from 2 percent to 5 percent, it produces shades of green, brown, and purple. Nickel is not used in low temperature glazes.

Uranium

Uranium is once more available to potters, but its high cost has reduced its popularity. Uranium produces colors ranging from bright orange to lemon yellow. At low temperatures in a high lead glaze, it is red; in an alkaline glaze, yellow. The forms usually used are black oxide of uranium (UO_2) and sodium uranate (Na_2UO_4). Between 5 and 8 percent is the right amount; an over-charge produces black. Uranium is good at all temperatures, but it cannot stand reduction.

Antimony

From 3 to 6 percent of antimony oxide (Sb_2O_3) will give a yellow color, but a glaze containing raw antimony is apt to blister; most potters prefer to obtain their yellows from yellow base or Naples yellow, which is made by calcining a mixture of red lead, antimony, and tin. (Red lead 15, antimony oxide 10, and tin oxide 4.)

Zinc

Zinc is not a colorant, but since it affects other colors we may consider it here. As mentioned above, it heightens the blue of cobalt and makes chromium turn brown. It also affects iron, turning it a mustard color. This is something to consider whenever you use a glaze containing zinc on a red clay, for the action of the zinc on the iron of the clay will tone down its color and produce a result which may or may not be pleasing. High zinc content in a glaze will make it semiopaque. The potter uses zinc as zinc oxide (ZnO).

Titanium (rutile)

Rutile, an impure form of titanium dioxide (TiO_2), gives a light buff color to glazes, but its main interest to the potter comes from the crystalline effects it produces. No two pieces glazed with a rutile glaze will come out of the kiln the same. Sometimes the effects are good, especially when the rutile is

241

used with copper or cobalt. Titanium is affected by chromium in the same way as tin, becoming pink when fired near it.

Tin

Tin is the strongest opacifier known to the potter. Instead of going into solution in a glaze, it stays in suspension, producing whiteness. The potter uses it as tin oxide (SnO_2), adding 10 percent to a glaze to make it opaque. With no other colorants present, tin produces a white glaze ideal as a background for majolica decoration. With colorants added, tin makes pastel shades which can be used even over dark clay bodies.

Zirconium

Zirconium is used as a substitute for tin. It is an opacifier but only half as strong as tin, so 20 percent must be used to make a glaze opaque. There are several forms of zirconium. Best for the potter are zircopax and ultrox.

Vanadium

Vanadium oxide produces yellow in a glaze when combined with tin. Potters usually use this metal in the form of a commercially prepared vanadium stain.

Commercially prepared colorants

An important source of color for the potter is the pigments sold by ceramic supply houses as underglaze color, overglaze color, and ceramic stains. *Stains* are used to color glazes and sometimes clay bodies. *Overglaze colors* won't stand high temperatures; at cone 07 they begin to fade, hence they are used only for decoration on top of a glaze which has been previously fired. They are then hardened in a third firing to cone 015 or 012.

Underglaze colors, as the name implies, are intended for decoration on bisque or raw ware which is then covered with transparent glaze. These colors must be able to stand any temperature the glaze will, and it is this flexibility in their temperature range which makes them useful for majolica decoration (designs painted on top of an unfired glaze) as well as for glaze colorants.

Commercial glaze stains in a wide variety of hues are available to the potter seeking brilliant colors. Most of these stains would be difficult for a potter to make for himself. Some of them can be fired to cone 10, whereas others are limited to the low fire range. Stains made of cadmium and selenium produce a bright red when fired in a fritted glaze to cone 07. Such a glaze should not be used on tableware because of the possible solubility of the glaze in weak food acids.

Good effects are often obtained by using two or more coloring oxides in a glaze. Table 13-2 lists a number of combinations.

Table 13-2. Coloring Action of Oxides in Glazes

Oxide	Percent	Color in Lead Glaze	Color in Alkaline Glaze	Color When Reduced
Chromium oxide	2%	Vermilion at cone 012 Brown at cone 06 Green at cone 02		
Cobalt carbonate	0.5%	Medium blue	Medium blue	Medium blue
	1%	Strong blue	Strong blue	Strong blue
Copper carbonate	0.5%			Copper red
	1%	Green	Turquoise	Deep red
	2–3%	Deep green	Turquoise	Red and black
	8%	Green with metallic areas	Blue-green with metallic areas	
Ilmenite	3%	Tan specks	Gray-black specks	Spotty brown
Iron chromate	2%	Gray-brown	Gray	
Iron oxide	1%			Celadon
	2%	Pale amber	Pale tan	Olive green celadon
	4%	Red-brown	Brown	Mottled green
	10%	Dark red	Black-brown	Saturated iron red
Manganese carbonate	4%	Purple-brown	Purple-violet	Brown
Nickel oxide	2%	Gray-brown	Gray	Gray-blue
Rutile	5%	Tan	Gray-brown	
Vanadium stain	6%	Yellow	Yellow	
Cobalt carbonate	0.5%	Gray-blue	Gray-blue	
Iron oxide	2%			
Cobalt carbonate	0.5%	Blue-purple	Aubergine	
Manganese carbonate	4%			
Cobalt carbonate	0.5%	Gray-blue	Gray-blue	Textured blue
Rutile	3%			
Copper carbonate	3%	Textured green	Textured blue-green	
Rutile	3%			
Ilmenite	2%	Textured brown	Textured gray-brown	Spotty brown
Rutile	2%			
Iron oxide	8%			Black
Cobalt carbonate	1%			
Manganese carbonate	3%			
Cobalt carbonate	3%	Mirror black		
Iron oxide	2%			
Manganese carbonate	2%			
Manganese carbonate	6%	Luster brown		
Iron oxide	3%			

243

Commercially Prepared Glazes

At the beginning of this chapter we said that glazes bought from dealers are more expensive than those a potter mixes himself. There are times, however, when the convenience of prepared glazes offsets their greater cost. Some potters who have analyzed production costs have learned that when the time spent in mixing glazes is considered, commercially prepared glazes actually prove more economical.

In some ceramics classes, especially those for young children, teachers plagued by the difficulty of storing bulk supplies, losses of material through errors in mixing, and similar problems prefer to rely upon commercial glazes.

Glazes can be bought in dry powder form or as liquids. Dealers offer an almost unlimited selection of colors and textures and special effects (illustrated in color in their catalogues). Some potters prefer to buy colorless base glazes in dry form and add their own colorants.

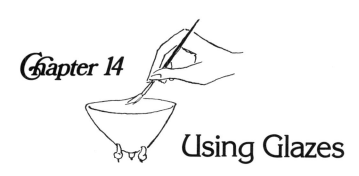

Chapter 14

Using Glazes

Mixing Glazes

Mixing a glaze is simple. You will need a scale for weighing out quantities in grams and a 100-mesh sieve. A mortar and pestle will be handy to have, although not absolutely essential, and for experimental work you should have a glass slab about 12 by 16 inches and a spatula for mixing small amounts of glazes for tests. And that, aside from bowls and glass jars, is all you really need. A ball mill with jars and pebbles is convenient but not really necessary—don't buy one unless you plan to mix large quantities of glazes.

The ingredients of a glaze are weighed out dry and then mixed with water—about one-half cupful for a 300-gram batch.

Using the ball mill

If you have a ball mill, put the ingredients and the water in the jar with a double handful of pebbles and let them grind for an hour—no longer. At the end of this time, dump the glaze and the pebbles into a bowl, then rinse the jar and pour the rinse water into another bowl. Remove the pebbles from the first bowl and wash them off in the second bowl, then pour the contents of both bowls into one and let the glaze settle. At the end of a few hours, the excess water may be poured off the top and the glaze put into a glass jar and labeled.

NOTE. This method does not work with alkaline glazes or any glazes containing soluble ingredients. With these you must be careful to add just enough water to make a thick creamy paste—no excess water can ever be poured off. For this reason it is best not to mix such glazes in a ball mill.

Ball mill

245

Without the ball mill

If you haven't a ball mill, you may grind the ingredients by hand, using a mortar and pestle. But even that much grinding is not absolutely essential. In most cases, you will find it satisfactory merely to mix the ingredients and the water thoroughly, shaking them in a covered jar, then screening them through a 100-mesh sieve. It may be necessary to use a paintbrush to rub the material through the screen. This sieving action not only removes coarse particles, but also makes the mixing more thorough.

Settling

Fritted glazes and glazes containing only small percentages of clay will settle to the bottoms of containers and cake into hard masses almost impossible to stir up. Adding 1 percent of bentonite will prevent this.

A teaspoonful of epsom salts dissolved in hot water and added to a glaze will act as a flocculating agent, making the glaze thicker, and thus reduce settling.

Gums

Sometimes glaze needs a binder to hold it in place on a pot until the pot is placed in the kiln. Gum arabic and gum tragacanth are good for this purpose, but most potters prefer the latter. Buy it in powder form. To prepare it, stir a teaspoonful in an ounce of alcohol, then add a half-pint of water. This will make a medium thick gum which can be added to glazes in the proportion of one tablespoonful to a pint of glaze. As we mentioned earlier, molasses can be used as a binder.

Organic gums such as tragacanth have one disadvantage; they will ferment after a short period of time unless a few drops of formaldehyde are added to the glaze.

Potters have recently turned to synthetic binders which will not ferment. The acrylic binders used with acrylic pigments in painting serve well as binders for glazes.

Other synthetic binders, such as CMC and the synthetic gums marketed under trade names of ceramic supply houses, are easy to use and do not spoil.

Experimenting with glazes

In past centuries all glazes were developed through trial and error, a process that is still good.

When you have had enough experience working with clay and glazes to know what kind of pottery you want to make, what kind of clay you like to use, and the firing range that suits you

246

best, then you will be ready to explore the possibilities of creating glaze recipes of your own.

There are several avenues of approach. One is to select a glaze recipe you have found to be pretty good and then try out substitutions.

If you start with a glaze that fires well on your pieces without crazing, you need not worry about making adjustments in the glaze fit. However, should you wish to make a glaze mature at a higher temperature you could do that by increasing the flint and alumina; to lower the maturing temperature you would do just the opposite—decrease alumina and flint, or increase the fluxes, or substitute a lower fluxing agent for a higher one. For example, substitute lead for zinc.

How much lead for how much zinc?

Let's consult Table 13-1 and look at the column headed "equivalent weight." The figure for zinc is 81; that for white lead is 258, roughly three times as great. This means that to maintain the same balance among the glaze ingredients, we must put back three parts of white lead for every part of zinc we remove.

But substitutions among fluxes are not made merely to alter the firing range of the glaze. As we learned in Chapter 13, the principal fluxes used in glazes—lead, sodium, potassium, calcium, zinc, barium, all produce different effects in glazes.

Suppose we wish to make a glaze more subtle by reducing its glossiness, thus giving it a more pleasing mat surface. This may be brought about by using barium carbonate in place of whiting. Again consulting Table 13-1, we see that barium carbonate has an equivalent weight of 197 while that of whiting is 100. Thus, for every part of whiting we remove from the recipe we would have to put back two parts of barium carbonate.

Other substitutions among fluxes may produce interesting results; for example, one part of zinc in place of three parts of lead, or one part of zinc in place of two parts of lead and one part of whiting.

To make a clear glaze somewhat opaque, try adding from 5 to 20 percent of zircopax. A series of tests of such additions should show various degrees of opalescence (zircopax is suggested instead of tin because it is cheaper).

Another avenue of approach is through substitutions in the clay in the glaze. See what happens when ball clay is substituted for kaolin; or try adding to the glaze the same clay used to make the object.

Try making a slip glaze out of a local clay by combining it with a flux; for example, a low fire frit with 10 to 20 percent of local clay might make a satisfactory glaze at cone 04. Equal parts

247

of local clay and flux might make a glaze that would fire well at cone 4.

Some of the materials listed in the section "Special glaze effects" later in this chapter should be tried out.

Another interesting approach is through trying out various combinations of colorants.

A line blend

Sometimes you will want to try mixing two different glazes to see the results when various proportions are used. To do this, make a line blend. This is a series of tests of mixtures in which proportions are systematically varied until all possible combinations are tried out. Thus if we have two glazes, A and B, the first test will be all A and no B, the second 4/5 A and 1/5 B, the third 3/5 A and 2/5 B, and so on. The complete line blend, with the proportions expressed decimally, would then look like this:

1	2	3	4	5	6
A—1.0	A—0.8	A—0.6	A—0.4	A—0.2	B—1.0
	B—0.2	B—0.4	B—0.6	B—0.8	

A way of trying out combinations of pairs of glazes is by making a diagram like the one on road maps which shows the distances between different pairs of cities. If we start with glazes A, B, C, D, and E, we put them on the top line. The second line starting under B will be AB, AC, AD, AE, and so on. When the tests are completed and arranged as in the diagram, the results of mixing equal parts of all pairs in the group will be shown at a glance.

A	B	C	D	E
	AB	AC	AD	AE
		BC	BD	BE
			CD	CE
				DE

If the series of tests shows an interesting result, a line blend may be made, thus—if the mixture BD seems good, then a line blend can be made of glazes B and D. Or if AC and BE both seem promising, a line blend can be made of those two mixtures.

A triaxial blend

A triaxial blend like the one illustrated can be used to test all combinations of three different glazes: A, B, and C.

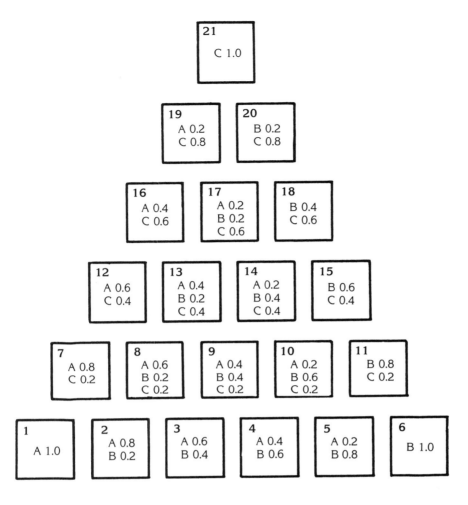

If you make such a series, number the tiles from 1 to 21 as shown. After the firing they may be easily arranged in triangle form and studied.

Test tiles

If you test your glazes on tiles which lie flat in the kiln, you won't get an accurate picture of how they work: a glaze which fires perfectly on a horizontal surface may run on a vertical one. Test tiles, therefore, should be fired standing on edge. Tiles should be made in an angle shape so that each tile provides a vertical surface on which to test the glaze. Such tiles can be made easily by throwing a ring shape on the wheel and cutting it into segments when it is leather hard (Fig. 14-1). Throwing ridges on the surface make for better tests.

249

Angular tile shows how much glaze runs

Clay ring thrown on wheel cut into tiles

Fig. 14-1   Making test tiles.

When you test your glazes you may find it helpful to paint a simple design over the glaze to see how much distortion is produced in the firing. Use underglaze colors for this purpose and follow the method described in the section on majolica.

Marking tests

All test tiles should be carefully marked and records kept of what went into the sample. Prepare marking fluid by mixing equal parts of transparent glaze and black underglaze and adding enough water and gum tragacanth so that you can paint with it easily. Use a small brush. This marking fluid may be used to label either raw or fired tiles, or it can be used to make designs on top of glaze tests, as described in the section above.

Applying glazes

The way you apply your glaze will have much to do with the beauty of the finished piece. It is important to get the glaze on in a smooth, even coat, thick enough so that it can flow into a satisfactory surface during the firing, but not so thick that it crawls.

Before applying a glaze, pour off the free water from the top of the jar, stir the glaze thoroughly and bring it to the right consistency by adding as much water as is needed; then screen it through a 100-mesh sieve. See that the glaze contains enough gum. Clean the piece to be glazed by wiping it with a damp sponge; dust on the surface will cause crawling, and so will any spots of oil or grease. Make sure that your hands are clean and take care in handling the piece.

Dipping or pouring

In glazing bisque ware by dipping, you can either saturate the piece with water first or have it dry. In the former case, the glaze must be quite thick. Soak the piece in a pail of water for several minutes, then take it out and wipe it with a towel. When there is no moisture left on the surface, pour on a little glaze as a test. You will be able to tell by the way the glaze piles up whether it is thick enough or if the piece is too wet. The trick is to get the proper balance between the moisture content of the ware and the thickness of the glaze. The wetter the piece, the thicker the glaze must be, and vice versa.

When you have the glaze and the piece adjusted to each other, glaze the inside by pouring in glaze. Roll the glaze around until the entire inside surface is covered, then pour out all excess which does not stick to the sides. Next turn the piece upside down and rest it on two sticks laid across the top of a bowl. The outside surface can now be glazed by pouring glaze over it.

If you have enough glaze to fill a large container, you may find it easier to hold the piece by the foot (a pair of three-pronged dipping tongs may help), dip it completely into the glaze, then lift it out and allow the excess glaze to drain off. Then the piece can be rested on two sticks until the coating of glaze dries. The places where the piece rests on the supports and where your fingers or the tongs grasp it will have to be touched up with a brush later. There will probably be too heavy a layer of glaze on the bottom; so when the piece is dry enough to handle, scrape the bottom clean with a spatula and brush on a thin layer of glaze. The foot should be completely free of glaze so that the piece can stand on the kiln shelf without the need of stilts.

Small pieces and tiles are especially suited to dipping. Practice until you become skillful. It is not always necessary to soak the bisque piece before glazing it. You can leave it dry if you wish. In this case the glaze must be much thinner and you will have to work quickly in order not to have it pile up in thick masses. Experience will be your best teacher.

Brushing

Applying glaze with a brush is not easy. It takes a delicate touch and, like everything else in pottery, requires practice. Use a flat brush with soft hairs, ½ to 1 inch wide. Work quickly, laying the glaze on with even strokes and avoiding thick deposits of glaze where strokes overlap. As long as the glaze coating is damp, you can brush over it; but once it has dried, another brush stroke is risky.

251

Spraying

This method is wasteful of glaze but it is the best way to apply even coats. It requires a spray gun, a compressor, and a spray booth (Fig. 14-2). The difficulty in spraying glazes is keeping the gun in good working order. Screen each glaze through a 150-mesh sieve before using it, and clean the spray gun carefully when you are through.

Fig. 14-2   Spray booth,
Amaco.

A simpler type of spray gun uses a replaceable can of propellant gas to provide pressure.

You can spray glaze with an ordinary flit gun if you have a lot of patience. The glaze has to be quite thin in order for the sprayer to be able to lift it, and it takes a long time to build up a thick enough coat of glaze; still it is worth trying if no better sprayer is available.

Wear a mask when spraying glazes.
Never spray a glaze containing raw lead.

Glazing raw ware (greenware)

Unfired pieces can be glazed in the same manner as bisque, but of course they cannot be soaked first; care must be taken in dipping to see that the piece does not absorb too much moisture. Glazes on raw ware are best applied by brushing or spray-

252

ing. If you use a brush you will find it helpful to paint the surface first with a coat of gum tragacanth. This will allow the glaze to be brushed on without having the piece act as a sponge.

Dry-footing with paraffin

An electric frying pan containing ½ to ¾ inch of melted paraffin is a convenient device for keeping the bottoms of pieces free from glaze. The current is turned on low and pots are dipped in while the paraffin is hot. Afterward, glazes applied by any method will not adhere to the paraffin-covered portion.

Some Glaze Recipes

Here are some glazes which you might like to make up and try. Recipes are given in percentages.

When a recipe calls for feldspar, any potash or soda spar may be used. When the recipe calls for clay, use any type of kaolin. Some recipes call for ball clay. This makes the glazes easier to apply. Some call for calcined clay. You can make this by putting some dry powdered clay into your kiln when you are firing.

Colorants can be added according to Table 13-2.

Low-fire glazes

1. Transparent lead glaze. Cone 06 to cone 02.

White lead	46.4
Whiting	11.4
Feldspar	19.5
Clay	7.3
Flint	15.4

2. Opaque white tin enamel glaze. Cone 06 to cone 02.
   This is made by adding 10 percent of tin or 20 percent of zircopax to glaze #1.

The three glazes which follow use frits. The numbers refer to the frits of the Ferro Enamel Company, Cleveland, Ohio

3. Transparent fritted glaze. Cone 07 to cone 04.

Frit 3304 (high lead)	90
Ball clay	10

4. White majolica fritted glaze. Cone 07 to cone 04.

Frit 3304	90
Ball clay	10
Tin oxide	10
or	
Zircopax	20

5. Alkaline majolica fritted glaze. Cone 07 to cone 04.

Frit 3124 (leadless)	90
Ball clay	10
Tin oxide	10
or	
Zircopax	20

6. Chrome red glaze. Cone 012

White lead	78
Clay	8
Flint	14
Chromium oxide	2

This glaze produces a bright vermilion red, but don't overfire it; it will turn brown if you do. It works best on a white body or on a piece covered with white engobe. Be sure that the piece is matured to the proper temperature before using this low fire glaze on it.

7. Raw alkaline glaze. Cone 08.

Soda ash	28
Whiting	10
Feldspar	51
Flint	11

Like all raw alkaline glazes, this must be ground by hand and applied immediately.

8. Lead glaze. Cone 07.

White lead	70
Flint	19
Clay	11

This glaze is particularly good on red clay. Use the same clay in the glaze that is in the body.

9. Purple glaze. Cone 05.

Soda ash	15
Magnesium carbonate	8
Boric acid	62
Flint	15
Cobalt oxide	2

This is an alkaline glaze and must be ground by hand and applied immediately. It is a tricky glaze which bubbles violently during the firing and is apt to produce some unexpected results.

10. Lead borosilicate glaze. Cone 06 to cone 02.

White lead	47
Feldspar	12

254

Ferro frit 3134	16
China clay	12
Flint	13
Tin oxide	5

11. Mirror black. Cone 04.

White lead	60
Whiting	7
Clay	9
Flint	24
Cobalt carbonate	3
Iron oxide	2
Manganese carbonate	2

12. Brown luster. Cone 04.

White lead	64
Feldspar	14
Clay	5
Flint	17
Manganese carbonate	6
Iron oxide	3

This glaze produces an attractive lustered surface. It is quite similar to the Rockingham glaze used by early American potters.

13. Oxidizing green glaze. Cone 04.

Soda ash	19
White lead	35
Zinc oxide	2
Feldspar	25
Flint	19
Tin oxide	5
Copper carbonate	3.5
Copper oxide	1.5

This glaze has an overload of copper. Parts of the surface of the glaze will have a metallic appearance after it is fired. This is a raw alkaline glaze, so grind by hand.

14. Raw alkaline glaze. Cone 04.

Borax	34
Feldspar	20
Whiting	9
Clay	3
Flint	25
Zinc oxide	9

Grind by hand and apply immediately. For turquoise, add from 1 to 3 percent of copper carbonate.

255

15. Borosilicate glaze. Cone 04.

Colemanite	21
Feldspar	38
Barium carbonate	20
Clay	4
Flint	17

16. Barium mat glaze. Cone 04 to cone 02.

White lead	40
Whiting	6
Barium carbonate	12
Feldspar	23
Clay	11
Flint	8

17. Rutile glaze. Cone 03.

White lead	67
Feldspar	10
Clay	2
Flint	15
Rutile	6

This glaze produces crystalline effects. It is especially good with the following colorants:

Copper oxide 3.0% produces green mat surface with light and dark stripes

Cobalt oxide 0.5% produces light blue mat surface with yellow and brown stripes

Iron oxide 5.0% produces brown mat surface with yellow crystals

This is an interesting glaze to experiment with. Try it with other colorants.

18. Alumina mat. Cone 03.

White lead	48
Whiting	12
Feldspar	24
Clay	4
Calcined clay	12

Middle range glazes

19. Cornwall stone glaze. Cone 2 to cone 4.

Cornwall stone	65
White lead	21
Whiting	10
Zinc oxide	4

This is an excellent glaze for Monmouth or Jordan clay.

20. Borosilicate glaze. Cone 4.

Colemanite	14
Feldspar	44
Dolomite	7
Whiting	8
China clay	3
Zinc oxide	4
Flint	20

21. Bristol glaze. Cone 4 to cone 8.

Zinc oxide	7
Whiting	10
Feldspar	68
China clay	8
Flint	7

High fire glazes

22. Feldspathic glaze. Cone 8 to cone 10.

Feldspar	56
Whiting	31
China clay	4
Zinc oxide	9

Harding Black, an authority on the glazes of ancient China, furnished the following recipes for this book. He adds 2 percent of bentonite and ½ percent of CMC to each glaze batch. Some tests of these recipes are shown in the color section.

23. Basic glaze. Cone 8 to cone 10. H.B.

Frit 3124	25
Potash feldspar	27
Whiting	7.5
Wallastonite	7.5
Barium Carbonate	5
Zinc oxide	5
Flint	23

24. Rutile glaze. Cone 6 to cone 8. H.B.

Frit 3304	27
Barium carbonate	30
Zinc oxide	11
China clay	12
Flint	20
Rutile	5

25. Alkaline glaze. Cone 8 to cone 12. H.B.

Potash feldspar	26.5
Whiting	6.5

Wallastonite	5.
Barium carbonate	5.
Zinc oxide	2.5
Ball clay	12.
Borax	13.
Sodium carbonate	2.5
Flint	27.

26. Oxblood glaze. Cone 10 to cone 12. H.B.

Potash spar	47
Whiting	3
China clay	3
Colemanite	19
Barium carbonate	11
Flint	17
Tin oxide	1
Copper oxide	1

Mix two batches, one with tin and copper, one without. Spray the second batch as a cover over the first. Reduce to cone 4, oxidize to cone 10.

27. Rutile glaze. Cone 8 to cone 10. H.B.

Nepheline syenite	75
Dolomite	15
Zinc oxide	5
Rutile	5

28. Frit glaze. Cone 8 to cone 10. H.B.

Frit 3124	25
Nepheline syenite	35
Zinc oxide	5
Barium carbonate	10
Flint	25
Tin oxide	1

29. Frit glaze. Cone 8 to cone 10. H.B.

Frit 3124	28
Soda feldspar	24
Whiting	8
Wallastonite	8
Barium carbonate	6
Zinc oxide	6
Flint	20
Tin oxide	1

30. Slip glaze. Cone 8 to cone 12. H.B.

| Feldspar | 30 |

EPK kaolin	5
Georgia kaolin	7.5
North Carolina kaolin	7.5
Kentucky ball clay	17.5
Tennessee ball clay	17.5
Flint	15

Additions: Copper oxide 5%

Pure red iron, Ferro 191. This produces the beautiful iron blue shown on a few of the test cups in the color section.

These slips require heavy application (three coats).

31. Porcelain glaze. Cone 10 to cone 12.
Feldspar	27
Whiting	20
Kaolin	20
Flint	33

Additions of 0.5 to 1.5 percent of iron oxide produce the light green tones of celadon in reduction.

32. Wood ash glaze. Cone 9 to cone 10.
Ashes, washed	33.3
Feldspar	33.3
Ball clay	33.3

33. Wood ash glaze. Cone 9 to cone 10.
Ashes, unwashed	35
Feldspar	35
Talc	15
Ball clay	15

Local reduction glazes

34. Copper red glaze. Cone 9 –10 Littlefield
Ferro frit 3191	13
Soda feldspar	45
Whiting	14
China clay	3
Flint	25
Tin oxide	1
Copper oxide	0.2
Silicon carbide FFF	0.2

For *celadon* replace the copper and the tin with 2 percent of iron oxide.

These glazes must be fired in an oxidizing atmosphere;

since the carbon has been introduced into the glaze a reduction atmosphere is not needed. They must be applied thickly. Results cannot be guaranteed; the recipes should be considered starting points for series of trials.

Glazes for raku

Now we come to an area where almost anything goes and daring experimentation is half of the fun! Because of the low temperature of raku firing, potters can use such things as lead all alone to make a glaze, but because of the hazards of raw lead, it seems wiser to use colemanite and various frits as fluxes.

Borax mixed into a paste with water and brushed thickly on a piece will form a glaze; so will Boraxo.

Interesting lusters often develop during reduction in glazes containing copper. Metallic lusters can be achieved by adding 5 percent of silver nitrate to glazes or 3 percent of tin chloride. The glaze colorants listed at the end of *Chapter 13* can be used in raku glazes.

Here are some raku glaze recipes:

Raw lead, glossy.
White lead	90
Clay (any)	10

Raw lead, mat.
White lead	75
Clay (any)	25

Add 3 to 6 percent chromium oxide to the above two glazes for red.

Clear raku glaze.
Frit 3134	40
Colemanite	60

Silvery white raku glaze.
Colemanite	70
Zircopax	30

Cloudy white raku glaze.
Colemanite	80
Feldspar	20

Yellow raku glaze.
White lead	60
Frit 3134	20
Flint	20
Lead chromate	1

Black luster raku glaze.

White lead	67
Whiting	7
Flint	26
Cobalt oxide	2
Copper oxide	3
Iron oxide	4

Luster glazes

This is a form of decoration developed by the early Persian potters who applied metallic salts to the ware, then fired it in a strong reducing fire. Here is a recipe:

Ferro frit 3195	90
Ball clay	10
Silver nitrate	1
Bismuth sub-nitrate	2

This glaze may be applied to greenware or to bisque. It is particularly effective over colored engobes (try it over black). Fire it to cone 04, then allow the kiln to cool to 010. At this point reduce the kiln as violently as you can, either by introducing organic matter into the chamber or by closing the dampers and shutting off the air at the burners so that the flame burns yellow. After 5 or 10 minutes of this, turn off the kiln and allow it to cool. When you open it, you should find some luster ware. You will also find a kiln black with soot, but don't let that worry you—it will burn out completely the next time you fire.

Fuming Lusters can be developed on glazes by fuming. This is done either during the cooling cycle or by reheating the glazed ware in the kiln. When the kiln is at cone 010, tin chloride is put into the kiln in small cast iron cups inserted through an opening in the kiln door. It is better to heat the metal cups to red heat (using a torch) before they are filled and put into the kiln. The kiln must be tightly sealed. Fifty grams of tin chloride is enough for fuming in a kiln of 10 cubic feet.

For stronger coloring in the luster, strontium nitrate and barium chloride may be added to the tin chloride in amounts of 10 to 20 percent.

Fuming also works with salt glazing. When the kiln has cooled to a dull red heat, the cast iron cups containing the fuming salts are placed among the pots.

Prepared lusters Commercially prepared lusters of gold, silver, copper, and other metals can be bought from ceramic dealers. These lusters contain their own reducing agents, so it is not necessary to reduce the kiln when using them. They are

261

painted over finished glazes with an oil medium, such as oil of lavender, and are then fired to cone 012.

To put a luster over a finished glaze, mix the luster glaze with cornstarch and put a thick layer on the piece to be lustered. Fire it up to cone 07, then allow the kiln to cool to cone 010 and reduce.

Egyptian paste

This is not really a glaze. Small objects such as ornaments and jewelry may be modeled of this paste and fired in the kiln at cone 07. Be careful when mixing the ingredients together not to lose any of the soluble materials. It is best to mix them with a spatula on a glass slab, using just enough water to make a workable material.

Feldspar	34
Flint	34
Clay	11
Sodium carbonate (soda ash).	5
Sodium bicarbonate	5
Copper carbonate	3
Dextrine	8

This produces turquoise. For other colors omit copper and add:

for green	1% chromium oxide
for blue	1% cobalt oxide
for yellow	10% Naples yellow

Special glaze effects

Variety is interesting. That is why potters experiment constantly with such things as mottling, specks, oversprays—anything, in fact—to give their ware individuality, to make it different from flat uniformity. Here are some things to try.

Specks

Whenever the coloring oxides in a glaze are not thoroughly ground, the glaze will have a speckled appearance. This is especially true of cobalt.

Common sand does interesting things in a low fire glaze. Try adding 10 percent to some of your majolica glazes screening it first through an 80-mesh sieve. The results in a lead glaze will be different from those in an alkaline glaze and, in either case, will be affected by the impurities which happen to be present in the sand. It is only by experimenting that you can find out what effects you can achieve. (Interesting results have come from putting bits of a copper scrubbing pad into a glaze.)

262

Fig. 14-3 Bowl, 9″ diameter, white mat glaze over
Albany slip; by Malcolm Norwood, head of the art
department, Delta State College, Cleveland,
Mississippi.

Other things which can be added to produce specks in glazes
are granular ilmenite (a titanium iron oxide, $FeTiO_3$), 100-mesh
carborundum (silicon carbide, SiC), and 80-mesh grog.

Mottling

The effects produced when colors put over one another at
random run together in a fluid glaze are sometimes pleasing,
but beware of overworking this trick and turning out ware
which is "arty."

Some of the early American potters were so fond of mottled
surfaces that they covered their pieces with a bright lead glaze
and then used a pepper shaker to sprinkle coloring oxides over
them before they were fired. Ware treated this way would
come out of the kiln covered with mingled flecks of green, blue,
yellow, brown, and orange. This type of glaze, called Flint
Enamel, was actually patented by the Bennington potters.

Crackle

A crackle glaze is one that has crazed, something much easier
to do than to avoid. You can make a crackle out of any glaze at all
just by forgetting to put in the flint or leaving out part of the
alumina; but remember, earthenware covered with such a glaze
won't hold water. When the Chinese potters put crackle glazes
on their porcelain vases, that was all right because the body was

263

vitreous anyway and would have held water without any glaze at all.

It is possible to create crackle effects and at the same time produce sound ware by means of an extra firing. Fire the glazed piece first to a point two or three cones below the temperature needed for maturity. As soon as the kiln cools, take the piece out and plunge it into a pail of water. This temperature shock will make the glaze craze over its entire surface. (It may also cause the piece to break, but that is one of the chances you must take.) Now rub some underglaze color over the surface of the piece so that it penetrates all the tiny cracks, and then wipe off the excess. The pattern of the crazing will now show in color. If you fire the piece again to its proper maturing point, all the cracks in the glaze will close and the crazing will disappear but its pattern will remain as a crackle. Since both glaze and body have now matured properly, the piece is good pottery.

Pooling

An extremely fluid glaze used in large amounts will form a pool on the floor of a shallow dish (it will also break the dish unless it is sturdily built, with thick walls). This pool, upon cooling, turns into a thick layer of glass which crazes considerably but which has beauty because of its depth. Colors may be introduced into such a glaze at random.

Bubbling

Much of the beauty of borosilicate and colemanite glazes is caused by the action of borax during the firing. This glaze ingredient boils violently, forming bubbles which disappear after the borax is melted. As the bubbles settle down and the glaze flows smooth, however, slight markings are left. These give a glaze an interesting texture. Other glaze ingredients which bubble violently during the firing are manganese and antimony. As an experiment, try the brown luster glaze, Recipe No. 12. Apply this to a piece of pottery and then brush a coating of white majolica glaze on top of it. The manganese in the brown luster glaze will bubble and break through the coating of white glaze.

A borosilicate glaze does interesting things to any design which is on top of it; the bubbling action breaks the lines slightly—not enough to destroy the design, but sufficiently to give an interesting texture to it.

Oversprays

The action of borosilicate glazes described above can be used to advantage by spraying a glaze of a different color over a borosilicate base. Again the bubbling action will give texture to the color on top.

Quite different effects are obtained by spraying a fairly viscous glaze on top of a highly fluid one. During the firing, the fluid glaze will run and will break up the glaze on top of it into patterns which may be pleasing.

Defects in Glazes

There is always an element of uncertainty in firing glazes. Lots of things can go wrong, and the source of trouble is sometimes hard to trace. It may lie in the glaze or in the clay itself. There may be a mistake in the formula or in the way the ingredients were weighed out. There may be faults of application or firing. Here are a few of the most common glaze defects, and some of the things which cause them.

Crazing

When a glaze crazes, it develops tiny cracks all over its surface. Sometimes these show immediately after the piece comes out of the kiln but often they do not appear until several months later. Crazing is an indication that the glaze does not fit the body.

Crazing can have many different causes. It is often a problem of the body rather than the glaze. Fire the ware higher, or add flint, or else add a body flux as described in Chapter 11 to increase the density. Bring the percentage of absorption down as far as possible—get below 10 percent. If you are using a native clay, it may be too coarse and sandy—try screening it through an 80-mesh sieve.

If the fault is not with the body, increase the alumina and the silica content of the glaze, running a series of tests of various additions until you have secured a better fit. Sometimes changing feldspars will help.

Crawling

When a glaze crawls, the piece comes out of the kiln with bare spots where the glaze has moved away, exposing the body underneath. This may be due to:
    a. Not enough gum tragacanth in the glaze, so that it cracked before going into the kiln.
    b. Dust on the surface of the piece when the glaze was applied.
    c. Oil on the surface of the piece.
    d. Too much grinding of the glaze.
    e. Too heavy application.
    f. Underfiring.

265

g. Firing before the glaze dried.

h. Too porous a body.

i. Too much plastic clay in the glaze.

The remedy for each of the above, except the last one, is obvious. If the trouble is caused by the shrinkage of clay in the glaze, try firing some of the clay in powder form and use it in the glaze calcined instead of raw.

Blistering

Blistering may be due to sulfur in the clay. To remedy, add 2 percent of barium carbonate to the clay when it is in slip form. Blisters or craters which are caused by sulfur will eventually burn out if the piece is refired.

If blisters appear in lead glazes and not in others, the trouble is reduction. Check the kiln and the burners.

Manganese often blisters in a glaze. Other causes are too heavy application, putting a second coat of glaze over the first, and underfiring. In most cases a piece which has blistered can be refired and cured.

Pin holes

Pin holes are often caused by air holes in the clay, especially in cast pieces. Other causes are too rapid firing or too rapid cooling. Painting over a glaze after it has dried is apt to cause this trouble.

Running

Too much flux in the glaze or overfiring will make a glaze run. Sometimes coloring oxides act as fluxes and cause running. To remedy, cut down on the flux or increase the alumina.

Dryness

Dryness is due to underfiring or not enough flux. In alkaline glazes, this often occurs through the loss of soda.

Sandpaper surface

A rough surface indicates that the glaze was not applied thick enough.

Shivering

Shivering occurs when sections of glaze lift off the piece. This is usually a body fault. To remedy, lower the silica in the body and increase it in the glaze. Another cause of shivering may be too rapid firing or cooling.

Discoloration

Discoloration may be due to reduction or to the presence of chromium in the kiln.

Chipping

Chipping usually results from lack of fit between glaze and body. The body may be too porous. Try introducing some feldspar.

Shiny surface on mat glaze

If a glaze which should be mat comes out shiny, the piece was fired too high.

Devitrification

Devitrification is a dull surface on a glaze resulting from the crystallization of silica. It occurs when the kiln cools too slowly. This is a defect which studio potters rarely encounter, for their kilns almost always cool too fast.

Some points on working with glaze

1. To get the full satisfaction of pottery, devise your own glaze formulas and make your own glazes.
2. Experiment, but know what you are doing. Keep accurate records of all the glazes you prepare and fire tests on carefully marked tiles.
3. Test every glaze before you use it on a piece.
4. Control your glaze effects; don't be satisfied with accidental results.
5. Work for glazes which fit your clay. Don't excuse crazing by saying you wanted a crackle anyway.
6. Let your glazes have translucence and depth. Avoid a paintlike quality.
7. Some mottled effects are pleasing, but beware of haphazard mingling of glazes.
8. Use the natural color of your clay.
9. Remember that form and color are both important; when you start to shape a piece of clay, have in mind the glaze which will be on the finished piece.

267

Chapter 15   Decoration

We have spoken about ways of decorating clay by carving, incising, and so on. Now a word or two about decorating in color.

Engobe

The most direct method of decorating pottery is by using clay of two different colors, inlaying one in the other or putting one on top of the other as a slip. Slip used this way is called *engobe*.

When you put liquid engobe on a leather-hard or bone-dry piece of clay, you face the problems of unequal shrinkage. If the engobe contracts more than the clay, it will crack off. To avoid this trouble, apply engobe decorations while the clay is still quite wet so that the engobe and the piece can shrink together. Another way of meeting the problem is to prepare an engobe with a high percentage of flux. Such an engobe is actually almost a glaze, but it can be used as a slip and may be applied to bone-dry ware or even to bisque.

Much can be done in slip decoration by using different colored native clays. Red and buff are harmonious when used together this way. For more brilliant colors, it is necessary to prepare a white engobe and color it with metal oxides.

Recipes

Here is a white engobe which can be used on wet clay:

	grams
China clay	25
Ball clay	20
Flint	30
Feldspar	17
Whiting	2
Magnesium carbonate	6

268

These ingredients should be mixed in the same manner as that described for glazes in Chapter 14.

The following engobe contains a high proportion of flux. It can be applied to bone-dry ware or to ware which has been fired. It will not work on wet clay. This engobe contains a soluble ingredient (borax), so mix it as you would an alkaline glaze.

	grams
China clay	6
Ball clay	6
Feldspar	10
Flint	20
Whiting	3
Borax	3
Nepheline syenite	12
Frit 3124 (Ferro Enamel Co.)	20
Zircopax	20

Both of the above engobes may be colored by adding metal oxides in the proportions listed for glaze No. 1 in Chapter 14.

Engobe can be painted on ware with a brush, applied with a tube, sprayed, poured, or dipped. Designs may be drawn directly with engobe or may be scratched through an engobe coating. They can also be made by using stencils.

Slip painting

It is not easy to use a brush with engobe. The material won't flow the way paint does, and so long brush strokes are impossible. During the firing some of the engobe goes into solution in the glaze which covers it; hence it must be applied thick—delicate strokes disappear. Pleasing brush decorations can be made with engobe, however, as long as the limitations of the method are understood. Since you cannot make long brush strokes, make short ones—compose designs with direct touches of the brush heavily loaded with engobe.

Slip trailing

More elaborate designs in engobe can be made by trailing the material onto the piece through a tube. The best and simplest tool for this work is a piece of glass tubing slightly narrowed at one end. The tube is filled by dipping it into the engobe and using it as a straw, drawing slip up into the tube by suction (be careful not to get a mouthful). The flow of slip can be regulated by changing the slant of the tube. When you hold the tube in a horizontal position, the slip will not run out at all. As you tip it up, the slip will start to flow, increasing in speed as the tube approaches a vertical position. A little experimentation will enable you to control the flow, producing thick or thin lines as you

269

wish. The slab-built box shown in Photo Series 9 was decorated this way.

Prepared engobe can be purchased from dealers.

Sgraffito

Sgraffito means scratched. In this type of decoration, designs are scratched in a coating of engobe so that the contrasting color of the body shows through. The coating of engobe may be put on the piece with a brush or may be poured or sprayed.

Another variation is possible in sgraffito design. Lines scratched when the engobe is still wet have a different character than lines scratched after it has dried. Different tools give different effects.

Another kind of sgraffito decoration is possible when pieces are poured in drain molds. Engobe of one color is poured into the mold and then poured out immediately so that a thin layer is left on the inside of the mold. Before this dries, casting slip of a different color is poured in. When the piece is removed from the mold, the engobe coating will cover the entire surface. A design cut through this outer layer will show the contrasting color of the body.

Another way of using slip as a decoration in connection with molds is to paint or trail a design on the inside of the mold before the casting slip is poured in. As the slip hardens, it will pick up the design and the finished piece will show the decoration as a colored inlay.

Spraying

Engobe may be applied with a spray gun. It is possible to put on even coats this way in preparation for sgraffito decoration, or designs may be sprayed through stencils.

Wax resist

Designs may be painted on greenware with wax resist emulsion (trade name, Ceramul). If engobe is then poured over the piece, it will stick only to those portions which are not covered by the wax resist, hence the design will show the color of the original clay body. This method is rather complicated and only simple designs should be tried.

Terra sigillata

The Romans had a way of treating their pottery to give it a hard, semiglossy surface almost as dense as a glaze. This surface treatment is *terra sigillata* (the words mean *sealed earth*). Terra sigillata is really an engobe made of very fine colloidal particles of clay which stay in suspension when the clay has been ground for a long period and deflocculated.

270

Fig. 15-1   Bowl, wax resist, by Jerry Friedman.

If you would like to experiment with terra sigillata, use 1000 grams of native clay, add 1000 grams of water and grind the mixture in a ball mill for 24 hours or longer. Remove the slip from the ball mill and put it in a tall glass container, then add water until the specific gravity of the mixture is 1.2 (you can measure the specific gravity of the slip with a hydrometer). Add 20 grams of sodium hydroxide, stir the slip thoroughly, and let it stand undisturbed for 24 hours more. At the end of this time, clay will have settled to the bottom of the container with an almost clear, colorless liquid above it. This liquid contains the colloidal particles of clay you are seeking. Carefully siphon off some of this liquid into another container. When this is sprayed on raw ware, the piece will come out of the kiln with an extremely hard coating having a slight shine.

A dry, unfired pot can be dipped into terra sigillata; dip it quickly in and out, just once.

The color of terra sigillata varies; sometimes it is quite different from the clay out of which it is made. It provides a good surface treatment for sculpture and may be used for various decorative treatments such as sgraffito or spraying over patterns.

Mishima

In this method of decoration, designs incised or carved in a leather-hard piece are filled with an engobe of contrasting color.

Another way is to bisque the piece, then glaze it by dipping or pouring. When the glaze has dried, the glaze is scraped away from the high portions of the piece and a second glaze is applied.

271

Ceramic Colors

There are many different ways of using ceramic pigments in decorating pottery. The colors may be painted on unglazed ware and then covered with a transparent glaze and fired (*under glaze* decoration), or they may be put on top of a coating of opaque glaze before it is fired (*majolica*). Colors may be painted on top of a glaze which has been fired (*overglaze* decoration) or they may be mixed in with the glaze itself and painted on the ware in decorative patterns (*polychrome*).

A good type of decoration for the studio potter is majolica. The method is simple (one firing of the piece is usually enough) and the results are highly satisfying, for the colors melt into the glaze and the design becomes part of the piece itself. Ware decorated this way has a true ceramic quality often absent from underglaze or overglaze work.

Prepared ceramic colors

It used to be that potters wishing to decorate with ceramic colors had to buy them in dry powder form, then mix them with a flux to make them fire properly, and use a liquid vehicle to make them flow from a brush. This is no longer necessary because dealers now sell prepared overglaze colors and underglaze colors, both in liquid form in jars ready for use and also in semimoist form (pans), in a metal box set which resembles the paint sets we used to get at Christmas when we were young. Dry colors are still available for use as glaze colorants, but the commercially prepared pigments eliminate a lot of work and may very well be cheaper.

Majolica

In this method of decoration, designs are painted with overglaze on top of an opaque glaze before it is fired.

The glaze may be put on either raw ware or bisque and it can be applied by dipping, brushing, or spraying. Try to get a smooth coat of even thickness.

Painting over a coating of glaze is tricky. When it dries, the glaze will absorb color rapidly and working on it will be just like painting on blotting paper. You will find it easier to apply your decoration while the glaze is still damp. If you have difficulty painting on the surface of the glaze, spray or brush a thin layer of gum tragacanth over the glaze before you paint.

You have planned your design well in advance, of course. The next step is to sketch the design on the piece. You can't use a pencil because this would mar the coating of glaze; so use a brush dipped in india ink. India ink will burn out completely during the firing and not leave any trace; you can be as free as

272

Fig 15-2 Majolica decoration painted with opaque
colors over a transparent glaze on a red body. The plate
was made on a drape mold.

you wish in using it. Sketching on the piece with a brush has the
added advantage of giving you a chance to practice the strokes
needed in the final design.

Now go ahead and paint. The quality of your brushwork is
most important here. Work quickly, painting with free direct
strokes. Avoid going over any portion of the design twice. Keep
your colors smooth and free flowing. Try to achieve character in
your line so that each brush stroke has beauty of its own.

For bands of color around the edges of plates, use the banding

Fig. 15-3 Majolica, dry brush
technique.

Fig. 15-4 Majolica, background
painted over a white glaze.

wheel or whirler. Center the piece carefully and spin the
wheel. Load your brush with color and touch it to the rim of the
piece as it spins, holding the brush steady until a complete band
is made. A brush with hairs about an inch long is best for banding, and the colors should be thin enough to flow freely.

Great variety is possible in majolica decoration through the
use of different glazes and different methods of painting. Designs may be made with smooth brush strokes, or a "dry brush"
technique may be used. In this method the brush is dipped into
the color, then squeezed almost dry and the hairs separated so
that tones rather than lines are painted. When designs are
painted over a borosilicate glaze which bubbles during the
firing, the effect will be quite different from that obtained when
they are painted over smooth lead glazes. If a glaze is sprayed
through a coarse nozzle so that it makes a pebbly surface on the
piece, brush strokes made over it will show a grain. To perfect
your skill in majolica decorating, paint a number of designs on
tiles. Try different methods and practice until you have full
command of the brush.

Majolica decoration is usually painted on top of an opaque
glaze but this is not the only way of doing it. Interesting results
are obtained by using a transparent glaze over a red clay body.
When you paint on top of such a glaze, mix liberal amounts of
tin oxide with some of the colors so that they will show up light
against the dark background of the piece. Other colors may be
used without tin.

Underglaze decoration

Designs may be painted with underglaze colors either on raw
ware or on bisque in the manner described in the section on

274

Fig. 15-5 Underglaze painting,
free brush strokes; by Pat Casad.

majolica; instead of using water as a vehicle, it is necessary to use glycerine or gum for raw ware and some oil medium for bisque.

The simplest method of underglaze decoration is painting directly on the raw ware. It is best to paint on ware which is still leather hard, for bone-dry clay is too absorbent and is apt to draw color from the brush, making it pile up in lumps instead of flowing as it should. If you have this trouble, try sponging the piece or else brush a thin coat of gum tragacanth over the surface to be decorated.

Sketch your design on the piece with a soft pencil or with brush and india ink. Sketches which don't turn out right can be removed with a damp sponge.

The quality of brushwork is important in underglaze painting as well as in majolica. Work freely and quickly. Keep the color from piling up in lumps, for these will stick out through the glaze and make ugly blemishes. If you make a mistake, don't try to correct it but sponge off the piece and start again.

Underglaze decorations can be made on bisque ware also—in fact, this is the usual method of commercial production. Painting on bisque requires an oil medium, but instead of using glycerine add a few drops of fat oil of turpentine and an equal amount of turpentine. If the mixture is too thick, use a little more turpentine to thin it.

Pieces with underglaze decorations can be glazed and fired in one firing if you are careful to apply the glaze without spoiling the design. It is best to spray the glaze over the decoration, although dipping is possible if you are skillful. Some potters prefer to fire the decorated piece to red heat before they glaze it.

275

This hardens the design on the piece so that it cannot be washed off when the glaze is applied. If you have painted on bisque ware using fat oil as a medium, it will be advisable to fire the piece to red heat before you glaze it in order to burn out the oil, which otherwise might cause trouble under the glaze.

Remember in underglaze decoration that the color of your clay will affect the colors of your design. If you want bright colors, it will be necessary either to use a white clay body for making your ware or else cover the ware with white engobe. If brilliance of color is not important, however, decorations may be painted directly on buff or red clay.

Overglaze painting

Designs can be painted with overglaze colors on ware which has been glazed and fired. The method involves an additional firing, but it has the important advantage of making available to the potter a range of colors not obtainable in any other way.

Overglaze colors will not stand high temperatures—most of them begin to disappear above cone 012. The piece to be decorated must, therefore, be glazed and fired to full maturing temperature before the overglaze colors are applied. The colors are then painted on and the piece is fired again, this time to a temperature just high enough to soften the glaze slightly. The colors are thus bound into the glaze.

Overglaze painting has one advantage over majolica: mistakes can be wiped off and decorations repainted as often as you wish.

Polychrome

Designs may be made on pottery by mixing colors with glaze and painting directly on the piece. Here the problem is to keep the colors of one area from flowing into another. Various devices are used to prevent this. Flat pieces, tiles, etc., are sometimes made with raised lines which separate areas where different colors will be placed. Sometimes color areas are outlined with a glaze made with insufficient flux so that it does not run. If care is used in preparing the glazes and in firing, however, it is possible to make decorations by direct painting with different colored glazes.

Polychrome decoration is better suited to sculpture and tiles than to plates and vases.

Overglaze printing with decalcomanias

The pictorially decorated tableware that became so popular in England during the last century involved making copperplate engravings. These were printed in ceramic colors on

276

Fig. 15-6   Polychrome
knick-knack.

Fig. 15-7   Kaleidoscope Fish, 19″ × 17″. Porcelain inlaid black
clay, with underglaze and decalcomania; by David F.
Silverman.

specially prepared transfer paper from which they went onto the ware.

Today ceramic designs are printed on decalcomania paper. Stock designs of birds and flowers, as well as trademarks and emblems, are commercially produced for use by manufacturers of tableware.

If you make your own design, a ceramic printing firm can reproduce it for you as a decal in one or several colors, including gold. Transferring such a decal to a ceramic piece is a simple process.

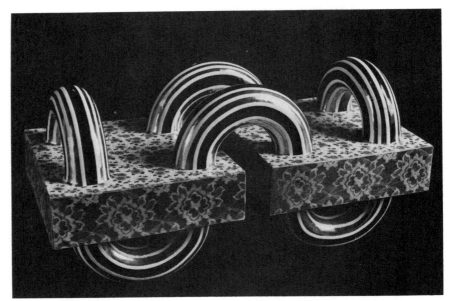

Fig. 15-8   Sunflower Segmentation, 28″ × 15″, underglazed, decaled, reduction; by David F. Silverman.

Some points on ceramic decoration

Think carefully before you decorate. Remember that what counts is the shape of the piece and the clay which forms it. Too often beautiful pottery is spoiled by overly elaborate ornamentation.

Tastes vary. Some people like gaily decorated pottery while others prefer plainer wares. We cannot say that one is right and the other wrong. We can say, however, that if decoration is used it must have a relation to the way a piece is made and the purpose it will serve.

Everything that is popular is not necessarily good. The fact that a piece of pottery is pictured in an expensive magazine or sold in an exclusive store does not mean that it is good.

Don't debase a piece of pottery by letting it serve merely as a background for painting.

As you work with clay your sense of design will improve. After a while you will realize that the most satisfactory decorations are usually the simplest—those which show what they are made of and how they are put on.

When you make a piece of pottery a bond is established between you and everyone else who has shaped clay ever since the world began. You are fellows in the same craft. Take a little time to study what others have done; let their work inspire you.

Drawing inspiration from potters of other times and other lands does not mean copying their work. The pottery you make must be your own, yet what you see in books on ceramic history or in museum collections can suggest ways of making your pottery more beautiful and more satisfying. After all it is not possible to be entirely original in ceramic work. A cup is a cup and a bowl is a bowl—you cannot make them completely different unless you enter the realm of the fantastic. Since that is so, be familiar with the best of what has been done so that your work may be a product of knowledge and understanding.

Chapter 16

Pottery as a Career

Now that we know some of the secrets of the potter, have mastered the wheel and learned how to control the fire, how about pottery as a career? It must be very pleasant to earn one's living creating beautiful things out of clay. Can it be done?

The answer is yes, it can be done and it is being done, but probably not exactly in the way you have in mind. Almost everyone who has worked with clay has dreamed of opening a small pottery shop by the side of the road, somewhere near a clay bank, where he could build his kiln, set up his wheel, and then throw pieces of ware all day long: like the man with the better mousetrap, the world would beat a pathway to his door. It is a romantic picture.

Places like that really do exist, but before you embark on such a venture, let's think about it.

We live in an industrial age. This gives us more efficient living, it is true, but at the same time it robs us of much satisfaction. The man who built his own home a few hundred years ago was not as well housed as our modern city dwellers, but his life had something which we miss. So much is done for us by machines today. Our clothes are made in factories, our food is cooked and frozen, we even have machines to sing our songs for us. Perhaps that is why so many of us turn to pottery with the hope that digging clay from the earth and shaping it to serve a purpose, decorating it in a way which seems good, may somehow supply a bit of what is lacking in our lives.

But earning a living from pottery is something else again. We cannot ignore the industrial era—just turn our backs upon it and, by wishing, return to the age of crafts. If you plan to make pottery your life work, you must face the fact that to support yourself and your family, you will have to sell a lot of pots; and throwing pots all day long is hard work. Remember too that when you make and sell pieces, you become a businessman; bothersome details of cost analysis, rent, invoices, bookkeeping, and taxes must not be overlooked.

The ceramic industry is a large one but, with a few exceptions, the workers in pottery plants are not much different from those on an auto assembly line. They do not make things, they perform operations. However, there are opportunities for the artist-craftsman in the industry; his creative talents are needed in all areas of design.

An industry which has burgeoned in the last twenty years is the one that supplies materials and equipment for ceramists. The potter's wheels made by scores of different companies were planned by artist-potters. Potters help to prepare the ceramic colors and stains used by other potters. There are many ways of earning a living through pottery besides the making and selling of individual pots. Here are stories telling about some people who are doing so.

A fourth-generation potter

Norman Smith is a potter of the old school. I met him many years ago when, while driving on a back road in Alabama, I came upon his shop and stopped for a visit. He nodded, said "howdy" and kept on throwing large crocks on a homemade kick wheel.

For my benefit he changed stride, "I'm fixin' to make a pitcher now" he said. In less time than it takes to tell it, he had shaped a form, rolled an edge, pulled out a spout, and attached a handle. In a few moments more, a smaller lump of clay became a mug.

The secrets of the potter's craft were handed down to Norman from his forefathers. His clay is dug from a nearby pit, mixed with water in the ground with the help of a mule. He used to make four hundred pots a day. About every two weeks his work was fired in a large down draft kiln (built by his great grandfather and repaired and enlarged during succeeding generations), using about three and a half cords of scrap wood from a nearby lumber mill as fuel. Some of his work is sold locally; some of it he takes to Birmingham, about sixty miles away, for sale by department stores.

Recently we revisited that back road and found to our amazement that Norman Smith was still there, still making sturdy functional pots. The road is now a county highway and customers come to his shop to buy large garden pottery, as well as ware for the kitchen and the pantry.

Norman is older now, but youthful as ever in spirit. He has a small tractor in place of a mule and he has cut his daily production in half. But he still loves the work he is doing.

Jugtown

This is a small area in North Carolina where clay is plentiful and potters are numerous. Pottery has been made there since 1750. Each year young people come as apprentices to learn the secrets of the craft with the hope of eventually opening their own shops. This area has become known and customers come from great distances to buy dinner ware, jugs, pitchers, bird houses, and candlesticks. It is good to know that one of the beautiful traditions of our culture is being preserved.

Marguerite Wildenhain

Most of the potters working in America today would fit into the artist-craftsman category. One of the best known and most respected among them is Marguerite Wildenhain, who began her career as a potter designing for a porcelain factory in Germany shortly after WWI. Before she emigrated to the United

Fig. 16-1   Footed bowl with two spouts, by Marguerite Wildenhain. Photo courtesy Luther College.

282

States in 1940, she had served an apprenticeship in pottery at the Bauhaus in Weimar, received instruction in sculpture, served as head of the ceramic department at a school of arts and crafts, and made models for mass production for the Royal Berlin porcelain factory.

In this country she has taught at colleges, given lectures, held seminars. At the present time she devotes the major part of the year to creative work in the shop she set up at Pond Farm near Guerneville, California, but during the summer months she teaches pottery courses. Her training in the tradition of European pottery and in the creative millieu of the Bauhaus has given her an awareness of the need for combining skilled craftsmanship with artistic design. Many young potters at work today owe their inspiration to Marguerite Wildenhain.

Lee Magdanz

Lee Magdanz built his shop, The Kiln Room, with the help of a loan from the Small Business Administration. During his college years he had training in crafts as well as in art education. He has taught for a dozen years in classes ranging from junior high school to college level.

He is now working to develop a studio which will be respected for the quality and integrity of the work, where, as he says, "I can develop in any direction I want to go and yet make a living." At the present moment he works alone except for a part-time college student who mixes his clay and helps with other chores. He has worked with apprentices but has found them a mixed blessing.

While he was teaching in college, he and his students made extensive tests of glazes. He is constantly searching for new glazes that are distinctively different. He likes to make functional pottery even though it seems to him that functional work is not the "in" thing. His work sells well; he has even had rejected work from shows sell out entirely before it could be sent back to him!

Avant-garde craftsman

After studying ceramics at a California university, he started looking for a job. This turned out to be more difficult than he had expected. After looking for almost two years, he ended up working for an architectural firm.

The job was ideal. He was given a free hand in creating ceramic adornments for buildings; he had his own shop and enough free time to do creative work of his own. He thought he was launched on a great artistic career.

The trouble was, he had difficulty selling what he made. He

283

sent work to all of the regional exhibits but results were not good. His entries were usually rejected; when accepted, they attracted little attention. He studied the situation, considered what work was winning prizes, and decided to change his style. "I realized," he said, "that to win acceptance I had to do something outrageous—something that would shock."

So he started to make things that would be the ultimate of the absurd, combining clay with scraps of metal from junk yards, rope fibers, fur, etc.

His plan worked. His next submission to a show won acceptance and an award—and most important, recognition by buyers. It made a big change in his thinking also. He decided to update his work without sacrificing his integrity. He is now making ware which sells and he is still winning prizes in ceramic shows. He still has his job.

"Is it alright if we tell your story like it is?" we asked.

"Sure" said he, "just don't mention my name."

Couples and clay

It is really great when husband and wife share artistic interests and cooperate in the designing, production, and marketing of their unique line of ceramic ware.

Lee and Dorothy Shank are such a couple and so are Steven and Susan Kemeneffy—with this difference: the Shanks work in a similar vein, while the Kemeneffys do work which is completely different from each others'. Steven builds and glazes—Susan glazes and paints.

Husband and wife help each other in so many ways. In some cases, one holds a job which pays the rent while the other pursues an artistic career. Even if one partner spends the greater part of the day in some completely different field, the sharing of experiences, the helpful criticism, and the encouragement are tremendously important.

Designing lighting fixtures

Another husband and wife team makes nothing but lamps. Their workshop is more a factory than a studio; it is a four-room structure built of concrete blocks with concrete floors on a lot adjoining their home. With the help of part-time workers employed on occasion, they produce a line of large, rectangular perforated globes that are suspended by chains from the ceiling. All of their work is made in plaster molds. Spherical shapes are slip-cast in two-piece drain molds; rectangular forms are made of slabs pressed into molds made of four large plaster slabs and held together by heavy rubber bands. While in the leather-hard state, pieces are pierced and incised by hand, then decorated with underglaze colors.

This small family industry is prosperous mainly because it is operated in a most efficient manner. Cost/time analyses have been made; waste motion is eliminated; labor-saving devices are used —a pug mill mixes clay, a blunger mixes slip, slabs are rolled by a mechanical device. They buy their glazes ready-made rather than take precious time to mix them. This couple works hard and puts in long hours but they like it that way.

Production/hobby shop

Neil and Dorothy Harper for many years operated a small ceramic production industry combined with a hobby shop. Neil was a dental surgeon who served overseas in WWII; Dorothy was a psychologist. After the war ended they moved to Florida, where they established their small industry. Neil experimented with Florida clays to produce a white casting slip with good working properties. The couple developed a lucrative business designing and producing custom tableware for hotels and res-taurants. One restaurant specializing in Polynesian food has some highly original ware produced by the Harpers. They also established a large mail-order business. They employed two or three helpers.

Dorothy sold supplies to ceramic hobbyists and conducted classes for beginners. Some of her former students have gone on to be successful producing potters.

A few years ago, they sold their shop and moved to a paradise on the Florida west coast where they designed and built their own home with a private dock for their boat and a workshop in which they continue ceramic activities. They still operate a mail-order business.

Businessman turned ceramist

Scion of a prominent industrial family, he was destined to enter the family business—or so his parents thought. But his interests lay elsewhere; after much persuasion, his parents con-sented to his going to Paris to study painting.

Before he completed his studies, however, some members of the firm died and top management was thrown into disarray. He was needed at home—desperately. Reluctantly he washed his brushes, closed his studio, and returned to assume the presi-dency of the firm. But on the way he made himself a promise.

After ten years the business was on its feet again; he had

285

inherited the family genius for industrial administration. At this point he kept the promise he had made to himself a decade earlier; he left the family business, never to return.

He did not go back to painting. During his stint as an executive he had learned about ceramics. The idea of combining his manufacturing and marketing skills with his interest in design was strongly appealing. He became a potter.

He spent some time studying the basic techniques of pottery making and some more studying the economic situation of the typical artist-potter. He was determined that any ware he produced would be a "quality" line, technically sound, beautiful and original in design—something people would want to buy and be happy to own.

Today he operates a small plant which he designed and built himself. He employs two fulltime workers and some parttime helpers, when they are needed, to produce a line of well-designed lamps, tables, and articles for interior decoration, as well as garden sculpture. The pieces are sold directly to hotels and through high class decorator shops. He is satisfying his creative urge; he does not earn as much as he did when he was president of the family firm, but he is happy.

Designing and manufacturing equipment

Ted Randall earned his graduate degree in ceramics with emphasis on the fine arts. Besides being a talented artist, he had the makings of an engineer. As he was throwing on a kick wheel in his ceramics class one day, he began to think about how the wheel could be made better. He had mechanical aptitude; he began to tinker. The result was a new type of wheel which has achieved great popularity (it is shown in Fig. 6-3).

Without giving up his career as an artist, Randall has developed a parallel career as a designer and manufacturer of wheels and other equipment for ceramists.

His sculptural works are known for their massive monumental qualities. (He designed and built his own kiln especially for the big pieces he models.) An example of his work is shown in the color section.

Research chemist

While earning his degree in ceramics he became fascinated by chemical research in the field of glazes. After graduation he went into partnership with a friend and began the manufacture of glazes and ceramic pigments especially for studio potters. The firm now does a multimillion dollar yearly business. Despite financial success, he still pursues his first great love—research.

Ceramics and architectural design

Charlene de Jori is an artist, a sculptor, a ceramist. She likes working in raku, has built a gas-fired kiln in the yard back of her studio. Her main interest, however, is ceramics for buildings, both inside and outside. With the help of a young woman assistant, formerly one of her students, she makes lamps: not the kind that stand on a table, but lamps that form an integral part of the area they illuminate—light as an element of sculpture. Much of her work is decorative plaques, name plates, and house numbers which are more than numerals—in her hands they become colorful embellishments of the buildings they identify.

Architects call on her frequently for special ceramic creations: wall dividers, patio sculpture, garden accessories.

Before accepting a job, Charlene makes a written agreement with the architect which specifies what the work will cost and when it is to be delivered. The agreement also states that the installation of the work is the responsibility of the architect. Experience has taught her that an agreement on these points is most important.

Charlene and her assistant work a full eight-hour day, six days a week, doing the kind of work they enjoy. They have all the commissions they can handle.

Designing for mass production

In the mid-thirties, Lee Rosen was teaching many branches of art in the New York City high schools. A gifted artist and inspiring teacher, she found herself the mentor of groups of talented young graduates who kept coming back—to show her their work, to ask advice, or just to talk. A year or two before WWII, she and her husband Sam, an engineer, started a cooperative workshop composed of professional craftsmen: silversmiths, potters, weavers, and sculptors. *Design-Technics* was established with the aims of selling good design to mass production industries and also training young apprentices in various crafts. WWII put an end to this plan.

Lee and Sam continued their work in ceramics. Sam was the technical and business expert, she the designer. Hard work and talent brought recognition. Lee resigned her teaching post to devote her time to designing ceramics, creating products from ashtrays to large-scale murals for architecture.

The husband and wife team moved their workshop to the country in Pennsylvania, where they built a shop and their home, but continued to operate their showroom in New York City where they sell their work on a custom basis to architects and interior designers. It is now called *Design-Technics Ceramics, Inc.* They produce quantities of ceramic lamps,

287

Fig. 16-2   Hand-thrown lamp; designed by Lee Rosen, Design-Technics.

planters, tables, wall surfacing, and various types of accessories both molded and wheel thrown. All are glazed and finished by hand in great variety of ceramic techniques; many are one-of-a-kind.

The Rosens' situation is ideal. They are doing what they like and they are making a valuable contribution to the aesthetics of our time.

Modeling figurines

A young sculptor I met abroad is not only a gifted artist, but a master mold maker as well. His skill at modeling delicate detail is amazing. I once watched him make a pair of statuettes 10 inches high, depicting a cavalier and his lady. They both wore hats with plumes; the lady carried a pair of gloves. The detail of their elaborate costumes was all there and all perfect. When the model was finished, a casting mold was made from it.

This sculptor is one of many talented artists who serve a large and important industry—the production of figurines. A fellow worker in the same plant spends her days painting figurines.

Neither of these two people has the freedom they would enjoy as independent artists working on their own; but they enjoy what they are doing, and that is what counts, isn't it?

Three merry jesters of Milan

Adriano Colombo, Toni Moretto, and Giovanni Duso met at a ceramics factory where they were doing work similar to that described in the section above. They were bored. They were ready to abandon the world of ladies and gallants in favor of subjects of more recent times. They left the ceramics factory

Fig. 16-3   Serenade, by Lo Scricciolo.

289

Fig. 16-4   Justice, by Lo Scricciolo.

and established a new one of their own; smaller, of course, but still a factory. They called it Lo Scricciolo.

The sculptures of Lo Scricciolo are caricatures of the professions, the amusements, and the social life of Italy during the period of transition when old forms were giving way to new. They make drawings witty, biting, satirical—of such things as a street photographer at work, a dentist treating a patient, a learned professor with a cluttered desk, a judge sentencing a miscreant, lovers in a drawing room. These drawings are then turned into clay. Thin slabs form backgrounds or are draped as clothing; thin coils shape arms and legs; balls form heads. Hair is produced by a small extruder as shown in Figure 16–5. They

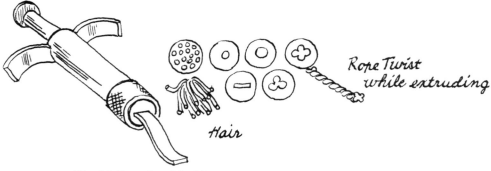

Fig. 16-5   A hand-held extruder is used to mold fine details.

use no molds, no armatures. They make editions of their subjects (environmental vignettes), but no two pieces are identical. Their work is avidly sought by collectors.

A painter discovers clay

Marguerite Drewry says that she literally owes her life to clay. She and her late husband were topflight artists on the Madison Avenue scene for many years. He was an art director, she an illustrator and fashion designer. A dozen years ago they moved to a place in the country. This was not retirement, for they kept their connections with the New York art world.

Then tragedy struck. One day as they were driving, a truck hit their small car head on. The car was demolished and Marguerite was so badly injured that doctors doubted they could save her. Her husband was killed.

But Marguerite survived. It was a long and painful process. Repeated surgery extending over three years was needed to save her right arm. Even so, the doctors feared that the arm would be paralyzed.

However, Marguerite is a woman of determination. While hospitalized, she began modeling clay with her left hand. The fact that she could create little figures gave her courage. After several months, she found that her right hand could help the left. As time passed, the right hand helped more and more until she finally became ambidextrous. "Clay has done so much for me," she says, "it helped me to get well and it has given me new insights into my painting. I see things differently; I can feel a third dimension in line. I wish I had discovered clay sooner."

Teaching

Most of us potters are teachers or have been at some time in our lives. It's a great experience—teaching a craft you love to students eager to learn.

Teaching ceramics full time in a high school or a college is especially rewarding. At those levels, teachers and students work together seeking information. Teaching becomes a two-way street; we learn from our students as they learn from us.

Well, there they are—a few dedicated people who have succeeded in making a living from some type of ceramic work.

Among these brief case histories, there may be a suggestion helpful to you.

These people differ in many ways; they work differently, like different things. Some are good business organizers, some like

291

the technical aspects of ceramics. Some prefer to make utilitarian ceramics in the classical tradition, others prefer the "way-out" forms of contemporary art. Despite all differences they have one thing in common—an understanding of clay, an appreciation of the close personal relationship between the potter and the materials through which he works.

There are many, many other ceramists who should have been included in this chapter: for example, the head designer for a large tableware firm, the curator of a ceramics collection in a museum, the potter who fires work for other potters, the young woman who makes ceramic jewelry, and her friend who makes lamps to order. While ceramics is not an Eldorado by any means, it does offer possibilities. And—oh yes, we must not forget—some people write books about it.

So long, good luck!

Glossary

Ceramic Terms

Abstraction—A work of art made without application to any particular object.

Agateware—Pottery that is veined and mottled to resemble agate.

Air floated—Sorted in particles of similar size by air separation.

Albany slip—A natural clay which melts at cone 8, used as a glaze on clay which fires at a higher temperature. Usually dark brown. Used by early American potters on stoneware and used today on porcelain electrical insulators.

Albarello—A cylindrical jar with concave sides, used for holding drugs. Decorated with majolica.

Alkali—Any substance having marked basic properties. For potters the term refers generally to compounds of sodium and potassium which act as fluxes in alkaline glazes.

Amorphous—Formless; in chemistry, without crystalline structure.

Argillaceous—Of the nature of clay or containing clay.

Armature—A framework used to support clay while it is being modeled.

Arretine ware—A red terra cotta, decorated in relief, made at Arretium in Italy, from about 100 B.C. to about A.D. 100.

Aventurine—A glossy type of glaze containing sparkling particles of copper or chromic oxide or ferric oxide.

Bag wall—A baffle wall in a kiln separating the chamber from the combustion area.

Ball mill—A device for grinding glazes, consisting of a porcelain jar in which glaze ingredients are placed along with a charge of pebbles and water. The jar is then rotated.

Banding wheel (also **whirler** or **decorating wheel**)—A turntable which permits work to be rotated while it is shaped or decorated.

Basalt ware—A type of black stoneware developed by Josiah Wedgwood.

Bat—A disk or slab of plaster of paris or fired clay, used to dry out clay or to work on.

Bisque—Unglazed fired clay.

Blanks—Pottery shapes, tiles, plates, fired but not glazed, used for applied decorations.

Blunger—A device for mixing clay slip, consisting of a container and rotating paddles.

Bone china—Hard translucent white ware containing bone ash (calcium phosphate). Originally produced in England.

Buccaro ware—A type of black pottery with ornament in relief, made by the Etruscans about 600 B.C., also called *buccero nero*. The black color was produced by reduction.

Burnishing—Producing a shiny surface on clay by rubbing it with a smooth tool when it is leather hard.

Butterfly—A small block of wood hung by a wire from the frame of an armature to support masses of clay.

Calcareous—Containing lime.

Calcining—A process of firing a material to expel volatile matter and to dehydrate it; done frequently with clay, borax and other material before they are used in glaze recipes.

Calipers—A device for measuring the dimensions of objects.

Calipers, proportional—A device for enlarging or reducing dimensions proportionately.

Cartoon—A full-size drawing for a mural.

Case mold—A mold from which other molds are made.

Casing—The process of making a case mold of a mold.

Casting—The process of pouring a liquid, either slip or plaster of paris, into a mold where it hardens.

Casting box—A device for constructing rectangular retaining walls when making plaster of paris molds.

Celadon—A pale green glaze produced by iron in a reduction fire.

Cheese state—The period during the setting of plaster of paris when it has the consistency of cream cheese.

Chemically combined water—Water which is combined in molecular form with clay to make it a hydrous aluminum silicate. This water is driven off in the kiln when the clay reaches red heat (about 900° to 1000°F.).

CMC—A synthetic gum for glazes.

Coefficient of expansion—The ratio of increase in size of a substance for a given rise in temperature.

Colloidal—Made up of extremely fine particles suspended in a fluid medium; gelatinous.

Cones, pyrometric—Small clay rods which indicate kiln temperatures.

Cottle—A wall set in place around a model when plaster of paris is to be poured over it.

Crackle—Tiny cracks in the surface of a glaze.

Crawling—A glaze defect in which the glaze rolls away from areas of the piece it is on, leaving bare spots.

Crazing—A glaze defect resulting from lack of fit between a glaze and the body it is on so that fine cracks appear in the glaze.

Crystallization—The formation of crystals. This occurs in glazes containing rutile, zinc, and other crystal-forming oxides.

Damp closet—A box, usually zinc-lined, for keeping work moist.

Damper—A device for closing the flue of a kiln.

De-airing—The process of subjecting plastic clay to a vacuum so that most of the air is drawn out of the clay. This makes it better for throwing. A de-airing device is usually attached to a pug mill.

Decalcomania—A process of transferring pictures and designs from specially prepared paper to china or glass.

Decant—To pour off liquid gently without disturbing the solid material which has settled.

Decomposition—The act of separating or resolving into constituent parts; disintegration. It is the decomposition of granite rock which forms clay.

Deflocculation—The addition of electrolytes to clay slip to reduce the amount of water needed to make it pourable.

Dehydration—The expulsion of water. Clay is dehydrated when the chemically combined water is driven off at about 1000°F.

Devitrification—Recrystallization on cooling, a defect in glazes.

Dipping—A method of applying glaze to a piece of pottery by immersing it in a container of glaze.

Draft—The taper on the sides of a model which permits it to be withdrawn from a mold.

Draw trial—A piece of clay drawn from the kiln during firing to judge the progress of the fire.

Dresden china—Decorated porcelain made near Dresden in Saxony, characterized by elaborate ornamentation and delicate figure pieces. Also called *Meissen ware.*

Dry footing—The process of removing glaze from the bottom rim of a piece so that it can be fired standing on a kiln shelf, without stilts.

Dunting—Breaking from strains in cooling.

Earthenware—Pottery fired to a temperature below 2000°F.

Electrolyte—An alkaline substance, usually soda ash or sodium silicate, added to a clay slip to deflocculate it.

Engobe—Clay slip, usually colored.

Epoxy cement—A strong adhesive good for attaching tiles to masonry walls.

Extruding—Process of shaping plastic clay by forcing it through a die.

Faïence—Earthenware covered with opaque glaze with decorations painted over the glaze.

294

Fat clay—Clay that is highly plastic.

Fettling—Removing the seams (fettles) of a cast piece.

Filler—A nonplastic material, such as flint, added to clay bodies to help drying and control shrinkage.

Filter press—A device for squeezing water out of clay slip to make it into plastic clay.

Firebox—The portion of a kiln in which the flame burns.

Fit—The adjustment between a glaze and the clay which it is on.

Flux—A substance which melts and causes other substances to melt also.

Frit—A glaze or partial glaze that has been fired and pulverized.

Frog—A device for cutting clay made by a wire stretched across two prongs.

Fuller's earth—An earthy substance resembling potter's clay but lacking plasticity, used in fulling cloth and as a filter medium. A colloidal hydrus aluminum silicate.

Fuse—To melt under the action of heat.

Glass—An amorphous substance, usually transparent or translucent, made by fusing together silica and soda and some other base.

Glass cullet—Finely pulverized glass used as an ingredient in glazes or as a body flux.

Globar—An electric element in the form of a bar, made of silicon carbide, capable of reaching extremely high temperatures.

Goldstone—Aventurine glaze.

Gombroon ware—Porcelain with pierced designs covered with flowing glaze so that no openings are left but light will shine through.

Greenware—Clay shapes that have not been fired.

Hard paste—True porcelain.

Igneous—Formed by the solidification of molten masses.

Infrared lamp—A type of electric light bulb whose light is good for drying clay.

Insulating bricks—Extremely porous, soft bricks used on the outside of kilns to reduce the loss of heat through the walls.

Jasper ware—A type of pottery made by Josiah Wedgwood, having a light-colored body with white figures and ornaments in relief.

Jiggering—The process of manufacturing pottery by means of convex molds and templates on a power wheel.

Jollying—A process similar to jiggering, using concave molds with the jigger template forming the inside of bowls and cups.

Kanthal—A metal alloy made in Sweden used as an element in electric kilns, capable of reaching temperatures of cone 6.

Kaolin—Pure clay.

Kiln furniture—Refractory shelves and posts used to stack a kiln.

Kiln wash—A mixture of china clay and flint with enough water added to make it brushable, used to protect kiln shelves from glazes that may fall upon them.

Lawn—To pass through a fine mesh screen.

Leaching—Subjecting to the action of percolating water or other liquid in order to separate soluble components.

Luster—A type of surface decoration made by depositing a thin layer of metal.

Luting—The process of joining two pieces of leather hard clay with slip or slurry.

Majolica—Earthenware covered with an opaque glaze containing tin with decorations painted on top of the glaze. Named for the island of Majorca.

Mat—Dull surfaced, not shiny.

Maturing—Reaching the temperature which produces the most serviceable degree of hardness. In the case of glaze, reaching the point of complete fusion.

Meissen ware—Dresden china.

Metamorphic—Changed in constitution by heat, pressure, water; said of rocks.

Muffle—A chamber in a kiln which protects ware from contact with the flame.

Nichrome—A chromium nickel alloy used as an element in electric kilns. Limited to temperatures of cone 2 and below.

Notches—Round depressions cut in one half of a mold so that the other half, when cast against it, will fit in place.

Opacifier—Material added to a transparent glaze to make it opaque; most commonly used are tin oxide and zircopax.

Organic materials—Vegetable or animal material sometimes present in natural clay.

Oxidation—The act of combining with oxygen, usually at high temperatures.

295

Patina—A surface appearance on objects, usually the result of age. Ceramic sculpture can be given a patina by treatment with wax, oil and other materials.

Peachbloom—A reduction glaze containing copper, with a pink color.

Peeling—A defect in which portions of a glaze or an engobe separate from the ware.

Petuntse—A type of feldspar found in China, combined with kaolin to make Chinese porcelain.

pH—The relative alkalinity or acidity of a solution.

Piercing—Cutting through the wall of a piece to create an open design.

Pinholes—A glaze defect caused by too rapid firing or by tiny air holes in the clay.

Pitchers—Porcelain grog.

Plaster of paris—Partially dehydrated calcium sulfate, made by calcining gypsum rock. Useful for bats and molds.

Plasticity—A quality of clay which permits it to be molded into different shapes without crumbling or sagging.

Polychrome—Many-colored; a term applied especially to Greek vases made in Athens during the 6th century B.C. The ground was often white with black, white, red, and yellow colors used in the decoration.

Pooled glaze—A fluid glaze which has flowed to the bottom of a bowl or a depression, forming a pool.

Porcelain—A hard white body, often translucent, composed chiefly of kaolin and feldspar, fired to cone 12 or higher.

Porosity—The quality or degree of being porous, filled with holes, capable of absorbing liquids.

Pressing—A method of shaping clay by squeezing it into molds or between the two halves of a press mold.

Pugging—Grinding and mixing clay in a pug mill.

Pug mill—A machine for grinding and mixing plastic clay. Usually has a vacuum attached.

Pyrometer—A device for measuring kiln temperature, usually operated by an electric thermocouple.

Raku—Japanese earthenware, used in the tea ceremony, rough, with dark glaze.

Raw glaze—A glaze that contains no fritted materials.

Reducing agent—Organic material put in a glaze or into a kiln chamber during the firing to bring about reduction.

Reduction—The act of removing oxygen from metal oxides; occurs during fire when not enough oxygen is present.

Refractory—Resisting high temperatures.

Reinforcement—Materials, such as burlap or metal lath, placed in plaster or cement castings for strength.

Relief—Sculptural form which projects from a background.

Representation—A picture or piece of sculpture made in the likeness of some material object.

Retaining wall—A cottle.

Reticulation—The netlike appearance which frequently occurs when a nonflowing glaze is put on top of one that flows more freely; also occurs in glazes high in boric oxide.

Rib—A flat tool, usually wood, used to refine shapes being thrown on a potter's wheel.

Rouge flambé—A type of copper-red reduction glaze, deep red with areas of green and blue.

Roulette—A wheel of wood or bisque with recessed designs in the rim, rolled over a plastic clay form to make a band of raised decoration.

Rubbing—Burnishing.

Running plaster—A method of shaping plaster by moving templates across it while it is going through the cheese state.

Sagger—A box made of fire clay in which glazed ware is placed for protection from the flames in a down-draft kiln.

Salt glazing—A method of glazing ware (usually stoneware) by throwing salt into the firebox of the kiln when temperature is at its highest point.

Samian ware—Same as Arretine ware.

Sand casting—A method of creating form by pouring a material which will set, such as plaster of paris, cement or clay slip, into a hollow scooped out of wet sand.

Sang de boeuf—Oxblood, a deep red copper reduction glaze.

Sedimentary—Formed by the deposit of sediment; said of rocks and clays.

Setting—the act of hardening as a result of cooling or chemical action.

Settling—A process by which materials in suspension, such as glazes, fall to the bottom of a container, often forming a hard mass.

Sgraffito—A method of decorating by scratching through a coating of engobe.

Shard—A pottery fragment.

Shims—Pieces of thin material used to separate portions of a mold.

Shivering—a glaze defect in which sections of a glaze lift off the piece.

Short clay—Clay that is not plastic.

Siccative—A drying agent.

Sinter—To harden by heat without reaching maturing temperature.

Slake—To soak with water.

Slip—Liquid clay.

Slurry—Clay of paste-like consistency.

Soft paste—An imitation of porcelain containing various materials, such as gypsum, calcium, bone, which act as fluxes, making the ware mature at a lower temperature than does true porcelain.

Spraying—A method of applying glazes with a spray gun.

Sprig—A relief decoration pressed in a sprig mold attached to ware with slip.

Stacking—Loading a kiln.

Stains—Pigments used for coloring clay bodies and glazes.

Stilts—Porcelain tripods on which glazed ware is fired. Stilts for low-fire work may have points of nichrome.

Stoneware—High-fired, vitreous ware, usually gray, sometimes shades of brown or tan.

Stylization—A form of design in which objects are represented according to a convention or style rather than realistically.

Taglietelle—A device for cutting clay into layers of uniform thickness.

Temperature—Intensity of heat measured in degrees Fahrenheit or centigrade.

Template—A pattern for shaping the profile of a piece.

Terra cotta—Low-fire earthenware, usually red, often containing grog, used for sculpture.

Terra sigillata—A surface treatment, developed by the Romans, that gives pottery a hard, semiglossy surface, made by spraying on an engobe of extremely fine colloidal particles of clay.

Tessera—A small piece of tile, glass, or other hard material, used to make mosaics.

Thread separation—A method of separating the two halves of a waste mold by pulling a thread through the plaster when it is in the cheese state.

Throwing—The process of shaping clay on the potter's wheel.

Tin enamel—A type of low-fire lead glaze containing tin, used in majolica work.

Trailing—Using a tube to apply a line of slip to clay.

Translucent—Transmitting light but not transparent.

Turning—Process of shaping leather hard clay by holding cutting tools against it as it turns on a wheel.

Turning box—A device for shaping plaster of paris by turning it on a spindle and holding templates against it.

Turntable—A rotating platform on which work may be turned; a banding wheel.

Viscosity—Resistance of a liquid to movement.

Vitrification—The act of becoming vitreous, that is, hard, glasslike, nonabsorbent.

Volatilize—To pass from solid through liquid to gaseous state under the action of heat.

Volclay—Bentonite.

Water smoking—the first portion of the firing cycle during which water is driven from the clay.

Wax resist—A method of decoration in which liquid wax is applied to portions of greenware after which engobe is brushed or sprayed over the piece. The wax repels the engobe.

Weathering—Decomposition under the action of wind, rain, heat, etc.

Wedging—The act of kneading or mixing plastic clay by cutting it in half and slamming the halves together.

Wedging board—A block of wood or plaster of paris with a post holding a wire so that a lump of clay may be cut in half and the two halves slammed together

Wedgwood, Josiah—The famous English potter, creator of Jasper ware.

Weep hole—A hole made in a depression in a piece of sculpture which is to be used outdoors so that rain water will not collect there.

Whirler—A banding wheel.

White body—A clay body which fires white, often at a low temperature, in which case it usually contains a high percentage of talc.

Wire, piano—Strong nonstretching wire used on wedging boards.

297

Ceramic Materials

Albany slip—A natural clay which, when fired above cone 7, melts to form a deep reddish brown glaze; used on stoneware and on porcelain electrical insulators.

Antimony—A source of color, opaque white in leadless glazes; semi-opaque yellow in lead glazes.

Arsenic—An opacifier, best avoided because it is extremely poisonous.

Barium—Barium carbonate ($BaCO_3$), used in clay bodies to make sulfides insoluble. Used in glazes for mat texture.

Bentonite—A highly plastic, very fine clay of volcanic origin; used in small quantities to make other clays plastic.

Bone ash—Calcium phosphate ($Ca_3(PO_4)_2$), added to china clay to produce bone china.

Borax—($Na_2O \cdot 2B_2O_3 \cdot 10H_2O$). Used as a flux in low-temperature glazes; highly soluble, almost always used fritted; produces beautiful colors, especially with copper oxide.

Cadmium—Used with selenium to produce red stains for glazes.

Calcium—An active flux used usually as whiting or calcium carbonate ($CaCO_3$) in glazes and clay bodies.

Cement—A product made by calcining and pulverizing argillaceous and calcareous materials; mixed with sand and water to form mortar.

Cement, Keene—A type of cement much like plaster of paris, made from gypsum, used to make a white mortar. Not waterproof.

Cement, Portland—A type of cement used for exterior work; waterproof.

Ceramispar—Crushed granite used in clay bodies.

Chromium—A source of color, used as chromium oxide (Cr_2O_3). Produces shades of green in lead-free glazes. At extremely low temperatures in lead glazes produces red in an oxidizing fire. Under reduction produces yellow in high lead glazes. In conjunction with tin oxide produces various shades of pink and maroon.

Cobalt—An important color source that produces a deep blue. Usually used as cobalt carbonate ($CoCO_3$). In combination with copper, manganese, and iron, produces black and gun metal glazes. Sometimes used as cobalt oxide (CoO) which is stronger, or as cobalt nitrate, a soluble salt used to add a slight bluish cast to a glaze or a body.

Colemanite—($2CaO \cdot 3B_2O_3 \cdot 5H_2O$). A natural source of calcium oxide and boric oxide. Used in glazes (called borosilicate glazes).

Copper—An important color source used usually as copper carbonate ($CuCO_3$) or copper oxide (CuO). In a lead glaze produces shades of green. In alkaline glazes produces turquoise blue. In a reduction fire produces colors ranging from purple to brilliant red.

Cornwall stone—A material resembling feldspar. Used as a flux in glazes. As a body ingredient tends to reduce warping.

Crocus martis—A color source producing reddish brown. Contains combinations of iron, oxide, and manganese dioxide.

Cryolite—(Na_3AlF_6). A flux used in enamels and glazes.

Dextrine—A binder for glazes.

Dolomite—($CaMg(CO_3)_2$). A source of magnesium oxide and calcium oxide used to replace part of the whiting in glazes and clay bodies.

Electrolyte—An alkaline substance, usually soda ash or sodium silicate, used to deflocculate clay slip. Other electrolytes include sodium alginate, sal soda, sodium tannate, and some water softeners.

Epsom salts—Used to prevent glazes, especially fritted glazes, from settling.

Fat oil, or **fat oil of turpentine**—A vehicle used in china painting.

Feldspar—In pure form $NaO \cdot Al_2O_3 \cdot 6SiO_2$, or albite. Rarely found in nature as a pure mineral but as a mixture of several types of feldspar which contain oxides of sodium, potassium, or calcium. The most important ceramic material next to clay. Used as a flux in clay bodies and in glazes.

Flint—Silica.

Fluorspar—Calcium fluoride (CaF_2), acts as an opacifier and a flux in glazes.

Frit—A glaze which has been fired and pulverized.

Glass cullet—Pulverized glaze used as a glaze ingredient or as a flux in clay bodies.

Grog—Clay which has been fired and ground. Used in clay bodies to control shrinkage and to give rough texture.

Groleg—An English plastic porcelain clay with a low shrinkage.

Gums—Binders used in engobes and underglaze decorations as well as in glazes. Most frequently used are gum tragacanth, gum arabic, CMC, V gum T, and various other prepared forms.

Gypsum—A naturally occurring material, hydrated sulfate of calcium ($CaSO_4 \cdot 2H_2O$), which is calcined, to make plaster of paris. In its pure form called alabaster.

Hydrastone—Similar to hydrocal. Sets even harder.

Hydrocal—A hard-setting type of plaster of paris.

Ilmenite—A titanium compound ($TiO_2 \cdot FeO$), used in granular form to produce specks in glazes.

Iron—An important source of color in bodies and glazes. In clay bodies produces shades from tan to brick red. In glazes produces shades of yellow, brown, and tan. In a high lead glaze at low temperature will produce iron red. An extra amount of iron produces a gold-flecked glaze called *aventurine*. In reduction, iron produces the beautiful green glaze *celadon*. Iron has three oxide forms—red (Fe_2O_3), black (FeO), and magnetite (Fe_3O_4).

Iron chromate—($FeCrO_4$). A source of color, especially for clay bodies; produces shades of gray.

Lead—The most widely used flux in low-temperature glazes, used as lead carbonate ($2PbCO_3 \cdot Pb(OH)_2$) or white lead. Red lead (Pb_3O_4) and litharge (PbO) mixed with molasses have been used to glaze primitive types of low-fired earthenware. Lead chromate ($PbCrO_4$), a source of color, produces shades of green in alkaline glazes, yellow in lead glazes. In the presence of tin, it produces shades of pink. *Poisonous*.

Lepidolite—($LiF \cdot KF \cdot Al_2O_3 \cdot 3SiO_2$). A flux used in high-fire glazes.

Lime—*See* Calcium.

Litharge—Lead monoxide (PbO), not as much used in ceramics as other sources of lead. *Poisonous*.

Lithium—(Li). A flux, similar to sodium or potassium in glazes, not frequently used—too expensive.

Magnesite—Magnesium carbonate ($MgCO_3$).

Magnesite cement—A white setting cement used in mosaics and in floor construction.

Magnesium—Used as magnesium carbonate ($MgCO_3$) as a flux in high-temperature glazes.

Magnetite—(Fe_3O_4). An oxide of iron.

Manganese—A source of color in glazes and bodies; produces shades of red, brown, purple, and black. Used as manganese carbonate ($MnCO_3$) or as manganese dioxide (MnO_2).

Maroon base—A prepared ceramic pigment made by calcining chromium in the presence of tin.

Minium—(Pb_3O_4). Red lead oxide, a flux in low-temperature glazes; can be used alone as a glaze on low-fired earthenware. *Poisonous*. (The word *miniature* originally meant a picture or manuscript illumination colored with minium.)

Nepheline syenite—A type of feldspar with a low fusion point; used in place of other feldspar as a flux in stoneware bodies to lower maturing temperature.

Nickel oxide, green (NiO) or **nickel oxide, black** (Ni_2O_3)—Sources of color in glazes; in the presence of zinc, produce shades of slate blue; with calcium, shades of tan; with barium, brown; with magnesia, green. Both oxides produce similar results. Useful in crystalline glazes.

Niter—Potassium nitrate (KNO_3). A source of potassium used in making frits.

Ochre—An iron ore used as a colorant for clay bodies to produce shades of yellow, red, or brown.

Opax—A commercial silicate of zirconium; acts as an opacifier in glazes.

Pearl ash—Potassium carbonate (K_2CO_3), used as a source of potassium in glazes, usually fritted.

Petuntse—A feldspar found in China. Early Chinese potters mixed it with kaolin to make porcelain.

Pink oxide—*See* Maroon base.

299

Plaster of paris—Calcium sulfate ($CaSO_4 \cdot \frac{1}{2}H_2O$). Made by calcining gypsum, used for making molds and casts.

Plastilene—Clay ground with oil so that it becomes nondrying. Used to model forms from which casts are made.

Potash—Potassium carbonate (K_2CO_3). Also called pearl ash, a flux, extremely soluble, rarely used except in fritted form.

Potassium dichromate—($K_2Cr_2O_3$). A source of color in glazes; produces yellow, red.

Pumicite—An ash formed by volcanic action, a kind of natural frit that can be used as a glaze ingredient.

Red lead—*See* Minium. *Poisonous.*

Rutile—An ore containing titanium oxide (TiO_2) and iron; produces light shades of yellow and tan in glazes; also produces broken color and mottled effects; with copper or cobalt, produces beautifully textured colors.

Salt, common—Sodium chloride ($NaCl$); produces a hard glaze on stoneware when thrown into the kiln at its highest temperature.

Salts, soluble—Metallic salts such as copper sulfate, silver nitrate, gold chloride, bismuth subnitrate, and others, used to produce lusters; also used to brush light washes of color over glazes.

Sand—Silica.

Selenium—A source of red in glazes and glaze stains.

Silica—(Si). Flint, most abundant substance in the earth's rocky crust, a major component of clays and glazes. Flint is used in glazes to change the coefficient of expansion and control crazing and shivering.

Silicon carbide—(SiC). Used very finely ground, as a reducing agent in glazes; coarse ground it produces lava-type glazes. Also used as an abrasive (carborundum) and an electric kiln element (Globar).

Size (potter's soap)—A neutral soap manufactured especially for ceramic work, used as a separator in mold making.

Soapstone—Talc.

Soda—Sodium oxide (Na_2O), an active flux, useful in glazes from the lowest to the highest temperature. Has some disadvantages—high coefficient of expansion; glazes are soft, easily scratched. Many feldspars contain soda. Glazes with high soda content have beautiful colors, especially the turquoise blue produced by copper.

Soda ash—Sodium bicarbonate (Na_2CO_3), a source of soda in glazes; soluble, hence usually fritted. Also used as an electrolyte.

Sodium chloride—($NaCl$). Common salt.

Spodumene—($Li_2O \cdot Al_2O_3 \cdot 4SiO_2$). A flux used in high-fire glazes.

Strontium oxide—(SrO). Acts in a glaze in a manner similar to calcium; rarely used—too expensive.

Talc—($3MgO \cdot 4SiO_2 \cdot H_2O$). Pulverized steatite, a flux used in glazes; its most important use is as a flux in low-fire bodies.

Tin oxide—(SnO_2). The most effective opacifier; 10% added to a clear colorless glaze will make it opaque white.

Titanium dioxide—(TiO_2). *See* Rutile.

Umber—A natural source of red iron oxide (Fe_2O_3), used as a colorant in clay bodies to produce shades of brown.

Uranium—Formerly used as a source of color in glazes; produces shades of yellow, orange, and red; used as uranium oxide (U_2O_3).

Vanadium—(V). Used to produce vanadium stain, a yellow colorant for glazes.

Vermiculite—Bloated mica, used as an insulator in kiln construction.

Volcanic ash—*See* Pumicite.

Wallastonite—A material resembling feldspar with a lower melting point. Used to lower the maturing temperature of clay bodies. Promotes resistance to thermal shock and to crazing.

Water glass—Sodium silicate.

Wax emulsion—A liquid wax used in making wax resist designs.

White lead—Lead carbonate ($2PbCo_3 \cdot Pb(OH)_2$). The usual source of lead in glazes. *Poisonous.*

Whiting—Calcium carbonate ($CaCO_3$), the usual source of calcium in glazes, used also as a flux in clay bodies.

Yellow base—Vanadium stain.

Zinc oxide—(ZnO). Used as a glaze flux in middle and high temperature ranges (above cone 1); added to low-fire glazes produces a mat surface; distinguishing ingredient of Bristol glazes; affects the colors of other oxides— Makes iron dull, makes copper turquoise green; promotes crystallization in glazes. Zinc oxide should be calcined before use, otherwise it tends to make glazes crawl.

Zirconium—An opacifier similar to tin but not as strong; 20% added to a clear colorless glaze makes it opaque white. Zirconium oxide (ZrO) is too refractory for most glaze use; Zircopax or Opax, commercial silicates of zirconium, are used instead.

Zircopax—*See* Zirconium.

Sources of Supply

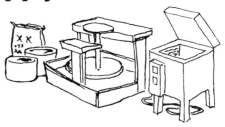

The studio potter can find most of his needs in the shops of local dealers in ceramic supplies (listed in the Yellow Pages).

If large amounts of clay are needed, try to find a nearby brickyard.

Manufacturers of kilns, wheels, and other studio equipment frequently have local distributors; check the advertising pages of *Ceramics Monthly* magazine.

Clay

American Art Clay
4714 West 16th Street
Indianapolis, IN 46222

Burns Brick Co.
Macon, GA 31200

Georgia Art Clay
Lizella, GA 31052

A. P. Green Fire Brick Co.
Mexico, MO 65265

V. R. Hood, Jr.
Box 1213
San Antonio, TX 78206

Kentucky-Tennessee Clay Co.
Mayfield, KY 42066

La Mo Refractory
323 Iris Avenue
New Orleans, LA 70121

Monmouth Natural Stoneware
Monmouth, IL 61462

Newton Pottery Supply Co.
Newton, MA 01432

Spinks Clay Co.
Box 929
Paris, TN 38242

Standard Ceramic Supply, Inc.
Box 4435
Pittsburgh, PA 15205

Stewart Clay Co.
133 Mulberry St.
New York, NY 10013

Trinity Ceramic Supply, Inc.
9016 Diplomacy Row
Dallas, TX 75235

United Clay Mines
Trenton, NJ 08608

Western Ceramic Supply Co.
1601 Howard Street
San Francisco, CA 94103

Westwood Ceramic Supply Co.
14400 Lomitas Drive
City of Industry, CA 91744

Jack D. Wolfe, Inc.
724 Meeker Avenue
Brooklyn, NY 11222

Zanesville Stoneware Co.
Zanesville, OH 43701

Kilns

A. D. Alpine, Inc.   Gas and
3051 Fujita Street   electric
Torrance, CA 90505

American Art Clay Co.   Electric
4717 West 16th Street
Indianapolis, IN 46222

California Kiln Co.   Gas
3036 Oak Street
Santa Ana, CA 92707

Craftool   Electric
1421 West 240th Street
Harbor City, CA 90710

Geil Kilns   Gas
P.O. Box 504
Hermosa Beach, CA 90254

Paragon Industries, Inc. Electric
Box 10133
Dallas, TX 75207

Skutt Ceramic Products Electric
2618 S.E. Steele Street
Portland, OR 97202

Stewart Clay Co.   Electric
133 Mulberry Street
New York, NY 10013

Raku kilns

Peach Valley Pottery
Route 1, Box 101
New Castle, CO 81647
303

Kiln Building Supplies

Refractories

Babcock and Wilcox Co.
161 East 42nd Street
New York, NY 10017

A. P. Green Fire Brick Co.
Mexico, MO 65265

La Mo Refractory
323 Iris Avenue
New Orleans, LA 70121

Insulation

Johns-Manville Co.
22 East 40th Street
New York, NY 10016

Superamics (Fiberfrax)
P.O. Box 89
Lawrenceville, GA 30245

Burners

Johnson Gas Appliance Co.
Cedar Rapids, IA 52405

Potter's Wheels and Other Studio Equipment

A. D. Alpine, Inc.
3051 Fujita Street
Torrance, CA 90505

American Art Clay Co.
4717 West 16th Street
Indianapolis, IN 46222

Craftool
1421 West 240th Street
Harbor City, CA 90710

Klopfenstein   Wheels
Route 2
Crestline, OH 44827

The Max Corporation   Wheels
P.O. Box 34068
Washington, DC 20034

Menco Engineers, Inc.
5520 Crebs Avenue
Tarzana, CA 91356

Randall Pottery, Inc.
P.O. Box 744
Alfred, NY 14802

Shimpo West   Wheels
P.O. Box 2315
La Puente, CA 91746

Skutt Ceramic Products
2618 S.E. Steele Street
Portland, OR 97202

Soldner Pottery Equip., Inc.
P.O. Box 428
Silt, CO 81652

Stewart Clay Co.
133 Mulberry Street
New York, NY 10013

Walker-Jamar Co.   Pug mills
365 South 1st Avenue
East Duluth, MN 55802

Pumps for Fountains

Canal Electric Motor Co.
310 Canal Street
New York, NY 10013

Little Giant Pumps
3810 North Tulsa Street
Oklahoma City, OK 73112

Ceramic Decalcomanias

Decals West
2521 West Burbank Boulevard
Burbank, CA 91505

304

Bibliography

Ball, F. Carlton and Lovoos, Janice. *Making Pottery Without a Wheel.* New York: Van Nostrand Reinhold, 1965. A comprehensive coverage of hand building, beautifully illustrated.

Berensohn, Paulus. *Finding One's Way with Clay.* New York: Simon and Schuster, 1972. A unique approach to making pinch pots.

Cardew, Michael. *Pioneer Pottery.* New York: St. Martin's, 1971. A book for potters who wish to make pottery using natural materials.

Kenny, John B. *Ceramic Design.* Radnor, Pa.: Chilton, 1963. A what-to-do book as well as a how-to-do book, lots of illustrations.

Kenny, John B. *Ceramic Sculpture,* Radnor, Pa.: Chilton, 1953. Covers methods and materials.

Kriwanek, Franz. *Keramos,* Dubuque, Iowa: Kendall, Hunt, 1970. New concepts in clay and in glazes.

Leach, Bernard. *A Potter's Book.* London: Faber and Faber; New York: Transatlantic Arts, 1940. An inspirational book, a combination of English and Japanese ideas on pottery.

Lewenstein, Eileen and Cooper, Emmanuel. *New Ceramics.* New York: Van Nostrand Reinhold, 1974. A comprehensive survey of contemporary trends in pottery world wide. Beautifully illustrated.

Newson, Glen C. *Ceramics, A Potter's Handbook.* New York: Holt, Rinehart and Winston, 1971. Comprehensive coverage of ceramics of the past and the present. Section on technical ceramic production.

Rhodes, Daniel. *Clay and Glazes For The Potter,* Revised Edition. Radnor, Pa.: Chilton, 1975. A most thorough coverage of the subject.

Rhodes, Daniel. *Kilns: Design, Construction and Operation.* Radnor, Pa.: Chilton, 1968. Everything a potter needs to know about kilns.

305

Rhodes, Daniel. *Stoneware and Porcelain.* Radnor, Pa.: Chilton, 1959. Materials and techniques used in high-fire pottery.

Riegger, Hal. *Raku: Art and Technique.* New York: Van Nostrand Reinhold, 1970. Complete coverage of clay, glazes, kiln building and firing.

Wettlaufer, George and Nancy. *The Craftsman's Survival Manual.* Englewood, N.J.: Prentice-Hall, 1974. How to sell the pottery you make.

Wildenhain, Marguerite. *Pottery: Form and Expression.* Palo Alto, Ca.: Pacific Books, 1959. A beautiful book, magnificent pictures.

Wildenhain, Marguerite. *The Invisible Core.* Palo Alto, Ca.: Pacific Books, 1973. An inspiring account of a potter's life and thoughts.

Ceramics Monthly. Columbus, OH, 43212. A valuable magazine for studio potters; articles on current trends, how-to-do projects, book reviews, exhibitions, and—best of all—a correspondence column where lively battles are waged between the devotees of "way-out" and those who favor classic traditions.

Ceramics Monthly Handbooks. A very practical how-to-do-it series. Titles include *Decorating Pottery,* by F. Carlton Ball; *Glaze Projects,* by Richard Behrens; *Underglaze Decoration* and *Brush Decoration for Ceramics,* by Marc Bellaire; *Throwing on the Potter's Wheel* and *Potter's Wheel Projects,* by Thomas Sellers; *Ceramic Projects,* edited by Thomas Sellers.

Index

Page numbers in italics indicate information in illustrations.

309

About the Kennys

JOHN KENNY served in the AEF in France during World War I. He studied painting at the Art Students League, New York City, and Ecole de la Grande Chaumiere, Paris. He earned his M.A. in Fine Arts (Ceramics) from Alfred University. Mr. Kenny taught art in the New York City public schools and worked as a draftsman for the Architectural Division of the New York Central Railroad. John Kenny is the founder of the High School of Art and Design, New York City; while serving as its first principal from 1941 until 1965, he was an active member of the Society of Illustrators. In addition to "The Complete Book of Pottery Making," he has authored "Ceramic Sculpture" and "Ceramic Design" (published by Chilton Book Company), and served as Contributing Editor, "Ceramics Monthly," from 1948 to 1974.

CARLA KENNY studied at the Art Students League, Grand Central School of Art, and Pratt Institute in New York. She taught fashion illustration at Pratt Institute, the High School of Art and Design and at the High School of Fashion, New York City. She worked as assistant to muralists Barry Faulkner and Dean Cornwell and from 1940 until 1965, worked as a freelance artist and designer for national advertising agencies. She is a life member of the Society of Illustrators and author of "Fashion Illustration" and "Advertising Layout and Design."

JOHN and CARLA KENNY met while working on a scholarship committee and have traveled extensively together. They lived for nine years in Mexico, where they conducted workshops for the International Cabaña, a worldwide organization of leaders of Girl Scouts and Girl Guides. Works by these artist-craftsmen are represented in private collections in this country, in Europe and in Mexico, and they have demonstrated their crafts many times on national television. John and Carla are co-authors of "The Art of Papier Mâché" and "Design in Papier Mâché," also published by Chilton. The Kennys have one daughter, Pamela, currently working for a college degree in foreign languages and in drama.

310